About Island Press

Since 1984, the nonprofit organization Island Press has been stimulating, shaping, and communicating ideas that are essential for solving environmental problems worldwide. With more than 1,000 titles in print and some 30 new releases each year, we are the nation's leading publisher on environmental issues. We identify innovative thinkers and emerging trends in the environmental field. We work with world-renowned experts and authors to develop cross-disciplinary solutions to environmental challenges.

Island Press designs and executes educational campaigns in conjunction with our authors to communicate their critical messages in print, in person, and online using the latest technologies, innovative programs, and the media. Our goal is to reach targeted audiences—scientists, policymakers, environmental advocates, urban planners, the media, and concerned citizens— with information that can be used to create the framework for long-term ecological health and human well-being.

Island Press gratefully acknowledges major support of our work by The Agua Fund, The Andrew W. Mellon Foundation, The Bobolink Foundation, The Curtis and Edith Munson Foundation, Forrest C. and Frances H. Lattner Foundation, The JPB Foundation, The Kresge Foundation, The Oram Foundation, Inc., The Overbrook Foundation, The S.D. Bechtel, Jr. Foundation, The Summit Charitable Foundation, Inc., and many other generous supporters.

The opinions expressed in this book are those of the author(s) and do not necessarily reflect the views of our supporters.

The Past and Future City

The Past and Future City

How Historic Preservation Is Reviving America's Communities

Stephanie Meeks

with Kevin C. Murphy

Washington | Covelo | London

Island Press is a trademark of The Center for Resource Economics.

Library of Congress Control Number: 2016938037

♲ Printed on recycled, acid-free paper

Manufactured in the United States of America
10 9 8 7 6 5 4 3 2 1

Keywords: Affordable housing, community revitalization, gentrification, green building, historic building, historic district, historic neighborhood, historic tax credits, inclusive communities, Jane Jacobs, National Main Street Center, Preservation Green Lab, public space, urban revitalization, walkable community

To Rob, for your inspiration and encouragement

A city is more than a place in space, it is a drama in time.
—Patrick Geddes

Contents

Acknowledgments

Just as historic places are the physical embodiment of countless Americans' stories, the act of writing a book is by no means solely the labor of one or two people. In crafting *The Past and Future City*, I am indebted to many hardworking staff at the National Trust for Historic Preservation and the wider preservation community as well as to other authors, thinkers, readers, friends, and family.

First, let me especially thank my colleague in composing this book, and the speechwriter at the National Trust, Kevin C. Murphy. He has proved invaluable in shaping, researching, revising, and editing the book before you. I also know he would feel remiss if I did not extend his deepest thanks to his patient fiancée, Amy, and dog, Murf.

This book immediately found a home and champion in Island Press, and I want to acknowledge Chuck Savitt, David Miller, and especially our keen and insightful editor, Heather Boyer, for their work in helping this project along.

I also want to recognize all the many dedicated and knowledgeable staff at the National Trust, whose hard work and passionate commitment to saving places inform so many of the stories throughout this book. Special thanks go to Tabitha Almquist, David Brown, Paul Edmondson, Sheri Freemuth, Tom Mayes, Germonique Ulmer, and Hannah White, all of whom contributed their invaluable thoughts and edits to this volume.

In addition, Mary Butler and her design team at the National Trust also went above and beyond what was expected in helping find and secure rights to the photographs, tables, and graphs throughout the book. Mary, Dennis Hockman, and others also helped us brainstorm the title and cover for this project.

This book relies particularly heavily on the groundbreaking empirical research conducted by the Preservation Green Lab, a small subset of the National Trust that carries an outsized impact on its work. With that in mind, I want to thank Jim Lindberg, Margaret O'Neal, Michael Powe, and Jeana Wiser as well as former directors Mark Huppert, Patrice Frey, and Liz Dunn. Jim, Mike, and Patrice also looked over this manuscript and made important suggestions.

I also want to thank the many writers and thinkers, in the preservation and planning communities and beyond, whose works inspired and informed this book. They include Kaid Benfield, Stewart Brand, Alan Ehrenhalt, Anthony Flint, Jan Gehl, Laurance G. Henderson, Sonia Hirt, Myrick Howard, Jane Jacobs, Ned Kaufman, James Howard Kunstler, Tom Mayes, Barbara McCann, Ed McMahon, Charles Montgomery, Max Page, Albert Rains, Donovan Rypkema, Jeff Speck, Carter Wilkie, and Richard Willson.

When I came to the National Trust from The Nature Conservancy in 2010, I knew I had big shoes to fill in replacing Richard Moe, the head of the National Trust for seventeen years. I extend many thanks to him, and also to my three board chairs, Clifford Hudson, Carolyn Brody, and Marita Rivero, as well as to all the members of the National Trust Board, National Trust Council, and advisors who have helped shape my thoughts on preservation over these past few years.

I am eternally in debt to my husband, Rob, for his insights as a real estate professional and planning commissioner, and to my three sons who (mostly) patiently endure our many trips to historic sites and neighborhoods.

Finally, I want to thank the fifteen million and counting preservationists in the United States, who are working each and every day in their communities to save the places that matter. This book—and all the work done at the National Trust—rests on their shoulders.

INTRODUCTION

The Powers of Place

WHAT ARE THE PLACES IN YOUR COMMUNITY that matter to you personally? Stop and picture one for a moment. You might see a park, a church, a school, a favorite restaurant. It might be a place where a significant event in your life happened, like a first date or an engagement. Or it might be a place that just brings you peace and contentment on a regular basis, like a favorite playground, movie theater, or watering hole.

What do such places mean to your life, and what do they say about who you are? How do they connect you to your friends, family, and neighbors? And how would you feel if they were gone?

We all have special places like that. Places that define us and our community. Places that bring people together and relate our history. Sometimes they are grand and beautiful buildings, like a church or local landmark. Just as often—maybe even more often—they are ordinary places that have become imbued with meaning by stories and memories.

Take the example of a simple grocery store and handball court in the East Los Angeles neighborhood of Maravilla, a diverse, primarily Mexican American community with a smattering of Irish, Japanese, German, and Armenian Americans.

At the end of World War II, a young woman named Michi Nishiyama moved there with her husband, Shigeru (or "Tommy" as he was better known), to start a new life after years in Minidoka, a Japanese internment camp in Idaho. The couple rented a grocery store on Mednick Avenue, next to a handball court that had been built by Maravilla residents in the 1920s using bricks from the nearby Davidson Brick Yard. Today, it is the oldest handball court in Greater Los Angeles. The El Centro grocery store—which everyone in the neighborhood knew as "Michi's," since she was always behind the counter—and the attached rooms where the Nishiyamas lived were added in 1946.[1]

Over the next several decades, Michi and Tommy worked to make the handball court a center of the Maravilla community, organizing dances, soap-box derbies, Christmas parties, food drives, and other events. The court was also home to the Maravilla Handball Club as well as the only place in Los Angeles where residents played "bola basca," or Basque Pelota. Although he only had one arm, Tommy was a well-known fixture on the court. And in 1971, the Nishiyamas bought the court and their store, and continued working to keep it the heart of the neighborhood.[2]

As the years went by, Maravilla had some rough edges, including gang activity, and the handball court also came to serve as an unofficial gambling hall. But, thanks to Michi and Tommy, it remained a safe haven for everyone in the community. "You could be shot by a stray bullet outside," said one longtime resident, "but this place was holy ground. It was special. It was treated with respect." "It was a safe place to come from the projects and from the police," recalled Ronnie Villegas, who used to live across Mednick Avenue from the court.[3]

Michi in particular is remembered as an underappreciated saint. "That lady was for me an icon for this community," said Villegas. "Here is a Japanese lady for gave to a community that was not part of her culture. . . . She would often be called upon to mediate in problems among the locals. The store was not making much money, but they kept it open for the sake of the community." Another neighbor recalled, "At the time when I met her, in the late '80s, I was homeless, but Michi would give us credit. She would talk to us, never chase us away." "The community didn't see them as Japanese," said Amanda Perez. "They were part of the neighborhood, part of the community."[4]

When Michi passed away in 2006, followed by her husband a year later, El Centro closed, the handball team dispersed, and the court initially began to fall into disrepair. "I could see the place falling apart," said Perez. "When I pulled over to check it out, it touched my soul. This is the heart of Maravilla, and it looked completely dilapidated." But Perez and other members of the community would not stand for it. They formed the Maravilla Historical Society and began working to save both the court and El Centro, and turn them into a community center. They enlisted a famous handball coach to begin giving classes there and held fund-raisers to draw attention to this neighborhood treasure, including one with demonstrations by local Mixteca Indians of other traditional forms of handball.[5]

Working with the National Trust for Historic Preservation and the Los Angeles Conservancy, the historical society was able to get a California landmark designation for the court and store in August 2012. "This place means a lot to a lot of people," said Virginia Sandoval, who grew up playing on the court and whose father worked at the Davidson Brick Yard. "I cried because those bricks were my father's life, that's how he supported us. And this handball court is part of our culture." "There are many good stories here," said Perez, summing up why places like the Maravilla Handball Court should be saved. "We want to preserve it as a landmark, so our children remember our history."[6]

Saving places like the El Centro and handball court—places that define a community so that future generations can know their past, feel a connection to those who came before, and build a foundation for the future—is the heart of historic preservation. We want these places to stand as beacons for us and for those who come after us. Said another way, historic preservation is about deciding what we want to survive into the next century.

There are many ways to go about it. When churchgoers pass the plate or a school holds a bake sale to raise money for needed renovations, they are doing historic preservation. When an abandoned industrial warehouse is converted into apartments, an events space, or a hip new restaurant or bar, or when an old, downtown commercial corridor sees a renewed influx of stores, shoppers, and new activity, historic preservation is happening there as well. When local activists work together to keep their neighborhoods affordable and sustainable in the face of rising rents and climate change respectively, they, too, are saving places that matter.

We all have places that matter to us—it would be almost impossible not to. In a survey of forty years of scientific literature into "place attachment," psychologist Maria Lewicka concluded that "development of emotional bonds with places is a prerequisite of psychological balance and good adjustment. . . . It helps to overcome identity crises and gives people the sense of stability they need in the everchanging world."[7]

Places, as philosopher Dylan Trigg put it, "define and structure our sense of self. . . . The memories we acquire of the places we inhabit assume a value that is both immeasurable and vital. Without the memory of places, memory itself would no longer have a role to play in our conscious lives."[8]

You don't have to have a PhD to know what they're talking about. "How hard it is to escape from places," author Katherine Mansfield wrote early in the twentieth century. "However carefully one goes they hold you—you leave little bits of yourself fluttering on the fences—like rags and shreds of your very life." Or, as four lads from Li٠ put it, "There are places I'll remember all my life," full o٠ with lovers and friends I still can recall." Places help shape us. They he٠p us understand ourselves, and they connect us to other human beings, even across centuries or millennia.[9]

I have felt that powerful connection myself. When I think of my own special places, I think of the Rialto Theater in my hometown of Loveland, Colorado, where I saw my first-ever movie, *Mary Poppins*. Built in the 1920s and renovated in the 1990s, the Rialto is still going strong as a performing-arts space today. I also think of, quite literally, a hole in the ground. When my father's ancestors came to the United States from Norway in 1869, my great-great-grandparents and their eight children lived in a dugout on the Kansas prairie, literally underground, for twelve years. That dugout in Kansas won't be on the National Register of Historic Places anytime soon. But that place connects me across generations to my ancestors as they made a new start on the Great Plains. It is where my own American story began.

It is these powers of place that draw me to the work of preservation. And it is a remarkable power, one that is fundamental to our well-being and sense of ourselves. It runs through every corner of our culture, from Judy Garland declaring, even in the magical land of Oz, that "There's no place like home!," to Kermit, Miss Piggy, Fozzie, and the gang trying to save their beloved theater in *The Muppets*, to the daily congregants of *Cheers* returning again and again to the bar "where everybody knows your name and are always glad you came." Famous journalist and social critic H. L. Mencken is remembered for being a cynic about just about everything, but on this subject he was unabashed. Writing of his home in Baltimore's Union Square, where he lived almost his entire life, he said: "It is as much a part of me as my two hands. If I had to leave it I'd be as certainly crippled as if I lost a leg."[10]

In 1943, psychologist Abraham Maslow articulated a theory of

human motivation called the hierarchy of needs, which is now usually portrayed in the shape of a pyramid: the most basic needs of men
and women form the base, and more aspirational concerns lay at the
top. After physiological needs like air, food, water, and personal safety,
Maslow argued, the most powerful need felt by us is belonging.

Certain places—especially, I would argue, old places—speak to that
need for belonging in a way that little else can. That is what I feel when
I think of that Kansas dugout where my ancestors made their home. It
is why visiting Colonial Williamsburg helps connect us across the centuries to the Americans of the colonial era, or Stonehenge connects us to
life thousands of years prior, or an old haunt connects us to the people
and memories of our own past—including even ourselves.

These places give us the chance to feel a connection to others. They
also connect us to the broad community of human experience, a community that exists across time. And they help us understand that the lives
we lead are not insignificant—that what we do will have an impact on
the future. "The sense of belonging. That's the feeling that noble, older
buildings give us when we see them on the street," argued Jaime Lerner,
renowned urbanist and former mayor of Curitiba, Brazil. "Another sensation an older building imparts is a contemplation of eternity. As if
someone up there were watching."[11]

That is why losing these places can be so extraordinarily traumatic.
"Being displaced," wrote Trigg, "can have a dramatic consequence on
our experience of who we are, and even leave us with a feeling of being
homeless in the world." Those who have been forced to leave their
homes, English professor Lily Cho has written, are "haunted by histories that sit uncomfortably out of joint. . . . It is to feel a small tingle on
the skin at the back of your neck and know that something is not quite
right about where you are now, but to know also that you cannot leave."
As the Oklahoma families displaced by the Dust Bowl lament in John
Steinbeck's *The Grapes of Wrath*: "How will we know it's us without our
past?"[12]

It is a sadness that refugees know all too well, but no one is immune to it. Fans of the television show *Mad Men* may remember Don Draper, in one of his many successful pitches, dwelling on the meaning of nostalgia—literally, "pain from an old wound"—for Kodak's Carousel slide projector. The Welsh word *hiraeth* and the Portuguese word *saudade*, neither of which have an exact corollary in English, also refer to the sadness over a place and time that no longer exist.[13]

The modern preservation movement in the United States actually has its roots in such trauma. As I'll talk more about in chapter 1, the destruction of landmarks, neighborhoods, and communities to make way for highways, monolithic housing complexes, strip malls, and other perhaps too-ubiquitous features of modern life today galvanized citizens to fight for the places that matter to them.

Places have other remarkable powers as well. It is well documented that our moods, emotions, and even health are dependent on the world around us. Studies have shown, for example, that people in hospitals recuperate more quickly if they have a window onto green space and natural light. Others have shown that people are happier and more social on lively streets than on drab, forlorn ones. "One of the great, but often unmentioned, causes of both happiness and misery," philosopher Alain de Botton argued in *The Architecture of Happiness*, "is the quality of our environment: the kind of walls, chairs, buildings, and streets we're surrounded by."[14]

In fact, this observation goes back to the father of medicine. In *On Airs, Waters, and Places*, composed two and a half millennia ago, Hippocrates argued that the key to ascertaining the health and disposition of a people was by looking into the air, water, soil, and layout of their city. On the other side of the world, Chinese scholars made similar inferences to craft the philosophy of *feng shui*. Although our medical techniques may have become slightly more refined over the years, the enormous impact of our environment on our well-being remains. "Those who create the world we are in," the former head of the Centers for Disease Control and Prevention's environmental health division has argued, "actually have more influence over our health than white coat doctors sitting at the end of the disease pipeline."[15]

All these points beg the question: If the places we live, work, and play help make up our identity, our community, our happiness, and even our health and well-being, shouldn't we work to make sure they're having a positive effect on us? At a time like today, when we are witnessing a profound transformation unfold in the way Americans are choosing to organize their lives, the answer to the question seems especially clear.

The Return of the City

In short, city living is making a roaring comeback. Already, 80 percent of Americans live in cities and urban areas, and that number is increasing. According to the last decennial census, the urban population in the United States grew at a clip of 12 percent between 2000 and 2010, faster than the nation's overall growth rate of 9.7 percent. The following year, urban growth even outpaced suburban growth, for the first time since the invention and mass production of cars. In addition, since 2000, home prices in city centers have outperformed those in suburbs by 50 percent. As a *Time* magazine headline put the new dynamic in April 2014: "The New American Dream Is Living in a City, Not Owning a House in the Suburbs."[16]

It is a particularly remarkable shift for those of us with longer memories. It had long seemed that the United States had embraced suburban living without looking back.

In the decades after World War II, housing developments bloomed in expanding concentric circles from former urban downtowns. Highways, declared a 1955 Disney short, *Magic Highway U.S.A.*, "will be our magic carpet to new hopes, new dreams, and a better way of life for our future." Historic neighborhoods were gutted to make way for these multiplying thoroughfares, so that suburban residents could travel back and forth from faraway homes to work with minimal fuss. "Our national flower," urban planner Lewis Mumford deadpanned of this cultural shift, "is the concrete cloverleaf."[17]

Meanwhile, as the center of commerce and culture for many communities moved to privately owned, often interchangeable shopping malls, downtowns and Main Streets fell into disrepair. "Either America is a shopping center," wrote Russell Baker, "or the one shopping center in existence is moving around the country at the speed of light."[18]

By the 1970s and early 1980s, films like *The Warriors*, *Escape from New York*, *Dirty Harry*, *Death Wish*, and *Taxi Driver* portrayed cities in the popular culture as disastrous cesspools of crime, poverty, homelessness, and urban blight. Meanwhile, the center of virtue, family, community, and the American dream became the suburban development, with its nuclear families living and growing up with a yard, a pool, and a two-car garage. "Suburbia," as historian Kenneth Jackson put it in 1985, "has become the quintessential physical achievement of the United States: it is perhaps more representative of its culture than big cars, tall buildings, or professional football."[19]

But as suburban sprawl continued to proliferate, many Americans began to feel that something critical was being lost in the name of late-twentieth-century convenience—that in building atomized neighborhoods structured around cars rather than people, we were losing so many of the aspects of place that comprised the building blocks of community.

"Many of our newer communities were essentially unplanned or minimally planned to provide the dream house on a large green lot far removed from schools, stores, and other community centers," Richard Moe, my predecessor as president of the National Trust, wrote in 1997. "The public spaces of these new communities more often than not are dominated by huge discount stores and/or strip malls along multilane highways. . . . The result of all of this is rampant sprawl, a phenomenon that has sucked the economic and social vitality out of traditional communities and filled millions of acres of farmland and open space with largely formless, soulless structures unconnected to one another except by their inevitable dependence on the automobile."[20]

Some observers expressed their feelings about the new national landscape even more vehemently. "Eighty percent of everything ever built in America has been built in the last fifty years," wrote James Howard Kunstler in *The Geography of Nowhere* in 1993, "and most of it is depressing, brutal, ugly, unhealthy, and spiritually degrading":

> the jive-plastic commuter tract home wastelands, the Potemkin village shopping plazas with their vast parking lagoons, the Lego-block hotel complexes, the "gourmet mansardic" junk-food joints, the Orwellian office "parks" featuring buildings sheathed in the same reflective glass as the sunglasses worn by chain-gang guards, the particle-board garden apartments rising up in every meadow and cornfield, the freeway loops around every big and little city with their clusters of discount merchandise marts, the whole destructive, wasteful, toxic, agoraphobic-inducing spectacle that politicians proudly call growth.[21]

Others noted that suburbia was, in fact, a tremendously inefficient way to structure a community. As Charles Montgomery outlined in his very worthwhile book *Happy City*, suburbs "take up more space per person, and they are more expensive to build and operate than any urban form ever constructed. They require more roads for every resident, and more water pipes, more sewers—more power cables, utility wiring, sidewalks, signposts, and landscaping. They cost more for municipalities to maintain. They cost more to protect with emergency services. They pollute more and pour more carbon into the atmosphere."[22]

In its complete dependence on the automobile, suburban living also ends up costing families more money—in the form of multiple cars, gasoline, and even health care. One study found that living in a suburb effectively subtracted four years from your life. Another determined that somebody who commutes from an hour away has to earn a full 40 percent more in salary to be as content as someone who lives right by his or her office. "In short," Montgomery noted, suburbia "is the most expensive, resource-intense, land-gobbling, polluting way of living ever built."[23]

Yet whether concerns about suburban living were measured, reflective, statistics driven, or expressed as a howl in the wind, there was still a prevailing sense that the ship had sailed, that the days of cities had passed, and that America's future lay in ever-expanding suburban development. "Nothing can be predicted quite so easily," sociologist Herbert Gans wrote in 1968, "as the continued proliferation of suburbia."[24]

Then a funny thing happened at the turn of the twenty-first century: cities began a remarkable comeback. "The truth is," argued Alan Ehrenhalt in his 2012 book *The Great Inversion and the Future of the American City*, "that we are living at a moment in which the massive outward migration of the affluent that characterized the second half of the twentieth century is coming to an end." This "great inversion"— whereby people with means soured on exurban living and returned to city centers—was not happening, Ehrenhalt wrote, because of "middle-aged commuters changing their minds." Instead, he argued, "it has far more to do with the emergence of new adult cohorts with different values, habits, and living preferences."[25]

The Kids Are Alright

As Ehrenhalt pointed out, the Americans driving this remarkable return to the city are those born between 1980 and 1997: the millennials, the largest and most diverse generation in the nation's history. A report by the Nielsen group found that 62 percent of millennials wanted to live in an urban, mixed-use environment, alongside shops, restaurants, and offices. Carol Coletta, former vice president of the Knight Foundation, has said their research suggests that a full 85 percent of this cohort— representing roughly one-sixth of Americans today—prefer city living to life in the suburbs.[26]

And they have been voting with their feet. The *New York Times* reported in 2014 that the number of college-educated people between the ages of twenty-five and thirty-four living within 3 miles of city centers surged by nearly 40 percent over the previous fifteen years. This isn't just happening in places like New York, San Francisco, and Los Angeles. It is a national phenomenon, boosting cities all over the United States, from Cleveland to Buffalo and Louisville to Pittsburgh. For example, Nashville saw a 37 percent bump in college-educated millennials living downtown between 2007 and 2013. Baltimore experienced a 92 percent increase, St. Louis a whopping 138 percent. Detroit, often considered a poster child for urban decay, saw its millennial population rise by almost 7 percent between 2010 and 2013.[27]

What is fueling this remarkable embrace of cities by young Americans? Experts offer a range of answers, from the impact of the housing crisis and Great Recession downscaling millennials' desire to own a suburban home, to the growth of what is known as the new economy. "The 25- to 34-year-old age group is focused on living near their peers," the National Association of Homebuilders's chief economist has suggested. "They want to be socially engaged and live near work. They want to reduce their automobile use. All of those things aim at high-density, urban-type living."[28]

There's also more to it than that. Time and again, when asked why they moved to the city, people talk about the desire to live somewhere distinctive, to be *some place* rather than *no place*. "Cities are volatile, cities are exciting," one young biotech engineer told the *Christian Science Monitor* about why he moved to Baltimore. "I feel for a while cookie-cutter [living] was a thing. Now people want a lot more authenticity—in what they wear, in what they eat, in where they live."[29]

"There was something about it—I can't even articulate it," another young woman interviewed said of her new home in Charm City, "but every time I was there I just felt this energy. I loved the art scene. I loved the culture. . . . I don't think I had a true sense of place until I moved here." Mencken would agree! "The old charm, in truth, still survives, in

Where the Population of College Graduates Is Growing

As metropolitan areas vie for these residents, some are attracting them at a higher rate than the national average. The rate over the last dozen years does not necessarily reflect the current percentage. For example, Denver's percentage in this age group is 7.5, higher than Houston's and more than the national average of 5.2 percent, but lower than that of Washington, the Bay Area and Boston.

Percent change in the number of college graduates aged 25 to 34, from 2000 to 2012

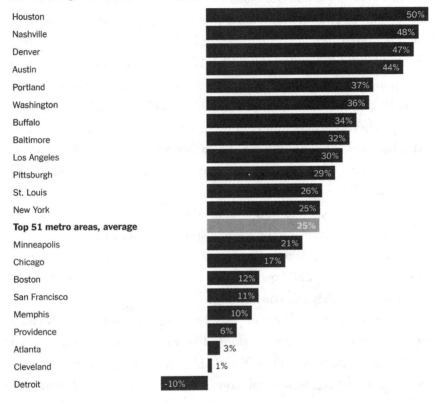

Houston	50%
Nashville	48%
Denver	47%
Austin	44%
Portland	37%
Washington	36%
Buffalo	34%
Baltimore	32%
Los Angeles	30%
Pittsburgh	29%
St. Louis	26%
New York	25%
Top 51 metro areas, average	25%
Minneapolis	21%
Chicago	17%
Boston	12%
San Francisco	11%
Memphis	10%
Providence	6%
Atlanta	3%
Cleveland	1%
Detroit	-10%

Source: Joe Cortright, City Observatory

The number of college-educated Americans between age twenty-five and thirty-four living in central cities has surged. (Data source: City Observatory; Graph from *The New York Times,* Oct. 20, 2014 © 2014 *The New York Times.* All rights reserved. Used by permission and protected by the Copyright Laws of the United States. The printing, copying, redistribution, or retransmission of this content without express written permission is prohibited.)

this town," he once wrote of his home city, "despite the frantic efforts of boosters and boomers who, in late years, have replaced all its ancient cobblestones with asphalt."[30]

Bernice Radle, a young preservationist who rehabs houses in Buffalo, has also seen her home become a thriving destination city for millennials. "The new American Dream is not owning a $200,000 house or owning a very expensive car," she said, "but owning something that matters to you." Secretary Richard Hall of the Maryland Department of Planning concurs. Today's generation has "seen the peak of suburban sprawl—they want something different," he told the *Monitor*. "They see their parents spending a lot of time driving for everything—for work, for education. They see a different path where they are able to more readily take control of their communities, and take an active role in the community."[31]

"Unlike their parents, who calculated their worth in terms of square feet, ultimately inventing the McMansion," another urban design professor wrote to *Time*, "this generation is more interested in the amenities of city itself: great public spaces, walkability, diverse people, and activities with which they can participate."[32]

Press reports abound of companies moving back into cities because their younger employees want things like windows that open, exposed brick, and walkable communities that no longer require an automobile to go anywhere. Millennials continually use words like "charm" and "authenticity" to describe the kinds of neighborhoods where they want to live and work. In short, Americans today want their homes and workplaces to be unique and distinctive—exactly the kind of distinctiveness, character, and sense of place that older buildings provide.

Happiness Is a Historic Building

What does "Happiness is a historic building" mean, exactly? Well, let's go back to our original thought exercise. What's the first thing that pops into your mind when you think of New York City?

Of course, different people will come up with different answers. Some born-and-bred New Yorkers may think of their favorite corner or coffee shop. Others, who know the city primarily from television and movies, may hear the distinctive opening of the *Friends*, *Seinfeld*, or *Law and Order* themes. But I bet many first thought of the Empire State Building, or the Statue of Liberty, or the bustle of Times Square, Fifth Avenue, or Grand Central Station.

Now, picture Washington, D.C. What do you see? Is it the White House, the Capitol, or the National Mall?

What about San Francisco? Did the Golden Gate Bridge pop into mind?

Here's an easy one: Paris, France. If you've been there, maybe you thought of the wide boulevards, the cafés, the banks of the Seine. But even if you haven't, the Eiffel Tower and the Arc de Triomphe have, in many ways, become our cultural shorthand for the City of Light, just as Big Ben represents London and the Colosseum is Rome.

You can do this same exercise with any city, all over the world. Cincinnati proudly features the Union Terminal, the template for the *Superfriends'* iconic Hall of Justice. Cleveland has the Terminal Tower and Seattle the Space Needle. Kansas City has the Liberty Memorial, and Philadelphia has the Liberty Bell.

Often these distinguishing urban landmarks are exciting neighborhoods. Miami boasts its Art Deco district, New Orleans the French Quarter. Sometimes, as in the case of Baltimore's historic row houses, the most distinguishing feature is the urban fabric itself. These landmarks and neighborhoods give our cities their distinctive character—they help make them feel like *someplace* rather than *anyplace*—and that distinctiveness helps fuel this welcome resurgence that cities are experiencing.

In 2014, the architectural firm Sasaki Associates conducted a 1,000-person survey in six cities—Austin, Boston, Chicago, New York, San Francisco, and Washington, D.C.—to determine exactly what residents loved about their respective homes. One of the surprising answers they discovered was historic buildings. According to Sasaki's survey, nearly two-thirds (57%) of city residents said they liked to stop and admire historic buildings while walking around, far more than those who said the same of modern buildings (19%) or skyscrapers (15%).[33]

When asked how architects could best improve the city's character, the most popular answer by far (54%) was working to renovate "existing historic buildings to retain character while making them more useable." Thirty-three percent said they loved their city as it is, and 30 percent said they wanted to see more pop-ups and community events. By contrast, only 17 percent—fewer than one in five—"felt their city was too quaint and would like to see more skyscrapers and iconic buildings." And—no doubt much to the consternation of many architects!—when asked what made a particular structure iconic, the top answer given (36%) was the building's history. Unique design came in third, at 24 percent.[34]

These findings accord with other studies on this subject. In her master's thesis on people's preferences for old places, Sandra Shannon found that 75 percent of respondents rated the appearance of older buildings higher than new buildings. (In addition, 88% of those Shannon surveyed thought historic places should be treated as community assets, and 83% thought historic preservation was extremely important and one of the top three services that communities can provide, along with economic development and public landscaping.) A 2007 Gallup poll on happiness and urban living, meanwhile, found the strongest positive correlation between happiness and those who felt they lived in a beautiful place.[35]

"A question I asked everyone while working on this book," author Stewart Brand wrote in *How Buildings Learn* in 1994, "was 'What makes a building come to be loved?' A thirteen-year-old boy in Maine had the most succinct answer. 'Age.' . . . The older a building gets, the more we have respect and affection for its evident maturity, for the accumulated

A street festival along the historic H Street corridor of Washington, D.C. (Photo by Ted Eytan)

human investment it shows, for the attractive patina it wears—muted brick, worn stairs, colorfully stained roof, lush vines." In fact, Brand noted, people like old buildings so much that new construction is often designed to look the part. "The widespread fakery makes us respect honest aging all the more."[36]

It's not just Americans who feel this way. Every year, the British conservation group Heritage Counts conducts a study to quantify the impact of old places on health, happiness, and well-being. In their 2014 study, they concluded that the positive benefit was equivalent to "£1646 per person per year for the average heritage goer," more than taking part in sports or viewing works of art.[37]

Even architects—whose livelihood often depends on constructing new buildings—feel this way. In 2011, the Melbourne newspaper *The Age* conducted a survey of 140 architects to determine the city's best and ugliest buildings; all ten of the ugliest were built after 1990, and five of them were built after 2000. As Brand observes, "Something strange happens when a building ages past a human generation or two. *Any* building older than 100 years will be considered beautiful, no matter what." Indeed, one of the ironies of historic preservation today is that communities are now fighting to save the same idiosyncratic modernist and brutalist buildings of the 1950s and 1960s that were once considered by many to be futuristic eyesores.[38]

In short, people love old buildings. They love their character, their history, and the sense of connection they provide—put simply, that power of place. "Place is more than a spot on the map," urban scholar Ed McMahon has said. "Place is what makes your hometown different from my hometown. . . . In the Old Economy, markets mattered. In the New Economy, place matters most. . . . In a world where capital is footloose, if you can't differentiate [your city] from any other place, you will have no competitive advantage. The same is true of a project or a community or a building."[39]

Statistics support McMahon's contention: Two-thirds of college-educated millennials say they pick the city they want to live in first and then look for a job. That is why, to take just one of countless examples, Columbus, Ohio, embarked on an ad campaign in 2014 to attract millennials away from cities such as Chicago and Washington, D.C.[40]

Old and historic places also bring tourists to cities. "Tourism is the biggest industry in the world," noted McMahon. "It is the first, second, or third largest industry in every single American state." And the biggest tourist draw in many states, he pointed out, is a historic neighborhood. For example, the French Quarter and Seattle's Pike Place Market are the number one tourist destinations in Louisiana and Washington, respectively. In Florida, Miami's Art Deco district lags only behind Disney World.[41]

As John Kenneth Galbraith once put it, "The great attraction of all travel is to see things that deliberately, by accident or by the continuity of institutions[,] . . . have been saved for the present generation. [Travelers] seek things that have been conserved deliberately in continuity with the past." Or as travel guide Arthur Frommer argued, citing numerous studies, "an interest in the achievements of the past" is one of the three main reasons people travel—along with R&R and to take in natural beauty. "Among cities with no particular recreational appeal," he wrote in 1988, "those that have substantially preserved their past continue to enjoy tourism. Those that haven't receive no tourism at all. It's as simple as that. Tourism does not go to a city that has lost its soul."[42]

Frommer's statement makes basic, intuitive sense. Travelers on a great American road trip do not stop at every fast-food restaurant or gas station along the way, nor do they take pictures of billboard after billboard. They stop to see places that are remarkable and different for some reason, like the venerable Wall Drug in South Dakota or the World's Largest Ball of Twine in Kansas. Most often, they make pilgrimages to places with some historic meaning, whether it's the birthplace of Abraham Lincoln in Kentucky, the final resting place of Dr. Martin Luther King Jr. in Georgia, or the Surf Ballroom in Clear Lake, Iowa, where Buddy Holly, Richie Valens, and the Big Bopper played their final show. "Tourism is about visiting places that are different, unusual, or unique," argued McMahon. "If every place was just like every place else there'd be no reason to go anyplace."[43]

The Promise of Preservation

That is why, for decades now, Americans have been working to save the places that enrich our environment and tell our story. Indeed, just as cities are experiencing a renaissance, so too has the field of historic preservation. Our research at the National Trust shows that 65 million Americans, led once again by the young and diverse millennial generation, believe that saving historic places is fundamentally important. Nearly a fourth of those—15 million—are already taking action in their communities to protect and preserve places that matter, even if they do not think of their advocacy as preservation.[44]

Why wouldn't they think of their work saving places as preservation? Well, it's safe to say that, in many circles, historic preservation has had a bit of a reputation problem. In popular culture, plenty of movies depict saving places as a positive good, among them *Who Framed Roger Rabbit* (where Toontown is threatened by a freeway project) and *Back to the Future* (where the Hill Valley Preservation Society's attempts to "Save the Clock Tower" are the reason Marty McFly can get home from 1955). More broadly, everyone from Captain America and *The Avengers* to Arthur Dent and the denizens of *The Hitchhiker's Guide to the Galaxy* have tried to save Earth—the ultimate place worth saving!—from scheduled demolition by various evil forces.[45]

Preservationists themselves are nonetheless often viewed as stuck in the past, unwilling to change—an archaic movement fond of doilies, plaques, and velvet ropes. To take a recent example, the long-running sitcom *How I Met Your Mother* featured for a season a preservationist, Zoey, as one of Ted Mosby's potential "mothers"-to-be. In a subplot focusing on the possible demolition of a historic hotel to make way for a skyscraper, both she and the Landmarks Commission are portrayed as fickle at best, crazy at worst. (Ultimately, the hotel is scrapped because, after Ted and the gang manage to steal a lion's head stonework from its front, it is suddenly deemed no longer historic.)[46]

It's not just pop culture. "The historic preservation community seems to be living in its own echo chamber," wrote one journalist in 2008. "To the rest of us it looks like preservationists want to preserve for preservation's sake, rather than for any larger community good." This view is also captured in a joke by historian David Lowenthal: "How many preservationists does it take to change a light bulb? Four—one to insert the bulb, one to document the event, and two to lament the passing of the old bulb."[47]

Sometimes, this stereotype of the typical preservationist takes on even uglier resonances. Preservationists, wrote one urban design blogger in 2007, are "busybodies, mostly. . . . It really is the urge to tell the neighbors how tall their grass should be, or what color to paint the windows."[48]

This unfortunate perception of preservationists as the "paint police" is partly because the first thing that comes to mind when many Americans think of our field is their local architectural or historic preservation review board. And although the members of these boards have the best of intentions, their interventions often have conspired to give preservation a bad reputation. As Catherine Buell, former chair of Washington, D.C.'s Historic Preservation Review Board, put it, speaking of how that board's work is viewed, "longtime preservationists are getting really uncomfortable with how unpopular they've become, and they haven't gotten traction with more and more audiences that are important."[49]

Review boards are a very small part of what encompasses our field, however, and this notion that the primary focus of preservation is telling people they can't have a back deck on their historic home is a cliché that is long past its sell date. Nor is preservation simply about preventing change from happening to old buildings and beloved places. These stereotypes simply do not reflect the ways in which preservation has grown and evolved over the years.

Rather, preservation is about managing change and helping ensure a smooth continuum between past, present, and future. It is about working to find new uses for the old buildings in our midst, so that generations to come can experience the special places that move us and tell our story.

Preservation is about ensuring that our urban landscape reflects more than just profit margins or the whims of developers and real estate speculators—that they address the real needs and concerns of communities. It is about working to see that we honor and reflect the full contours of our past, including the complex and difficult chapters. It is about unleashing the enormous potential of historic buildings to address the critical problems we face, bring us together, and make us happy.

Happiness may seem like too abstract a concept to build a city around. But, in fact, there is a growing movement all over the world to reorganize the way we live so as to maximize contentment and community. "Cities must be regarded as more than engines of wealth," Charles Montgomery wrote in *Happy City*. "They must be viewed as systems that should be shaped to improve well-being."[50]

To accomplish this goal, he put forward the following checklist:

- The city should strive to maximize joy and minimize hardship.
- It should lead us toward health rather than sickness.
- It should offer us real freedom to live, move, and build our lives as we wish.
- It should build resilience against economic or environmental shocks.
- It should be fair in the way it apportions space, services, mobility, joys, hardships, and costs.
- Most of all, it should enable us to build and strengthen the bonds between friends, families, and strangers that give life meaning, bonds that represent the city's greatest achievement and opportunity.
- The city that acknowledges and celebrates our common fate, that opens doors to empathy and cooperation, will help us tackle the great challenges of this century.[51]

Montgomery's book is a valuable overview of how our urban environments are being reshaped in the twenty-first century to achieve these priorities. Another such work is city planner Jeff Speck's *Walkable City: How Downtown Can Save America, One Step at a Time*. "As growing numbers of Americans opt for more urban lifestyles," Speck wrote, "they are often met with city centers that don't welcome their return." As such, he offers a number of worthwhile fixes to make "downtown living attractive to a broader range of people" and "transform a city and the lives of its residents."[52]

Both of these invaluable works describe how our cities are being transformed today, and the ways they must continue to change to achieve further health, happiness, and sustainable growth. But they also mostly overlook one critical component guiding and accelerating this urban renaissance: the power and potential of older buildings.

In all the ways described above and many more, historic buildings and the preservation movement are helping make our cities more desirable, and urban residents happier and healthier.

Historic buildings can spur economic growth, nurture start-up businesses, and create jobs. They can reduce energy costs and environmental impact and can encourage healthy living practices like walking and cycling. They help provide solutions to critical challenges like access, affordability, displacement, and climate change. They help turn diverse neighborhoods into communities and help us know who we are, where we come from, and where we must continue to go to achieve the full promise of the American dream. They are building the foundation of America's future and keeping our communities vibrant and strong.

The pages that follow provide a sense of the many ways these changes are already taking place all over the country, and what we can all do to see that the urban America of tomorrow is made up of happy, walkable, equitable, sustainable, thriving, and yes, historic cities. Along the way, I will talk about the many ways historic preservation is revitalizing communities by encouraging economic growth, bringing families and neighborhoods together, improving our health and well-being, making our cities more livable, and helping us better understand ourselves.

Chapter 1 begins by looking at why and how much of our current urban landscape came to take the shape it did, and how the contemporary preservation movement emerged as a creative response to these sometimes traumatic transformations. Chapter 2 provides a short overview of recent and innovative empirical research conducted by the National Trust's Preservation Green Lab into how, exactly, older historic fabric benefits our neighborhoods.

Building on this continuing research and the work of other scholars and urbanists, chapter 3 offers ten steps that city residents—be they municipal officials, developers, community advocates, or ordinary citizens—can take to unleash the potential of historic buildings in their cities and neighborhoods. Chapter 4 examines in further detail how creative adaptive reuse projects—the heart and soul of contemporary preservation—are enhancing cities all across the United States.

In chapter 5, I take a look at how preservation has evolved to reflect and encompass a more diverse American story, and why it is so important for our future that we come to terms with the entirety of our past. Chapter 6 delves more deeply into some of the complicated issues that have attended today's urban renaissance—namely, affordability, inequality, gentrification, and the displacement of existing residents—and assesses how preservation and other tools can help mitigate these trends. Finally, chapter 7 explores how the preservation and reuse of existing historic fabric can help address two of the biggest challenges before our cities and our future: environmental sustainability and the accelerating threat of climate change.

Growth, diversity, equity, sustainability—preservation can positively influence all these virtues when applied to our towns and cities. The best part is that, all across the United States, the buildings that will drive these changes are already there. All we need to do to transform our lives for the better is unlock their amazing potential.

As you will see in the ensuing chapters, that's something that preservation has been working on for decades now. Today, we are better at it than ever before, with new tools, research, technology, partnerships, and priorities guiding our work.

First, though, we need to debunk the misguided belief that older buildings are problems that should be demolished rather than tremendous opportunities for growth. To help make that case, let's return to the middle of the twentieth century and the work of a pioneering urban activist, one who knew a thing or two about the death and life of great American cities.

CHAPTER 1

Downtown Is for People: Competing Visions of the Ideal American City

Cities have the capability of providing something for everybody, only because, and only when, they are created by everybody.
—Jane Jacobs[1]

AMERICA'S WELCOME URBAN REVIVAL invites important questions: What makes a city successful? Why does one neighborhood thrive and another fail? What are the key urban ingredients for prosperity and happiness?

In 1961, one theory was offered by a remarkable writer and observer who celebrated her centenary in 2016: Jane Jacobs. At the height of an "urban renewal" movement that demolished many richly textured historic neighborhoods in the name of progress, she argued that, in fact, older buildings provide critical and necessary space for entrepreneurs, small businesses, and a diversity of residents to thrive. Their destruction meant that neighborhoods were being drained of economic opportunity, culture, and life. As she wrote, "Cities need old buildings so badly, it is probably impossible for vigorous streets and districts to grow without them."[2]

We may take historic neighborhoods for granted now. But, as author Anthony Flint has pointed out, this declaration was as revolutionary in its own way as 1960s treatises like Betty Friedan's *The Feminine Mystique*, Rachel Carson's *Silent Spring*, and Ralph Nader's *Unsafe at Any Speed*. Jane Jacobs's contention stood against not just the entire direction cities were moving at the time, but against the deeply held philosophy and well-funded ambitions of the era's master builders, most notably the shaper of modern New York, Robert Moses.[3]

Before we talk about the important implications of Jacobs's arguments for cities today, we should look back at how her views challenged the established orthodoxies of the time. Doing so reveals much about how our cities were shaped in the twentieth century, how historic preservation rose up in response, and what we should try to accomplish going forward.

Building "The Radiant City"

Suffice it to say, urban planners before Jane Jacobs felt rather differently about the old buildings in their midst. "Our world, like a charnel-house, is strewn with the detritus of dead epochs," observed the enormously influential architect Charles-Édouard Jeanneret Gris, better known by his adopted moniker, Le Corbusier. "The great task incumbent on us is . . . clearing away from our cities the dead bones that putrefy in them."[4]

Le Corbusier instead envisioned a "Radiant City" made up of gleaming skyscrapers, surrounded by vast lawns, connected by elevated superhighways, and organized along a grid. Because "it is essential that motors can travel as directly as possible," he argued, all curved roads would be banished, and all paths would be made straight. As for older buildings, they would all obviously have to go—they were "not worthy of the age; they are no longer worthy of us." In 1925, at a design exposition in Paris, Le Corbusier even proposed tearing out the city's entire Marais

District and converting it into a real-life prototype of his ideal metropolis. (His countrymen, while intrigued by his ideas, said no thanks.)[5]

In the end, Le Corbusier only ever built one building in the United States, the Carpenter Center at Harvard University, but his grand ambitions inspired generations of city planners in the United States. The "Radiant City scheme became the only model for urban redevelopment in America," wrote James Howard Kunstler in *The Geography of Nowhere*. "From the late forties through the eighties, thousands of [projects] in the Radiant City mold went up all over America: housing, office complexes, hospitals, colleges. The defects of the concept quickly became apparent—for instance, that the space between high rises floating in a superblock became instant wastelands, shunned by the public—but this hardly stopped anyone from building them."[6]

If Le Corbusier was the thinker who most helped shape the modern urban environment, Robert Moses was the one who best translated his ideas into action.

Robert Moses's plan for New York's future—with its enormous housing projects, vast green spaces, and cross-cutting highways—accorded very closely with the vision of the Radiant City. Over the course of decades—primarily as the head of his own municipal fiefdom, the Triborough Bridge and Tunnel Authority—Moses built 637 miles of highways, 658 playgrounds, 17 miles of beach, thirteen bridges, two tunnels, and state and city parks in and around the city, doubling the city's green space. Like Le Corbusier, Moses believed that, in our "motorized civilization," "cities are created by and for traffic." So in 1945, he proposed more miles of superhighway in and around New York than existed at that time in all the other cities of the world combined. "What will people see in the year 1999?" he once declared. "The long arteries of travel will stand out."[7]

To make this vision real, the existing fabric of New York often paid a heavy price. Moses demolished eighteen city blocks on the Upper West

Side to make way for his Lincoln Center for the Performing Arts (after which, he argued, "the scythe of progress must move northward"). His Cross-Bronx Expressway, built over fifteen years at a cost of $128 million, in Flint's words, "broke up thriving and diverse immigrant enclaves and jump-started the economic and social decline of the Bronx." In total, to forge a more Radiant New York City, Moses is estimated to have displaced 250,000 people from their existing homes.[8]

One can argue, as Moses did, that you cannot make an omelet or remake a city "without breaking eggs." Indeed, Moses is responsible for many New York landmarks that are now woven into the fabric of the city and considered historic in their own right, such as the United Nations, the World's Fair Pavilion, and the Central Park Zoo. He was also a stalwart defender of urban living at a time when suburbia was in full flower.[9]

Even Moses's allies, however, concede that "if it came to a project or people, he'd take the project." And even as more voices raised the alarm about how he was transforming the city, Moses continued pushing New York—and the many other cities inspired by him—ever closer to Le Corbusier's vision. In his desire to remake the modern metropolis, Moses was an unstoppable force. But there was also an immovable object, and she happened to live on 555 West Hudson Street in Greenwich Village, right in the path of Moses's grand designs.[10]

Queen Jane

A writer and journalist by trade, Jane Jacobs had no formal schooling in urban planning or architecture. She was brilliant, iconoclastic, and, most important, possessed the laudable ability to see the world as it is, not as theory or conventional wisdom said it should be. Even before Moses's ambitions threatened her home, she began to wonder if urban planning had not gotten lost somewhere in its own designs.[11]

Given an assignment to write about urban renewal in Philadelphia in 1954, Jacobs met with the executive director of the city's Planning Commission, Edmund Bacon. Along with Edward Logue, who occupied a similar role in Boston, Bacon was another of the era's master builders and is still hailed today as the Father of Modern Philadelphia. (For those who enjoy the "Kevin Bacon game," he's also the father of the famous actor.)[12]

Unlike Le Corbusier's "all skyscrapers and no history" aesthetic, Bacon worked to maintain the historic character of neighborhoods like Society Hill and fought to ensure that no building rise taller than the William Penn statue atop City Hall, in the heart of Philadelphia. (He lost that fight in 1987, inaugurating a curse that haunted Philly sports fans for two decades.) Otherwise, he shaped the City of Brotherly Love in much the same way as Moses changed New York City. Often through liberal bulldozing of the existing fabric, Bacon helped forge places like Independence Mall, JFK Plaza, Market East, and Penn Center, and he was the driving force behind the three major highways bisecting the city today: the Schyulkill, Vine Street, and Delaware Expressways. A fourth—the Crosstown Expressway—was envisioned but ultimately never built.[13]

At the time of their meeting in 1954, Jacobs was a great admirer of Bacon and generally thought positively about "urban renewal." As they toured Philadelphia together, however, she quickly noticed a fly in the ointment. "First, he took me to a street where loads of people were hanging around on the street, on the stoops, having a good time of it," she wrote later, "and he said, well, this is the next street we're going to get rid of. That was the 'before' street. Then he showed me the 'after' street, all fixed up, and there was just one person on it, a bored little boy kicking a tire in the gutter. It was so grim that I would have been kicking a tire too. But Mr. Bacon thought it had a beautiful vista."[14]

When Jacobs asked the planner where all the people had gone, Bacon responded, in very Le Corbusier terms, about the need for an underlying order and clear sight lines in a modern city. The buzzing of people going about their daily business on the street left him cold. To Bacon, it was a bug that needed fixing. To Jacobs, it was the whole point.[15]

In a 1958 article for *Fortune* focused on the American city, "Downtown Is for People," Jacobs began to articulate, for the first time in writing, her comprehensive critique of "master builders" like Moses and Bacon. First, she explained, it did not do just to plan out a Utopia on paper. Any planner worth his or her salt should begin by leaving the office and touring the city on foot. "He should insist on an hour's walk in the loveliest park, the finest public square in town, and where there is a handy bench he should sit and watch the people for a while." In this manner—through "an observant eye, curiosity about people," and humility rather than hubris—a builder "will understand his own city the better—and, perhaps, steal a few ideas." He or she will also find "that many of the assumptions on which the projects depend are visibly wrong."[16]

Foremost among them was the idea that older buildings were bad. "One of the beauties of the Fort Worth plan," Jacobs wrote, citing a city she thought was doing renewal right, "is that it works with existing buildings. . . . This is a positive virtue, not just a cost-saving expedient. Think of any city street that people enjoy and you will see that it characteristically has old buildings mixed with the new." These old buildings, she argued (a point she'd later develop further), provided affordable space for both new enterprises and low-overhead, socially minded concerns. By contrast, she wrote, "notice that when a new building goes up, the kind of ground-floor tenants it gets are usually the chain store and the chain restaurant."[17]

Older buildings were important for more than just economics: they gave streets and neighborhoods character. "A sense of place is built up, in the end, from many little things too, some so small people take them for granted, and yet the lack of them takes the flavor out of the city; irregularities in level, so often bulldozed away; different kinds of paving, signs and fireplugs and street lights, white marble stoops." As it was, however, urban planning was proceeding in a completely wrongheaded fashion. "Great tracts, many blocks wide, are being razed" in city after city, all with "no hint of individuality or whim or surprise, no hint that here is a city with a tradition and flavor all its own." What will be built in their place "will be spacious, parklike, and uncrowded. They will feature long green vistas. They will be stable and symmetrical and orderly. They will be clean and impressive and monumental. They will have all the attributes of a well-kept, dignified cemetery." Such projects "will not revitalize downtown; they will deaden it," Jacobs concluded. "For they work at cross-purposes to the city. They banish the street. They banish its function. They banish its variety."[18]

If Jacobs's *Fortune* piece wasn't already incendiary enough to those in planning circles, she also disparaged a number of grand projects by name, among them Robert Moses's Lincoln Center. "This cultural superblock is intended to be very grand," she wrote, "but its streets will be able to give it no support whatsoever." "My God, who was this crazy dame?" exclaimed the publisher of *Fortune* upon reading the piece. "Of all things to attack, how could we give aid and comfort to critics of Lincoln Center?"[19]

In fact, the disagreement between Robert Moses and Jane Jacobs was already well on its way to a full-fledged feud by then, moving beyond magazine think pieces and into the streets. In the 1950s, Moses made a renewed push to extend bustling Fifth Avenue right through Washington Square Park, the heart of Greenwich Village and not far from Jacobs's home on Hudson Street. Once the stomping grounds of Edith Wharton and Henry James, the park was in Jacobs's day a hangout for beatniks and small children alike, and already fast becoming the center of the '60s folk revival. Now, Moses wanted to make it yet another forlorn stretch of four-lane highway—his "temple to urination," as Jacobs's husband quipped.[20]

The opposition to Moses's plan (and to his subsequent compromise to run the road under the park instead) was already established before Jacobs got involved. With her background in public relations and incisive ability to read a situation, however, her hard work against what she called a "monstrous and useless folly" helped propel the neighborhood movement to new heights. Jacobs brought on local celebrities like Eleanor Roosevelt, Margaret Mead, and her editor William Whyte. She enlisted up-and-coming New York politicos like John Lindsay and Ed Koch. She put local kids (including her own) at the forefront of the backlash, as petitioners, pamphleteers, and photo opportunities for the newspapers. She also studied up on her new nemesis and helped journalists connect the dots between Moses's plans for the city and the wealthy developers and other financial interests who stood to gain from them.[21]

These efforts paid dividends. "The American city is the battleground for the preservation of diversity," exclaimed Columbia professor Charles Abrams, "and Greenwich Village should be its Bunker Hill." "Washington Square . . . has a claim to our historic respect," wrote Lewis Mumford in his own letter, "a respect that Mr. Moses seems chronically unable to accord any human handiwork except his own." The local paper of record, the *Village Voice*, opined that "any serious tampering with Washington Square Park will mark the beginning of the end of Greenwich Village as a community" and make it just "another characterless place." When these respected voices helped change the minds of powerful city officials, Moses stood down. "There is nobody against this," he grumbled in retreat. "Nobody but a bunch of mothers."[22]

It would not be the duo's last heavyweight bout. In February 1961—in what might well have been one of Moses's political retributions—Jacobs opened the *New York Times* to discover that fourteen blocks in the West Village—her exact neighborhood—was "blighted" and had been slated for "urban renewal." Once more she took the reins of a neighborhood organization and worked to defeat the proposed overhaul of her home, taking the fight all the way to the New York Supreme Court.[23]

Jane Jacobs, chairwoman of the Committee to Save the West Village, at a press conference at Lions Head Restaurant at Hudson and Charles Streets, December 5, 1961. (*World Telegram* and *Sun* photo by Phil Stanziola; Library of Congress Prints and Photographs Division LC-USZ-62-137838)

Not long after, she was enlisted by desperate Little Italy residents to help them defeat Moses's proposed Lower Manhattan Expressway, or "Lomex." Proposed to run along Broome Street—once a thriving nineteenth-century commercial district and site of many historic and beautiful cast-iron buildings—this particular superhighway would have carved through SoHo, Chinatown, the Lower East Side, and Little Italy and would have resulted in 416 buildings demolished, 365 stores closed, and 2,200 families displaced. During this fight, Jacobs ended up getting arrested and charged with "inciting a riot and criminal mischief." In part because of these obviously overblown charges against a now public figure, Jacobs and her allies defeated Moses a third time. The buildings saved as a result are today some of the most desirable in Manhattan.[24]

Death and Life

Jacobs's most enduring victory over Moses and his ilk was *The Death and Life of Great American Cities*, since described by the *New York Times* as "perhaps the most influential single work in the history of town planning." "What I would like to do is create for the reader another image of the city," she said before embarking on the 1961 book, "not drawn from mine or anyone else's imagination or wishes but so far as this is possible, from real life." To do that, she first had to smash the reigning false idols. "To put it bluntly," Jacobs began, the city planners of her time "are all in the same stage of elaborately learned superstition as medical science was early in the last century, when physicians put their faith in blood-letting. . . . Years of learning and a plethora of subtle and complicated dogma have arisen on a foundation of nonsense."[25]

What was the fatal flaw in all their grand designs? Planners fundamentally didn't understand people. "They operate on the premise that city people seek the sight of emptiness, obvious order, and quiet. Nothing could be less true. People's love of watching activity and other people is constantly evident in cities everywhere." As such, planners were only succeeding in creating a "Great Blight of Dullness." It was more than just an aesthetic problem. Although "dull, inert cities . . . contain the seeds of their own destruction and little else[,] . . . lively, diverse, intense cities contain the seeds of their own regeneration, with energy enough to carry over for problems and needs outside themselves."[26]

In trying to understand what makes good neighborhoods work, Jacobs followed her own advice. She walked around America's cities, hoping to figure out why Boston's North End flourished while the Pruitt-Igoe towers in St. Louis—another public housing complex in the Corbusier mold—was a disaster from the start. Most of all, she watched the rhythm of West Village life unfold from her window on 555 Hudson Street, attempting to uncover the "complex order" beneath "the seeming disorder of the old city," an order "composed of movement and change . . . the ballet of the good city sidewalk."[27]

After countless acts of this ballet, Jacobs formulated her diagnosis. The primary characteristics of a healthy urban environment, she argued, were "lively, well-used streets and other public spaces" where people felt safe, secure, and engaged. "In cities, liveliness and variety attract more liveliness; deadness and monotony repel life." Jacobs then posited four essential conditions of lively streets: mixed use (to ensure foot traffic at all hours of the day), short city blocks (to encourage walking), a high density of people, and "buildings that vary in age and condition, including a good proportion of old ones." All four conditions "in combination are necessary to generate city diversity," she explained, and "the absence of any one of the four frustrates a district's potential."[28]

On behalf of older buildings, Jacobs put forward several arguments. First, their lower overhead spurs the diversity of uses so necessary to lively streets. "Chain stores, chain restaurants, and banks go into new construction," she wrote. "But neighborhood bars, foreign restaurants, and pawn shops go into older buildings. . . . Hundreds of ordinary enterprises, necessary to the safety and public life of streets and neighborhoods, and appreciated for their convenience and personal quality, can make out successfully in old buildings, but are inexorably slain by the high overhead of new construction."[29]

Because they were relatively inexpensive, older buildings also contributed to the vibrancy of cities by being incubators of innovation. "Old ideas can sometimes use new buildings," she observed. "New ideas must use old buildings" because when it came to "really new ideas of any kind—no matter how ultimately profitable or otherwise successful some of them might prove to be—there is no leeway for such chancy trial, error, and experimentation in the high-overhead economy of new construction."[30]

Older buildings—built at different times with different materials for different purposes—also contribute to urban vitality through their idiosyncratic nature. "Large swatches of construction built at one time are inherently inefficient for sheltering wide ranges of cultural, population, and business diversity," she warned. Citing her home of Greenwich Village, she contended that "there is no place for the likes of us in new construction. . . . The last thing we need is new construction. What we need, and a lot of others need, is old construction in a lively district, which some among us can help make livelier."[31]

Finally, older buildings help give places a distinctiveness that attracts people's interest. "Landmarks," for example, "emphasize (and also dignify) the diversity of cities; they do this by calling attention to the fact that they are different from their neighbors, and important because they are different," Jacobs wrote. This sense of character was threatened by the massive incursion of highways. "Automobiles are hardly inherent destroyers of cities," said Jacobs, especially because they were quieter and cleaner than the horse-drawn carriages of earlier times, but "we went awry by replacing, in effect, each horse on the crowded city streets with a half a dozen or so mechanized vehicles, instead of using each mechanized vehicle to replace half a dozen or so horses." As it was, "the Great Blight of Dullness is allied with the blight of traffic congestion." In addition, because the city was now being transformed to prioritize the needs of cars over people, "city character [is] blurred until every place becomes more like every other place, all adding up to Noplace."[32]

In all these ways, Jacobs argued, older buildings help neighborhoods grow, prosper, and persevere. If they are all demolished, the ensuing neighborhood "shows a strange inability to update itself, enliven itself, repair itself, or to be sought after, out of choice by a new generation. It is dead. Actually, it was dead from birth, but nobody noticed this much until the corpse began to smell." Indeed, cities razed existing historic fabric at their peril. Although money can always be leveraged toward new construction, "the economic value of old buildings is irreplaceable at will. It is created by time. . . . Vital city neighborhoods can only inherit, and then sustain [it] over the years."[33]

As with so much else in her book, this advocacy of older buildings did not go over well with planners of the time. Boston's Edward Logue called the book "a plea for the status quo." Another quipped that "it was as if Mrs. Jacobs had visited Pompeii and concluded that nothing makes a city so beautiful as covering it with ashes." The director of the American Society of Planning Officials declared it "will be grabbed by screwballs and reactionaries and used to fight civic improvement and urban renewal projects for years to come." Robert Moses, who received an advance copy from the publisher's cofounder, deemed it "intemperate and inaccurate [and] libelous. . . . Sell this junk to someone else."[34]

At the same time, Jacobs's "brashly impressive tour de force," as the *New York Times* called it, also struck a chord with the public at a moment when more and more Americans were beginning to question the received wisdom of 1950s elites. Soon Jacobs was being written up in *Newsweek*, photographed by Diane Arbus, deemed "Queen Jane" by *Vogue*, and feted by Lady Bird Johnson at the White House. The book gained particular traction among the many families whose homes and neighborhoods were being upended by "urban renewal." "We don't live in no slum," said one woman at New York's City Hall, cradling a copy of Jacobs's work. "We don't want to live in no project. We want to stay where we is, but we want it fixed up in the way she says."[35]

In short, Jacobs's criticism of the way cities were being remade, and those who would remake them, hit a national nerve. And even as she continued to defend her neighborhood from bulldozing, others were working to enshrine her principles into federal law and shepherd into creation a national grassroots movement, dedicated to preserving America's disappearing historic fabric for future generations.

With Heritage So Rich

Even as the ink dried on *Death and Life*, another decisive moment for the future of cities unfolded in the nearby New York offices of the Pennsylvania Railroad. Facing serious budget problems for several years running—in no small part because of competition from the nation's expanding highway system—the desperate railroad company agreed to sell one of its most prized assets to the owners of Madison Square Garden, who wanted a new arena: the site of New York's Penn Station. The Beaux Arts railroad station at 34th Street and 8th Avenue was a little more than fifty years old at that point, but it had already become a beloved feature of the New York City landscape. Now it too stood to be demolished.[36]

Soon, Jane Jacobs and many other concerned New Yorkers, among them Norman Mailer and architect Philip Johnson, were out in front of the endangered civic landmark, holding signs emblazoned "ACTION NOT APATHY" and "SAVE OUR HERITAGE," and urging the railroad to reconsider. "Penn Station, one of our finest structures," was in mortal danger "to make room for more profit-making square footage," read a 1962 public letter signed by Jacobs and many others. "It may be too late to save Penn Station . . . but it is not too late to save New York. We the undersigned—architects, artists, architectural historians, and citizens of New York—serve notice upon present and future would-be vandals that we will fight them every step of the way. New York's architecture is a major part of our heritage. We intend to see it preserved."[37]

But not even Jane Jacobs could win every fight. Demolition began in October 1963, and all traces of the beloved station were gone within three years. "Until the first blow fell," lamented architecture critic Ada Louise Huxtable, "no one was convinced that . . . New York would permit this monumental act of vandalism against one of the largest and finest landmarks of its age." Something was deeply wrong, she wrote, when such a landmark could be destroyed. "The final indictment is of the values of our society. Any city gets what it admires, will pay for, and, ultimately, deserves. . . . We want and deserve tin-can architecture in a tin-horn culture. And we will probably be judged not by the monuments we build but by those we have destroyed."[38]

The razing of Penn Station became a potent symbol of loss for Americans across the country. If such a beloved landmark could be erased solely in the name of profit, it seemed, anything could go. As such, even as Penn Station was coming apart brick by brick, a national conference of preservationists came together in Williamsburg, Virginia, in 1964. This gathering inaugurated several years of meetings and high-level discussions about how historic places could be better protected in an age of rampant demolition.[39]

Shocked by Penn Station's ignominious end, New York led the way: in 1965, Mayor Robert Wagner Jr. signed the city's brand-new Landmarks Law into effect. It created an eleven-person Landmarks Commission, made up of architects, historians, planners, real estate brokers, and citizens of every borough, to protect the places in the city that mattered from further demolition. By 2015, the law's fiftieth anniversary, it had helped protect 1,400 individual landmarks and more than 100 historic districts in the city.[40]

On the national front, a group of concerned preservationists from the Williamsburg meetings, with the blessing of Lady Bird Johnson, formed a Special Committee for Historic Preservation, led by Congressman Albert Rains of Alabama and lobbyist Laurance G. Henderson. This committee toured Europe to determine best practices, identified potential shepherds of a new preservation law in Congress, and ultimately contributed to a remarkable and eclectic volume of essays, poetry, photography, and policy recommendations called *With Heritage So Rich*.[41]

"We on the committee . . . have tried to discover what we must do to rescue from certain destruction what remains of our legacy from the past," wrote Rains and Henderson in the opening essay to *With Heritage So Rich*. Rescue work was desperately needed: The committee found that nearly half of the 12,000 listings on the Historic American Buildings Survey of 1933 had been demolished. "This is a serious loss," wrote the First Lady in her foreword, "and it underlines the necessity for prompt action if we are not to shirk our duty to the future. We must preserve and preserve wisely."[42]

Coupled with New York's Landmarks Law, *With Heritage So Rich* helped jump-start the push for stronger federal protections of historic properties. On October 15, 1966, President Lyndon Johnson signed the National Historic Preservation Act, officially enshrining into federal law the values, tools, and benefits of saving historic places. It created an Advisory Council on Historic Preservation and a National Register of Historic Places, similar to the tools created in New York. The very same day, he also signed legislation creating the Department of Transportation, which among its provisions included the vitally important Section 4(f). It requires federally assisted transportation projects to "use all possible planning to minimize harm" to historic resources.

Almost immediately, preservationists began using these new tools to prevent historic places from being destroyed. One of the most critical parts of the Preservation Act was Section 106, which requires federal agencies to evaluate the impact that their proposed actions would have on historic properties and mandates that the newly created Advisory Council be given time to weigh in. In one of the very first tests of this Section 106 review, the Advisory Council recommended against a proposal to run an elevated highway along the waterfront of New Orleans' French Quarter. Preservationists later invoked Section 4(f) to stop a highway from smothering Baltimore's Fort McHenry, which had moved Francis Scott Key to pen the national anthem during the War of 1812. In cities like Atlanta, Washington, D.C., and Pasadena, these tools helped safeguard historic neighborhoods from being converted into giant highway cloverleaves.[43]

This resurgent and transformed preservation movement—animated by Jacobs, devastated by the loss of places like Penn Station, and deeply concerned by the national embrace of even more superhighways and Radiant Cities—became the vanguard of, in author Stewart Brand's words, "a quiet, populist, conservative, victorious revolution." Preservation, wrote another historian cited by Brand, became "the only mass popular movement to affect critically the course of architecture in our century." In 1990, James Marston Fitch declared that "preservation is now seen as being in the forefront of urban regeneration, often accomplishing what the urban-renewal programs of twenty and thirty years ago so dismally failed to do. It has grown . . . [into] a broad mass movement engaged in battles to preserve 'Main Street,' urban districts, and indeed whole towns."[44]

If anything, that has only continued in the years since. Across the United States, fifteen million Americans and counting are taking action in their communities to save places they love. Historic preservation now has a seat at the table in discussions of urban planning, zoning policy, and municipal growth. And the go-to urban planning theory now studied, quoted, and dissected by every student of the subject is by none other than Jane Jacobs.

With *Death and Life* now the conventional wisdom about urban redevelopment, today's planners have been reassessing her work with a more critical eye. Many have come to believe she missed the boat on the issue of gentrification and that her vision of the ideal city inevitably leads as readily to the displacement of existing families as Moses's bulldozing, an issue we will look at more deeply in chapter 6.

There also has been an extant question as to how much of her prescriptions and criticisms were simply aesthetic in nature. In the decades since *Death and Life*, we simply haven't had much in the way of empirical data to assess her claims about the social and economic impact of older buildings on cities.

That is, until now.

CHAPTER 2

Older, Smaller, Better:
How Older Buildings Enhance Urban Vitality

In the city, time becomes visible.
 —Lewis Mumford[1]

EVER SINCE *THE DEATH AND LIFE OF GREAT AMERICAN CITIES*, preservationists have been using Jacobs's arguments to make the case for
retaining historic neighborhoods and older buildings. To be sure, her
reasoning *feels* right, primarily because we all sense that historic places
feed our soul and connect us to our past and our community over time.

In the intervening years, some excellent studies have been written on
the economic value of retaining older buildings, most notably *The Economics of Historic Preservation* by Donovan Rypkema, researcher, consultant, and founder of PlaceEconomics. "To make a new brick today
to build a building on a site where there is already a building steals from
two generations," Rypkema has argued. "It steals from the generation
that built the brick originally by throwing away their asset before its
work is done, and it steals from a future generation by using increasingly
scarce natural resources today that should have been saved for tomorrow."[2]

Now, with new tools and technology at our disposal, we can empirically assess the economic dimension of Jane Jacobs's case: that older buildings help neighborhoods flourish by nurturing new businesses, spurring innovation, and generating activity at all times of day.

So in 2013, the research arm at the National Trust for Historic Preservation—the Preservation Green Lab—went to work assessing her claims. Using state-of-the-art big data analytics, the Green Lab developed a comprehensive geospatial analysis of the fabric of three major US cities—Washington, D.C., San Francisco, and Seattle—and is now in the process of applying the same analysis to dozens of other US cities.

What we found in the initial cities is that Jacobs's observations were correct: areas with a mix of older, smaller buildings perform better than districts with larger, newer structures across a range of economic, social, and environmental outcomes.

As historic preservationists, you can imagine how happy we were to be able to quantify that! Still, what we found surprised even us. The power of older buildings is far more than just aesthetic. They are tremendous engines of economic growth, vitality, and quality of life. And more than just providing useful empirical evidence for Jacobs's theories, the Preservation Green Lab's *Older, Smaller, Better* report demonstrates how cities all over the United States can use their older commercial districts and corridors to generate jobs and dollars, attract more families and businesses, and jump-start the revitalization of blocks and neighborhoods.

The Green Lab Goes to Work

In fashioning the *Older, Smaller, Better* report, the first challenge for the Green Lab was to develop a methodology that could test Jacobs's arguments about older buildings while controlling for other factors that might affect urban vitality, such as residents' income levels, investment in construction, and the accessibility of mass transit. The researchers also wanted to look at more than just buildings and districts that were designated as historic and consider the age and size of buildings across an entire city.

To do that, they paired a common tool of archaeologists the world over—a grid survey—with a very new one: geographic information system (GIS), or geo-mapping, technology. GIS software, which can organize multiple layers of data into one highly useful map, has revolutionized dozens of industries, particularly as more and more of the world's data have been digitized. A 2013 study in *Foreign Affairs* estimated that although only 25 percent of existing information was in digital form in 2000, today only 2 percent is *not* digital. As such, business meetings in professions like urban planning and conservation now routinely begin with a GIS map of whatever area is being discussed, featuring layers of pertinent data that are critical to informed decision making.[3]

Until very recently, however, and perhaps as befitting a cause that seeks to honor and maintain the charms of the past, preservationists have been slow in adopting twenty-first-century tools to facilitate our work. For the Green Lab, which wanted to bring together many disparate data sets to measure urban performance, GIS technology was the key to the entire project.

For the initial study, team members chose three US cities that boasted both extensive older fabric and strong real estate markets: Washington, D.C., San Francisco, and Seattle. They first combed through county assessor records and census data to figure out three key pieces of information about all the buildings in these cities: their ages, the diversity of those ages in a particular neighborhood, and their "granularity," meaning the overall compactness along a block. So, for example, a commercial block with several two-story town houses would have higher granularity than one with a large big-box store.

But they didn't stop there. The team also found metrics that could be used to measure the social, economic, and cultural performance of these areas. They included business listings and registries of new businesses, rental housing ads on Craigslist, photo submissions to Flickr, walkability and bicycle friendliness scores via the website Walk Score, and cell phone usage data.

With these key statistics at the ready, the Green Lab then overlaid a 200 meter by 200 meter square grid—equivalent to about one to two square city blocks—across each city so that "apple-to-apple" comparisons could be made across diverse areas. Although blocks might seem a good measure initially—and, indeed, much of the existing census data was organized by blocks—block size can vary enormously between and even within cities. A grid, by definition, remains the same size and allows visual and statistical comparisons much more readily than block size.

After making sure the assembled data conformed correctly to this new grid division, the Green Lab team isolated the squares that represented mixed-use and commercial areas for intensive further study—adding up to roughly 17 percent of Seattle, 21 percent of Washington, D.C., and 30 percent of San Francisco. (To qualify, a given cell on the grid had to have at least three businesses, one full-time job, ten commercial square feet, 1% of non-single-family housing, and at least one complete record of a building.) Each of these boxes was then assigned a composite "character score" based on each area's building age, diversity of age, and granularity, respective to the averages across the city.

Now, with each part of the city divided into boxes of equal size and judged by a common measure, the Green Lab could evaluate the relative success of each sector. Team members employed what is called a spatial regression analysis, which allowed them to check the performance of each area against the norm along forty different economic, social, and cultural metrics while controlling for other mitigating factors like income, investment, and mass transit.[4]

What they found is neighborhoods with a mix of older and newer

Our Methodology

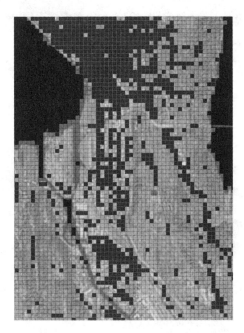

- Overlaid 200m x 200m grid
- Focused on mixed-use corridors
- Measured key features of the built fabric: building age, diversity of building age, granularity

The Preservation Green Lab's *Older, Smaller, Better* methodology. (© National Trust for Historic Preservation)

buildings have a "hidden density", with more people and businesses per commercial square foot than areas with just new buildings. Such neighborhoods often have more small business jobs, more creative jobs, more new and women- and minority-owned businesses, fewer chain businesses, and more diversity in housing costs, meaning more opportunities for families of all incomes. Per Jacobs's arguments about new ideas needing old buildings, innovative and creative economy positions like media production, software publishers, and performing arts companies in particular seem to flourish amid a diverse historic fabric.

These neighborhoods are also more walkable and show more activity on evenings and weekends than other neighborhoods, with greater cell phone activity and more businesses open late. And although the median

LOW CHARACTER SCORE

HIGH CHARACTER SCORE

- Newer buildings
- Larger buildings
- Less age diversity

- Older buildings
- Smaller buildings
- Greater age diversity

The difference between high and low character scores. (© National Trust for Historic Preservation)

age of residents is lower than in new-building-only areas—as we've seen, young people love old buildings—these neighborhoods exhibit significantly more diversity across age groups as well.

Historic Neighborhoods in Bloom

Take Washington, D.C., our nation's capital and the home of the National Trust for Historic Preservation. Many visitors to the city, after walking around the National Mall, spend their time in the neighborhoods of the Northwest—famous hangouts like Georgetown, Dupont Circle, and Foggy Bottom. In the less well-known Northeast quadrant of the city, however, there is an emerging, twelve-block area known as the H Street corridor, located near the Union Station train depot. It is nationally recognized as a valuable historic place, but after the assassination of Martin Luther King Jr. in 1968, H Street experienced heavy

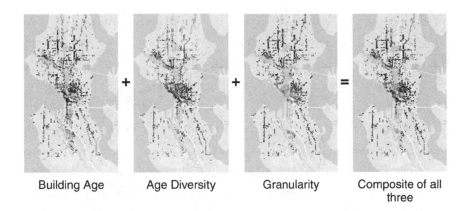

| Building Age | Age Diversity | Granularity | Composite of all three |

Our composite measure = "Character Score"

The various measures of city fabric undertaken by the Green Lab. (© National Trust for Historic Preservation)

rioting that left the area distressed and despondent for decades. Today, a diverse building stock is aiding the robust transition of this former "riot corridor" into one of Washington's fastest growing communities and a place where both longtime residents and new arrivals are enjoying an economic renaissance.

What H Street has going for it are fine-grained blocks with buildings of various ages, most of them (85%) built before World War II. The corridor is lined with narrow, century-old two- and three-story homes and commercial blocks housing local retailers, restaurants, and bars. They include places like the H Street Country Club, a restaurant with a miniature golf course inside; the Atlas Arcade, a pub filled with classic 1980s video game machines; and The Pursuit, a wine bar renowned for its gourmet grilled cheese sandwiches. Nearby are the Rock and Roll Hotel and the Atlas Theater, two local performing arts venues.

In fact, H Street was recently ranked among "ten great urban neighborhoods" by *USA Today* and was featured at number six on a *Forbes* magazine's list of "America's Best Hipster Neighborhoods" in 2012. And these rankings ring true, particularly after the sun goes down. The neighborhood's residents have a median age of about thirty-five, which is younger than in areas of the city with the newest, largest buildings.[5]

H Street is far from just a hipster enclave for new arrivals, though. The older, smaller buildings found there help support people across the economic spectrum, allow for a variety of uses and income levels within the corridor, and accommodate the ever-changing needs of society—from clothing stores to an outreach center. They also house a higher concentration of new businesses, women- and minority-owned businesses, and nonchain businesses than Washington, D.C., as a whole. H Street's Walk Score—which measures proximity to basic neighborhood amenities such as stores, parks, and restaurants—and its population density are also higher than the local average. In addition, a revived streetcar service to connect the corridor to other neighborhoods launched in the spring of 2016.

Entrepreneur Erin Losie partnered with her brother to introduce a fitness gym in the neighborhood and said before launch day: "We were hoping to have 20 clients when we opened. Now, as soon as we open, we're going to have to look to expand." In total, the H Street corridor created more than 250 new businesses and added close to 3,000 jobs in just over a decade. This result was in keeping with the general findings in the report that older business districts provide affordable, flexible space for entrepreneurs from all backgrounds.[6]

In Southeast DC, a similar story has been unfolding in the neighborhood of Barracks Row, an old commercial corridor so named because of its proximity to both the Navy Yard and the marine barracks that run along 8th Street (and not, as some visitors initially suspect, after the forty-fourth president!). Part of the Capitol Hill Historic District, Barracks Row features many two- and three-story commercial buildings dating to the turn of the twentieth century. The six-block area is home

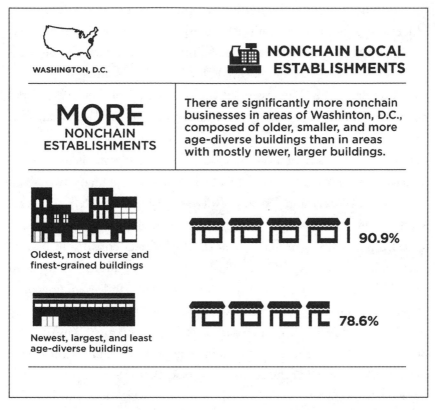

Washington, D.C.'s mixed-older fabric enjoys more independent, nonchain businesses. (© National Trust for Historic Preservation)

to stores, apartments, and dozens of restaurants and eateries, such as Ted's Bulletin, renowned for its homemade pop tarts, and Rose's Luxury, named America's best new restaurant by *Bon Appétit* in 2014. The strip is particularly well-trafficked on weekends during the baseball season, when it becomes both a staging area and after-game destination for Washington Nationals fans.[7]

Barracks Row's redevelopment and performance according to the *Older, Smaller, Better* metrics have been a little more uneven than the H Street corridor, in part because the neighborhood was, long ago, bisected by Interstate 695. The area north of the highway and closer to Capitol Hill enjoys about five times more businesses per commercial square foot than the side of the neighborhood caught on the other end of the overpass, but that too is changing. In 2014, a local church bought the Navy Yard Car Barn, the "blue castle" that anchors the southern end of the neighborhood and was once a repair facility for the local streetcar. This acquisition, coupled with the continued expansion and development of the Navy Yard area right around Nationals Park, suggests the rest of 8th Street may soon catch up with the blocks north of the highway.[8]

In fact, H Street and Barracks Row are just the tip of the iceberg. Washington, D.C., is seeing neighborhoods rejuvenate across the district, from Shaw, Logan Circle, and the 14th Street corridor in Northwest DC, Petworth and Columbia Heights in the North, Navy Yard and "Hill East" in Southeast and Northeast DC, and even Anacostia and Capitol Heights, which are separated from the rest of the city by the Potomac River. This rejuvenation is in part because Washington, being home to the federal government in good times and bad, has been insulated from some of the economic shocks that accompanied the collapse of the housing bubble and ensuing Great Recession. But it is also because, thanks to a quirk of law, Washington has been gifted with a citywide historic fabric that facilitates entrepreneurship, innovation, and vitality.

In 1899 and again in 1910, and in response to the then-enormous Cairo Hotel, built in 1894 near Dupont Circle, Congress passed the Height of Buildings Act that declared that no commercial building can stand taller than the width of the street it faces plus 20 feet, with a maximum cap of 110 feet (later 130 feet). As a result, the city's historic neighborhoods are filled with one- to four-story buildings that are engines of revitalization. "These sections of the city," confirmed the Green Lab, "consistently emerged as [Washington, D.C.'s] most active and vital places, especially by measures related to entrepreneurship:

percentages of nonchain businesses, new businesses, and women- and minority-owned businesses. . . . The sections of the city with the tallest buildings, most notably the blocks just north of the White House and the National Mall, have a substantial number of the city's businesses and jobs on an aggregate basis, but they are outperformed by older buildings on a per square foot basis."[9]

In recent years, some planners and economists have called for eliminating the height act (as well as height restrictions in other cities), or at the very least amending it to allow buildings to rise to 200 feet. As I will discuss more in chapter 6, to such economists, it is a simple market demand problem: small buildings mean fewer apartments, so giant skyscrapers should reduce the exorbitant and increasing rents experienced in Washington, D.C., and many other cities across the United States. This "reactionary government policy from 1899," argued Vox writer Matthew Yglesias in a June 2015 essay on the Height of Buildings Act, has helped make the city "an American Versailles, an exclusive community dedicated to ruling a country rather than being an integral piece of the country it rules." Getting rid of this low-slung historic fabric and adding skyscrapers, he declares, would make DC "a beating heart of prosperity for the entire country rather than the refuge of a narrow elite."[10]

There are a few problems with this line of reasoning, however. For one, Yglesias's assertion runs exactly counter to the empirical findings of the *Older, Smaller, Better* report. In fact, as just noted, these smaller buildings are providing more opportunities for local and diverse-owned businesses to take root. For another, as urban planner (and former Washington, D.C., resident) Jeff Speck noted, "economists don't seem to have fully processed one thing the designers know, which is how tremendously dense a city can become at moderate heights. Boston's North End, in Jane Jacobs's day, achieved 275 dwelling units per acre with hardly an elevator in sight."[11]

In fact, according to Speck, Washington, D.C.'s low-level building stock is its genius. Rather than railing against Congress (again), he
wrote, we should be talking about "how tremendous the District of
Columbia's height limit has been for the city and its walkability. . . . [It]
has caused new development to fill many more blocks than it would
have otherwise. The strategy has created street after street of excellent
urbanism." Skyscrapers aren't necessarily inhospitable to livable cities,
he concluded, but they often end up reflecting developers' desires to
"sell luxury condos" more than they do any true attempt to achieve
better affordability. His point is well taken, as discussed in more detail
later on.[12]

San Francisco

On the other side of the country, the Green Lab also ran its *Older,
Smaller, Better* analysis in San Francisco. Research found, once again,
that areas with older, smaller fabric had a significantly higher percentage
of small business jobs than newer areas.

One of the most notable stories in San Francisco is the Mid-Market
neighborhood (also known as Central Market), which runs along Market and Mission Streets from 5th to 10th Streets and is in the midst of
a profound high-profile transformation. Once decimated by the 1906
earthquake and fire and then quickly rebuilt—such that, even today,
more than half the buildings there date to before World War II—Mid-
Market is dotted with low- and midrise early twentieth-century commercial buildings, including theaters, government buildings, and hotels.
For many years, it was known as a down-at-the-heels area of social service delivery sites and single-room-occupancy hotels, and it clearly still
has some rough edges. In January 2015, for example, the neighborhood
received some unfortunate national press when a suitcase of dismem-
bered body parts was found a block from the new downtown headquarters of Twitter.[13]

Older, smaller parts of San Francisco have more small business jobs. (© National Trust for Historic Preservation)

Mid-Market is nonetheless evolving rapidly to include tech firms, arts organizations, and market-rate housing among its gritty mix of restaurants and retailers. It exhibits more residential density and evening activity than the city as a whole and remains more racially and socioeconomically diverse as well. And although Mid-Market has not yet proven to be the powerful incubator of small-business start-ups that H Street in Washington, D.C., is, it has provided a potent case study for how old and historic buildings can help an area revitalize by attracting innovative tech and new economy firms. As Todd Rufo, an economic development officer in San Francisco, put it, "A once vacant and blighted area . . . is now a gravitational center for some of the most innovative companies in the world."[14]

The turnaround began in earnest in 2011 when the city of San Francisco began offering tax incentives to encourage businesses to move to neighborhoods like Mid-Market and the Tenderloin. Twitter was one of the first to take advantage of an exemption from the city's payroll tax: the social networking service fell in love and moved into the Merchandise Mart Building at 10th and Market, an art deco wholesale furniture store dating to 1937 that had been vacant for five years. Twitter was soon followed by companies like Square, the merchant services and mobile payments firm; Spotify, a digital music service; and Dolby, the audio specialist, all of whom have now relocated in historic buildings. Together, their presence has sparked new, high-density development on vacant parcels and surface parking lots, and led to an influx of vibrant new small businesses and arts groups.[15]

The numbers really do tell the story. Just a few years ago, Mid-Market had a vacancy rate hovering around 30 percent, which has since dropped to under 6 percent and falling. The area has also experienced a 21 percent increase in sales tax revenue, more than making up for the original business tax benefit. (This benefit, viewed as a tax giveaway for rich companies by some San Franciscans, is becoming moot, since the payroll tax from which Twitter and others were excluded is being phased out, in lieu of a gross receipts tax, by 2018.)[16]

At the same time, the city of San Francisco has worked with the new high-tech employers in the area to create community benefit agreements, or CBAs, that work to make sure that the neighborhood's improving fortunes do not leave out existing low-income residents. (CBAs are an important and emerging tool to ensure equity that I will discuss more in chapter 6.) For example, Twitter has opened a $3 million, 4,000-square-foot community center called NeighborNest across the street from its offices that includes computer classes, child care, and support for the homeless in finding housing and jobs. Per the CBA, the company has also donated $360 million to local nonprofits and $3 million in future grants to those working in the Mid-Market community.[17]

Another recent arrival, Microsoft-owned Yammer, has given away $60,000 in grants and millions in free computers to local children in the Mid-Market and Tenderloin neighborhoods. Yet another, the Danish software company Zendesk, has been called the "gold standard" by local residents and city officials. Along with building a website to help local residents access jobs, medical care, housing, and other services on their phones, 93 percent of Zendesk's employees volunteer in the community every week—including the CEO, who serves food regularly at the local soup kitchen. "Their perspective was, 'We are neighbors, and neighbors help neighbors, so what do you need?,'" said the head of one of Mid-Market's largest service organizations of Zendesk.[18]

Some might argue that companies like Zendesk are more the exception than the rule, and that we shouldn't predicate our urban revitalization strategies on the neighborly goodwill of private-sector corporations. Nonetheless, the trend unfolding in Mid-Market is also playing out in cities all over the United States: the innovative companies that underpin the new economy seem to have a natural affinity for older and historic buildings. In New York City, for example, a surge of tech companies and start-ups have popped up in and around Union Square and the Flatiron District—most notably Google, which made a big splash by purchasing the historic Port Authority building at 111 Eighth Avenue in Chelsea. Google has helped turn that immense 1932 structure into a hub of the twenty-first-century economy. Over in Los Angeles, Google recently leased the former airplane hangar of Howard Hughes in the neighborhood of Playa Vista, once home to the "Spruce Goose," the largest airplane ever built. The company is converting that into one of its flagship offices as well.[19]

This trend isn't just a phenomenon of the Internet; indeed, it goes back to Jacobs's argument about new ideas and old buildings in *Death and Life*. In *How Buildings Learn*, author Stewart Brand pointed out that one of the most beloved structures on the campus of the Massachusetts Institute of Technology is a giant wood box hailing from 1943 known as Building 20. Originally built to test the development of radar, this particular lab has played an innovative role in scientific experiments ever since. "Unusual flexibility," noted the MIT museum, "made the building ideal for laboratory and experimental space." Similarly, Brand interviewed the head of Apple, John Sculley, in 1990 as they were expanding from five to thirty-one buildings. "Do you prefer moving into old buildings or making new ones?" Brand asked him. "Oh old ones," Sculley replied. "They are much more freeing." "Even in rich societies," Brand concluded, "the most inventive creativity, especially youthful creativity, will be found in Low Road buildings taking full advantage of the license to try things." That's true in Mid-Market, Silicon Alley, or anywhere else.[20]

Before moving on from the Bay Area, it's important to note that, with the possible exception of Manhattan, San Francisco has become the tip of the spear in the United States for what threatens to become a nationwide crisis in urban affordability. Reports conducted by the real estate website Zumper found that San Francisco was the nation's most expensive city for renters in 2015, with the average one-bedroom clocking in at $3,500 a month. (Nearby Oakland and San Jose didn't offer much relief either; they were ranked number four and number six, respectively.)[21]

Here again, as I will discuss more extensively in chapter 6, many urban economists blame policies like historic preservation and height acts for restricting the quantity of affordable housing. In fact, the answer is complicated. San Francisco's particularly extreme housing crisis has roots in the politics, ideology, history, and bureaucracy of the city going back to the mid-twentieth century, when thousands of African American residents of the Fillmore neighborhood—once the "Harlem of the West"—were evicted en masse in the name of "urban renewal." Ever since that mass displacement in the 1950s and '60s—and a similar, contemporaneous attempt to upend the Mission neighborhood—San Francisco has been particularly wary of new development. The city has one of the strictest permit processes in the United States, requiring a six-month preliminary review even for projects that conform to all laws and standards. (As a result, of the top ten tech hubs in the country, San Francisco has allowed the fewest new construction permits per 1,000 units since 1990.) And, unlike New York City—which enjoys one municipal government that oversees all five boroughs—the Bay Area is home to many municipalities, from San Jose to Mountain View, all of which would prefer that their neighbors sort out this housing shortage instead.[22]

It is clear that San Francisco is in need of more affordable housing, and local nonprofits like SPUR (formerly the San Francisco Planning and Urban Research Association) have been working with local preservation groups such as San Francisco Architectural Heritage to facilitate it through appropriate infill development, creative adaptive reuse, and other methods. Again, this issue is very important for cities and for preservation, and I will take it up further in chapter 6.[23]

Seattle

Just as in San Francisco, Seattle is seeing several twenty-first-century tech businesses take advantage of the flexibility of older buildings. (In fact, the city's new and pioneering outcome-based energy code—which I will discuss more in chapter 7—was first piloted in a former commercial laundry, dating to 1906. That structure is now leased by Amazon, which has shown a growing affinity for older building stock to supplement its newer offices.) And just as in Washington, D.C., many of Seat-

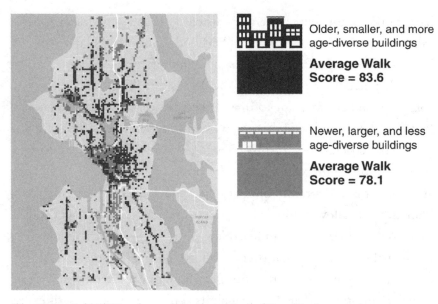

Older, smaller, and more age-diverse buildings

Average Walk Score = 83.6

Newer, larger, and less age-diverse buildings

Average Walk Score = 78.1

The Green Lab's GIS-enhanced determination of Seattle's character score. (© National Trust for Historic Preservation)

tle's most vibrant and thriving neighborhoods are renowned for their dense, mixed-use historic fabric—places like Ballard, Belltown, Capitol Hill, Fremont, and Pioneer Square.[24]

Although a considerably smaller percentage of Seattle's buildings are pre–World War II compared to Washington, D.C.—37 percent as opposed to 70 percent—the same overall findings applied. Areas with older fabric saw more businesses, jobs, and creative jobs per square foot, more cell phone activity and foot traffic, and more cafés and fewer chain stores. Mixed-vintage blocks combining old and new buildings also saw more women- and minority-owned businesses, lower rents, and higher racial, ethnic, and economic diversity than newer neighborhoods.[25]

One of the neighborhoods the Green Lab examined in particular detail was its home base, in an area known as the Pike/Pine corridor (bordered on the south and north by Pike and Pine Streets, respectively). Once the setting for the grunge rock scene in the early 1990s, this twenty-six-square block is now a cultural hive of restaurants and

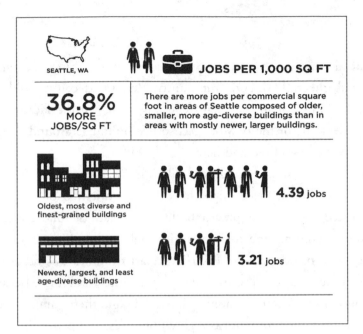

Seattle's older neighborhoods have a greater job density than newer areas. (© National Trust for Historic Preservation)

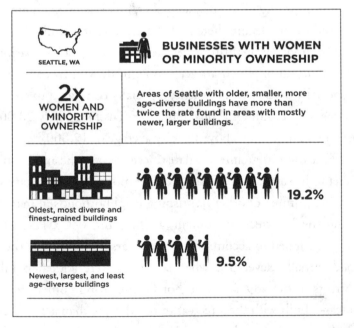

These older Seattle neighborhoods also have more women- and minority-owned businesses than newer neighborhoods. (© National Trust for Historic Preservation)

nightclubs and is the center of Seattle's lesbian, gay, bisexual, transgender, and queer (LGBTQ) community. Renovated century-old apartment buildings, many of them retaining their historic façades, stand alongside some of the newest green office buildings around, blending together the best of old and new.

In the early twentieth century, Pike/Pine was known as "auto row" because of the car dealerships and other car-oriented businesses that dominated the area. Its prewar buildings—made of solid concrete or masonry, standing one to two stories high and equipped with large garages and bay doors—set Pike/Pine apart from Seattle's other neighborhoods and serve as the area's signature architectural form. Because of this once utilitarian, now more whimsical design, these garage buildings have been adapted for reuse as nightclubs, cafés, and coffee shops.

Take, for example, the Elliott Bay Book Company, which occupies space in a historic Ford warehouse dating back to the early 1900s. "The neighborhood is one of incredible vitality," said its owner, Peter Aaron, who moved the bookstore there in 2010. Indeed, it is. Elliott Bay shares its neighborhood with thrift stores, record shops, tattoo parlors, and karaoke spots, all of which attract people in droves. In fact, Pike/Pine is an especially dense part of Seattle, especially compared to streets with more large, new buildings. The population density is nearly 20,000 people per square mile, well above the city average of 12,000.[26]

Pike/Pine owes its architectural distinctiveness to the automobile, but the secret to its success may lie in an earlier mode of transportation. Like a surprising number of other flourishing neighborhoods in major cities, including the H Street corridor in Washington, D.C., Pike/Pine was originally designed to accommodate streetcars. (In this case, the neighborhood initially developed when streetcars were added to Pike and Pine Streets in the 1890s.) As author Charles Montgomery has noted, such areas—built with the streetcar in mind more than a century ago—seem to have inadvertently stumbled on exactly the right size and layout to facilitate happiness and encourage urban vitality. "As it turned out," he wrote, so-called "streetcar suburbs . . . created a near-perfect scale of happy living. . . . Without modern suburbia's massive yards, wide roads, and a strict segregation of uses, almost everything you needed was a five-minute walk or a brief streetcar ride away."[27]

In recent years, many cities have caught on to the tremendous benefits of streetcars and have been adding them (or returning them) to the urban fabric. Seattle is no exception. The First Hill Line, which began operations in 2016, has restored street services to a number of historic Seattle neighborhoods, including Pioneer Square, Capitol Hill, and the Chinatown-International District.[28]

This last-mentioned area—home to Seattle's Chinese, Japanese, Filipino, and Vietnamese communities—boasts historic fabric that dates to the early twentieth century, when Chinese settlers first arrived in Seattle to help build the railroads and staff the timber mills, yet it is an outlier when it comes to the usual *Older, Smaller, Better* metrics. Unlike Pike/Pine and other historic neighborhoods, there are fewer jobs, businesses, and creative jobs per commercial square foot in this neighborhood than the city average. In addition, the average resident is a decade older (48.6) and substantially poorer (making $27,000 less) than the average Seattle resident (38.5 years old, making $59,241 a year).[29]

Some of these differences are likely due to the challenges that ethnic communities in particular face in preserving the cultural character of their neighborhood. They also reflect another reality about the *Older, Smaller, Better* report: it is effectively a snapshot in time. When the Green Lab surveyed Seattle, the Chinatown-International District was still suffering from higher crime and commercial and residential vacancy rates. Many of its existing businesses had been negatively affected by the temporary traffic difficulties that accompanied construction of the restored streetcar lane. Perhaps most important, because the upper floors of many of the historic buildings in the neighborhood do not meet Seattle's building codes, they were sitting vacant and were effectively wasted historic assets.[30]

But, either for good or ill, this current state of affairs looks to change relatively soon. For one, major new development is taking place on both sides of the Chinatown-International District, in nearby Yesler Terrace and close to the Seahawks and Mariners stadiums. Along with the completed streetcar, this development could spur further investment and historic rehabilitation of Chinatown-International District properties.[31]

For another, two recent changes in municipal policy will help decide the fate of these many empty second floors. In July 2015, *New Yorker* writer Kathryn Schultz frightened the entire Pacific Northwest with a compelling, well-researched, and award-winning essay about an upcoming cataclysmic earthquake—"the worst natural disaster in the history of North America"—set to hit the region at some point in the future. ("Our operating assumption," one director of the Federal Emergency Management Agency is quoted as saying, "is that everything west of Interstate 5 will be toast.") The city of Seattle, well aware of this grim geologic destiny, has been developing an unreinforced masonry building program for commercial districts and encouraging homeowners to conduct seismic retrofits.[32]

Another recent law requires that all landlords register their properties and undergo inspections from now on. This Rental Registration and Inspection Ordinance (RRiO) should mean better building maintenance and upgrades across Seattle. It also provides an opportunity to revamp the irreplaceable historic assets of the Chinatown-International District and put them to work. Taken together, these policies will either spur the necessary investments to rehab these buildings or will mean they will be replaced. As with so much else, time will tell, but all evidence suggests that demolition will further complicate attempts to restore urban vitality while maintaining the unique cultural fabric of the Chinatown-International District.[33]

A third recent municipal policy decision may well affect older buildings all over the city. As part of efforts to tackle the growing problem of climate change, Seattle has committed to becoming completely carbon neutral—meaning the city would emit no net greenhouse gases—by the year 2050. As I will discuss further in chapter 7, one of the best and easiest ways to achieve this worthy goal is to make more use of the existing historic fabric. It takes a considerable amount of energy to demolish old structures and put in place new buildings, even green buildings. The fastest way to achieve carbon neutrality is through historic preservation.

Other Cities

As I'm sure many readers can attest, the Green Lab's findings about the importance of older buildings to thriving cities are by no means confined to Washington, D.C., San Francisco, and Seattle.

In November 2016, the Green Lab released a new atlas of older and historic buildings and blocks, exploring characteristics of the built

Older building fabric in downtown Louisville. (Photo by Andy Snow)

environment in more than fifty cities across the country through the *Older, Smaller, Better* rubric. Included are great metropolises like New York, Boston, Chicago, and Houston; midsize cities such as Raleigh, Tulsa, Tampa, and Portland, Oregon; and smaller but growing cities like Greensboro, Tacoma, Tempe, and Boulder. (The atlas is now available online at http://savingplaces.org/atlas.) The Green Lab saw the same exact story unfolding all over the United States.

In Baltimore, neighborhoods like Fells Point, Federal Hill, or Hampden have seen remarkable transformations in the past few years. Once vacant or underutilized structures are now humming with activity, and scores of historic buildings are seeing new lives as brewpubs, coffee shops, and offices. In fact, 83 percent of the *Baltimore Sun*'s top fifty bars in 2013 and top fifty restaurants of 2014 reside in buildings built before 1920. (In total, only half the buildings in Baltimore are that old.) The really important factor, of course, is not quality dining as much as good available jobs. Areas in Baltimore with older, smaller buildings have more than twice the number of small business jobs (and more young people) than areas with large, new structures.[34]

Philadelphia is experiencing a similar revival in neighborhoods like Center City, Fairmount, Fishtown, and Northern Liberties. There, neighborhoods with older, smaller fabric have 50 percent more creative jobs and are more than twice as likely to have a substantial population of eighteen- to thirty-four-year-olds as the rest of the city. As with Baltimore, nearly two-thirds of *Philadelphia* magazine's top fifty restaurants and bars are located in pre-1920 buildings, compared to 50 percent of commercial businesses in older buildings in total, suggesting these neighborhoods are home to creativity and innovation.[35]

In Louisville, a midsize city that boasts many historic distilleries and one of the largest collections of Victorian-era homes in the country, residents are working to make their city a national leader in smart, preservation-based development.

In Detroit, historic buildings are now being rehabilitated, a critical first step in transforming barren streets back into thriving places.

In Tucson, the Green Lab discovered not only the usual connections between historic fabric and urban performance, but further promising lines of study. Compared to newer neighborhoods there, older neighborhoods have more tree canopy and lower average surface temperatures, also enjoy more top-rated restaurants, and are most likely to have both Tucson's oldest and newest businesses.

In Chicago and Minneapolis, the *Older, Smaller, Better* methodology also unearthed similar connections between historic fabric and urban vitality in, respectively, Logan Square and Lincoln Park, and Uptown and Downtown West.[36]

Even in Los Angeles—once the quintessential automobile city—the past is driving the city toward a more vibrant future. In 1999, a partnership between neighborhood groups, city leaders, developers, and preservationists in downtown Los Angeles led to the Adaptive Reuse Ordinance, which lowered regulatory barriers and made it easier—and cheaper—for developers to convert vacant, older commercial buildings into residential use. As a result, the population in downtown neighborhoods has tripled, and the area is now a thriving residential and commercial hub with an astonishing 14,000 new housing units in older buildings.

All across the United States, the story is the same: old buildings are helping cities grow, develop, and become stronger communities. We now have empirical evidence that these buildings are necessary to civic and municipal health and are the key to long-term success.

Of course—and as we saw in Seattle's Chinatown-International District—they can't always just do it on their own. To unleash the full potential of the historic fabric all around us, we need to employ sound and effective public policies that put vacant and underused buildings to work.

CHAPTER 3

Making It Work for Your City: Unleashing the Power and Potential of Historic Fabric

How can you lose?
The lights are much brighter there
You can forget all your troubles, forget all your cares
So go downtown
Things will be great when you're downtown
No finer place for sure, downtown
Everything's waiting for you
    —Petula Clark[1]

"WE'VE KNOWN FOR THREE DECADES how to make livable cities—after forgetting for four," wrote Jeff Speck in *Walkable City*, "yet we've somehow not been able to pull it off." Jane Jacobs's arguments have long won over urban planners at this point, Speck noted, but "the planners have yet to win over the city. . . . In the small and midsized cities, where most Americans spend their lives, the daily decisions of local officials are still, more often than not, making their lives worse."[2]

It doesn't have to be this way. As our *Older, Smaller, Better* research underlines, in city after city, neighborhood after neighborhood, the road to revitalization and stronger, more vibrant communities is often just sitting there, waiting to be harnessed. In many cities, even as less than 5 percent of older buildings are designated historic, a vast percentage of the existing building stock dates to before World War II and is ripe and ready for reuse.

Indeed, the cities across the United States that are really taking off now—attracting businesses, creative innovators, and millennials back to their fold—are the ones where mayors, city council members, and other municipal officials "get it": where historic preservation is already being used as an important planning tool to leverage older buildings toward equitable and sustainable growth.

In short, smart policies can make the difference between a stagnant neighborhood at risk and a thriving community. So, building on what we have learned in the *Older, Smaller, Better* research, the Green Lab has been working to encourage systemic solutions that allow for more older buildings to breathe life into our neighborhoods.

As such, in 2012 the National Trust joined together with the Urban Land Institute, the nation's largest real estate development organization, to form the Partnership for Building Reuse. In Los Angeles, Chicago, Detroit, Baltimore, and Philadelphia, this partnership talked extensively with developers, architects, contractors, property owners, municipal officials, and community organizations to figure out the specific obstacles and opportunities for reusing older buildings in each city. The partnership then collected extensive data, mapped development trends, brought disparate groups together, and developed an action plan of recommendations tailored to each specific urban environment.[3]

Some of the neighborhoods they studied were white-hot, whereas others were dealing with declining populations and a surplus of vacant buildings. Along the way, however, the partnership uncovered some recurring problems and solutions that can help cities across the United

Moving Beyond the 5% Solution
Most cities protect fewer than 5% of their buildings

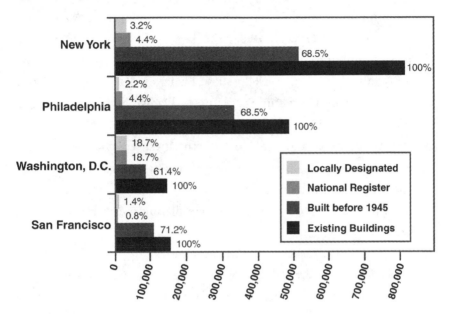

Although less than 5 percent of older buildings are officially designated as historic in many cities, a much larger percentage of the existing building stock dates to before World War II. (© National Trust for Historic Preservation)

States, whatever their circumstance, do more with their existing buildings. Based on this research as well as the work of other preservationists and planners across the country, here are ten steps that communities can take to maximize the advantages of their older buildings.

Step 1: Make Data-Driven Decisions

Let's begin with Jane Jacobs's most essential argument: "The best way to plan for downtown is to see how people use it today; to look for its strengths and to exploit and reinforce them." We can imagine a better future for our city, but we must first spend time critically observing the city as it is. Any successful attempt at spurring urban growth must be rooted in an informed understanding of how neighborhoods are performing today and which ones exhibit particular potential for historic revitalization.[4]

How do we accomplish this task? Jacobs's emphasis on walking through neighborhoods and really getting to know their particular rhythms and needs is an excellent start. That was also the secret of one of today's most influential urban planners, Danish architect Jan Gehl. When he graduated from architecture school in 1960, Gehl had mainly learned, in his words, how to "do modern cities, with high-rises and a lot of lawns and good open space—good windy spaces." Soon thereafter, though, he met the love of his life, a psychologist named Ingrid, and his work took quite a different focus than planning ever-more Radiant Cities.[5]

In 1965, the Gehls visited Italy and undertook their first "Public Space, Public Life" survey; in simple terms, they walked around the city, counted how many people were in various areas, and described what those people were doing. This experience transformed Jan Gehl's understanding of his profession. Instead of building cities "to make cars happy," he instead decided to figure out—through critical observation—"how cities are used by people" and how one could help design a place "that people would be happier using."[6]

Six years later, Gehl compiled his findings in a 1971 book called *Life between Buildings*. "Life between buildings is not merely pedestrian traffic," he argued therein; it is the barometer of a city's health and what makes "communal spaces in cities and residential areas meaningful and attractive." In fact, "life between buildings is both more relevant and more interesting to look at in the long run than any combination of colored concrete or staggered building forms." In short, it is the entire point of living in a city at all. To capture and enhance that life, one must first observe the city in its natural state and design neighborhoods so that they reflect the needs and rhythms of their residents.[7]

Over the years, *Life Between Buildings* has become a classic of the profession, and Gehl and his firm, Gehl Architects, have been leading voices on behalf of more people-friendly and livable cities, especially in the Gehls' hometown of Copenhagen. *Walkable City*'s Jeff Speck is one of the many urban planners who've taken up Gehl's vision. Whenever he is called on to help a city, Speck first moves his family there for at least a month because "it allows you to truly get to know a place. . . . Shuttling between a hotel and a meeting facility is not what citizens do. They take their kids to school, drop by the dry cleaners, make their way to work, step out for lunch, hit the gym or pick up some groceries, get themselves home, and consider an evening stroll or an after-dinner beer. . . . These are among the many normal things that nonplanners do, and I try to do them." In sum, there is no substitute for knowing a city in your bones. Working to gain this sort of intuitive understanding of how a community actually functions can help mitigate unwise and uninformed decision making about its future.[8]

At the same time, today we enjoy observational tools that Jacobs's generation could only dream of. In the twenty-first century, we are swimming in useful data and metrics, from rents to parking spaces, energy performance to bike-share usage, job numbers to restaurant reviews. Almost all these data are (or should be) readily available. And, through the magic of GIS mapping, we can now organize all this valuable information geographically and thus evaluate the performance of a given building, street, city block, or neighborhood along any number of critical social, cultural, and economic indicators, as the Green Lab did in *Older, Smaller, Better*.[9]

Even back in the day, as Jane Jacobs well noted, it didn't make much sense that a city's future was being fashioned according to the whims of a Robert Moses without any regard to how particular neighborhoods were actually functioning. Today, there is no longer any excuse for such haphazard planning. Simply put, in the Information Age, information should drive urban policy. Stewards and planners of cities today have a responsibility to examine the pertinent data, develop and calibrate sensible performance metrics, and make informed decisions about land use, infrastructure, transit, redevelopment, and related issues accordingly.

Where this information does not already exist, it should first be acquired. A good place to start would be to conduct a citywide survey of historic resources and neighborhood character to figure out the places most primed for revitalization. It doesn't need to be a costly enterprise. Today, through mobile technology, such surveys can even be accomplished with a handful of dedicated volunteers.

To take one recent example, to help influence where and how demolitions occurred, committed citizens in Detroit used a mobile phone app in January 2014 to conduct a speedy survey of historic properties in that beleaguered city. Unfortunately, after the housing crisis, more than $100 million in federal funding that was meant to be dedicated to mortgage relief was redirected to the state of Michigan to pay for mass demolitions. With half that amount going directly to Detroit, Mayor Mike Duggan committed to four hundred demolitions a week. Designated historic neighborhoods were off the chopping block, but eligible historic districts were not. In addition, there was no chance of a federal preservation review—a Section 106 review under the National Historic Preservation Act—to save a place that had been scheduled for demolition.[10]

In this challenging environment, the Michigan Historic Preservation Network and Preservation Detroit quickly organized fifty volunteers to survey 18,000 historic properties in just two weeks—in the dead of a Michigan winter. They first worked with a company called Local Data to create an easy-to-use tool that allowed surveyors to record basic information about a property on their phones to derive a "historic preservation score." Walking around the neighborhoods, the volunteers—primarily preservation professionals—answered questions about each parcel's architectural integrity, neighborhood character, the condition of the block, and whether further research was needed. Once they hit "enter," the parcel changed color to show that the survey was complete, and they moved on to the next house. In the meantime, the team could watch the surveys adding up in real time through a Dashboard view. When aggregating all this information, they could create a comprehensive view of a block or neighborhood.[11]

This information was then converted into a GIS layer, with color-coded historic preservation scores, and given to a group called Motor City Mapping that was collating other data to help decision makers assess their demolition options. Preservationists found that this historic survey and the technology that created it were powerful tools for securing a seat at the table in guiding demolition decisions. It also gave them a chance to show they understood the realities facing the city and were not going to demand that every single building be saved. In fact, a first-pass overlay of the data from Motor City Mapping and the historic resource survey showed just eight properties where the judgment of preservationists led to a larger discussion about the properties' future.[12]

In Los Angeles, a similar mobile tool—called the Field Guide Survey System, or FiGSS ("Figs") for short—has been helping residents and municipal officials complete a citywide survey of historic resources across more than 880,000 parcels of land and almost 500 square miles. Begun in 2010 and completed this year, SurveyLA has been a very successful partnership between the city's Office of Historic Resources, which has managed the project, and the J. Paul Getty Trust, which has partially funded and supported it.[13]

Previously, according to the Getty Conservation Institute, also part of the Getty Trust, only around 15 percent of Los Angeles had ever been surveyed for historic resources. Now, anyone who is interested can obtain a much more comprehensive map of the city's historic assets than ever before simply by visiting the SurveyLA website. As a result, this

n is being used not just for planning future renovation, zon-
development, but for encouraging cultural tourism, facilitating
r response and environmental reviews, furthering local under-
ding of Los Angeles history and ethnic heritage, and even finding
film locations.[14]

Making these data public is exactly the right thing to do, and I hope
that other cities and communities will follow suit, both with their own
historic resource surveys and with any other municipal data they have
on hand. As many a computer programmer and software engineer can
tell you, open-source data spur innovation. The Green Lab could never
have conducted the *Older, Smaller, Better* report without accessing
diverse data sets, both from the city and from other organizations. Making survey data accessible in digitized form allows members of the community to use the data to create apps and websites that solve problems
and make life easier—say, apps that help find affordable apartments,
track bike-share stations or snowplows, or direct visitors to historic sites
of note.

Digitized, publicly available survey data also help city planners and
developers take advantage of renovation opportunities. In April 2014,
as part of the Buffalo Building Re-Use Project, Buffalo's mayor, Byron
Brown, released a CD containing the data from the city's Preservation-
Ready Survey. It identified more than five hundred historic buildings
downtown that were eligible for preservation tax credits and other reinvestment incentives and that were primed for reuse. The information—
in effect, a treasure map to Buffalo's most valuable historic assets—was
shared with local, state, and national real estate developers so that they
knew exactly where the best redevelopment prospects in Buffalo were
waiting.[15]

Through open data, businesses can make more informed choices
about new construction as well. A few years ago, the National Trust

and other preservation allies met with Wal-Mart executives to encourage them to stand down on a proposed 138,000-square-foot megastore 15 miles west of Fredericksburg, Virginia, right in the heart of an important Civil War battlefield. The proposed site had once been "the nerve center of the Union Army during the Battle of the Wilderness," in historian James McPherson's words. It was now going to be a giant box store and parking lot.[16]

Once the joint awareness campaign with the Civil War Trust and others convinced Wal-Mart of the site's importance, the company agreed to give up their original proposal and donated the land to the state of Virginia. It then asked us how we could prevent similar such problems in the future. One good answer is a publicly available digital survey of important Civil War battlefields so that Wal-Mart and other businesses can know beforehand if their proposed development would affect an important historic place. Put simply, I believe most companies want to do the right thing—or at the very least, they want to avoid a costly battle with concerned residents. Access to data makes it easier for them to do it.

Finally, open-source data also help generate accountability, transparency, and a sense of civic engagement. The more people who have access to this information, the less likely it is that a municipality will move in a direction that runs counter to the interests or desires of affected residents or neighborhoods. If anything, cities should partner with community organizations to help analyze their findings and should encourage them and other residents to share theirs as well. Access to more data means more informed and less arbitrary decisions, which profits everyone.[17]

Of course, figuring out the neighborhoods that most stand to gain from historic revitalization is only the first step. We also have to make sure older buildings are free to work their magic and a city's zoning and building codes are up to date.

Step 2: Pursue Regulatory Solutions, Not Obstacles

For roughly five millennia now (and perhaps for far longer), our urban environment has been partially shaped by municipal regulations. "If ever any person living in the city pulls down his old house and builds a new one," King Sennacherib of Assyria told residents of Nineveh in 3000 BC in one of the first-known building codes, "and the foundation of that house encroaches on the royal processional way, they shall hang that man upon a stake over his own house." Other examples of early building regulation can be found in Hammurabi's code (shoddy builders will be put to death), and the Old Testament (among the many other rules therein, the book of Leviticus decrees how structures should be appropriately inspected for disease-causing mold).[18]

Thousands of years later, while the laws have proliferated (and the punishments have become considerably less severe), the contours of our urban landscape are still predominantly determined by building and zoning regulations. "Code is to the city what an operating system is to a computer," wrote Charles Montgomery in *Happy City*. "It is invisible, but it is in charge." In the words of another expert, Sonia Hirt, zoning "conveys to us messages of the places in the city where we can and should meet each other, the streets we can and should travel on, how many cars we can and should have, and the kinds of homes we can and should live in. It tells us about the activities we can and should perform at home and the kinds of people we can and should live near." In short, Hirt argued, regulation "imposes a moral geography on our cities."[19]

These regulations are often good and necessary. History books are rife with terrible, readily preventable tragedies that were caused or exacerbated by the lack of (or flouting of) sensible regulations. To take just one particularly notorious cautionary tale, consider the 1911 Triangle Shirtwaist Fire in New York City, in which 146 garment workers died because of inadequate fire codes and workplace protections. Locked inside a ninth-floor sweatshop in a building that had only one pitiful and inadequate fire escape, the workers—overwhelmingly young women—were forced to jump to their deaths to avoid the flames.[20]

It's also safe to say that the American preservation movement over the years owes much of its success, if not its very existence, to regulatory constraints enacted by towns, cities, states, and the federal government to protect historic and treasured places.

For example, dismayed both by the disappearance of older homes and Standard Oil's mass building of gas stations at the time, Charleston, South Carolina, created the first-ever historic district in 1931, along the famed Charleston battery, to promote "the preservation and protection of historic places and areas of historic interest." This 1931 law established a five-member Board of Architectural Review, made up of knowledgeable architects, planners, and artistic-minded citizens, that gently (so as to avoid a legal challenge) offered advice to builders and residents within the designated district on issues such as paint colors, mantels, and paneling. The board didn't protect old buildings from demolition, even within the district boundaries—it couldn't delay demolitions until 1959, or prohibit them until 1966—but the law still helped ensure that the exterior features of new and renovated construction were compatible with the existing environment.[21]

Five years later, in 1936, New Orleans passed a similar zoning plan to protect the Vieux Carré, a.k.a. the French Quarter. (It is no coincidence that today the Battery and the French Quarter are two of the South's biggest tourist draws, a direct result of these wise interventions.) Soon thereafter, many other cities created their own local historic districts—including Alexandria (1946), Winston-Salem (1948), Santa Fe (1953), and Boston (1955)—to ensure that new construction didn't disrupt historic character. Two hundred cities had passed similar preservation laws by the 1970s. By the 1990s, that number had leaped to 1,800.[22]

These local historic districts—as well as state and national registers, Section 106 and 4(f) reviews, national monuments, and protected public lands—are all examples of worthwhile regulation that have made our homes and cities more interesting and desirable.

At the same time, we have to make sure that our codes and zoning regulations reflect what we now know about the successful city. They should help rather than hinder vibrant cities by allowing for high densities, mixed-use buildings, and the effective reuse and adaptation of existing historic fabric. As it is, many places across the United States, as one developer in Los Angeles put it, still suffer from "obsolete zoning that was put in place for a lifestyle that is no longer relevant"—a lifestyle of megahighways, strip malls, separation of uses, and expanding suburban development.[23]

This situation is mainly because conventional American zoning methods, for reasons ranging from protecting the public health to maintaining property values, often segregated buildings by use: houses should be by houses, factories by factories, stores by stores. As Hirt pointed out in her 2015 book *Zoned in the U.S.A.*, this strict segregation of uses is a uniquely American phenomenon. "The U.S. model" of zoning, she noted, "focuses on strictly separating the basic land-use classes (residential, commercial, industrial, etc.) in ways we don't commonly find in other countries . . . [and] gives a highly preferential treatment to a particular spatial form—the single-family home with the private yard— in ways we don't easily find elsewhere." The result of this tendency is "urbanized environments that are strikingly low in population density, from an international point of view."[24]

Put another way, this uniquely American "zoning tendency finds its apotheosis," wrote Jeff Speck, "in suburban sprawl, where an elephantine regime of separated activities enforces the bankrupting hyper-mobility that has been so destructive to our national civic life."[25]

To put their historic fabric to work, cities need flexible zoning policies that allow for old industrial warehouses to be readily converted into lofts or offices, former corner stores to become restaurants or breweries, and old, single-family townhouses to become multifamily apartments without undue and unnecessary red tape. They need policies where setback regulations—which dictate how far buildings must be from the street or one another—aren't mandating useless empty spaces that are diminishing density and thwarting creative infill. In addition, they need codes that are flexible enough to recognize the distinct character of older structures, which may have been built before the automobile and assuredly don't need a panoply of parking spaces surrounding them now.[26]

Los Angeles is in the middle of a much-anticipated five-year overhaul of its zoning codes, the first in seventy years. Many of the cities leading the way in urban revitalization of and through historic neighborhoods—places like Denver, Miami, Nashville, and Washington, D.C.—have been revamping their regulations as well to ensure that they are fostering dense, walkable, self-regenerating neighborhoods rather than additional sprawl.[27]

In Baltimore, for example, city officials have been working on TransForm Baltimore, a comprehensive rewrite of the city's zoning code (the first since 1971). Among other things, the TransForm Baltimore plan simplifies and streamlines the regulations and approval process surrounding the renovation and repurposing of historic buildings. It also creates neighborhood commercial districts that would more readily allow for commercial and nonresidential uses in certain older neighborhoods, as well as more mixed-use zone districts to speed along the adaptive reuse of the city's extensive industrial infrastructure. Philadelphia has undertaken similar reforms.[28]

Similarly, recognizing that historic structures often have distinct features and needs that make them incompatible with cookie-cutter, one-size-fits-all regulation, California passed a State Historic Building Code into law in 2013. It works to provide "alternative building regulations for permitting repairs, alterations, and additions necessary for the preservation, rehabilitation, relocation[,] . . . change of use, or continued use" of historic structures while ensuring that they are still fire- or earthquake-safety compliant. Currently, the alternative code only applies to buildings that have been landmarked or put on a historic register, but preservationists and reformers are working to expand its scope to include older buildings in general.[29]

Sometimes when I mention ongoing work like this in speeches or interviews, people blink and ask me, aren't you the preservationists? They say, I thought you *enacted* codes and regulations, not relaxed them! But rules are not all that preservation is about. Preservation is about keeping buildings alive, in active use, and relevant to the needs of the people and the cities that surround them. To best accomplish this purpose, zoning and building regulations often need to be modernized and made more flexible, and regulatory barriers to building reuse need to be lifted. When done correctly, these steps can elevate and accelerate cities' efforts to remake themselves through their existing historic fabric.

Another way forward that has been gaining traction is form-based zoning, an idea first put forward by the founders of the New Urbanism movement: planners, designers, and architects who aimed to combat America's ever-expanding sprawl by creating higher-density, walkable, mixed-use communities. Instead of emphasizing *use*, form-based zoning puts *form* first, meaning both the form of the buildings themselves and their physical relationships to one another and to the street. A good form-based code is context-sensitive. It starts with a careful analysis of historic development patterns, tailoring zone districts and development regulations to align better with the character of valued older neighborhoods. This type of zoning tends to accord better with both the rhythms of older blocks, where uses were often mixed, and the lively neighborhoods cities now want to create. In addition, because zoning is such a powerful tool, it allows for urban transformations at scale.[30]

Believing in the necessity of good regulation and believing that our regulatory apparatus could be streamlined in some important ways are

Opportunity: A BiggerToolbox
Percent of Buildings Impacted

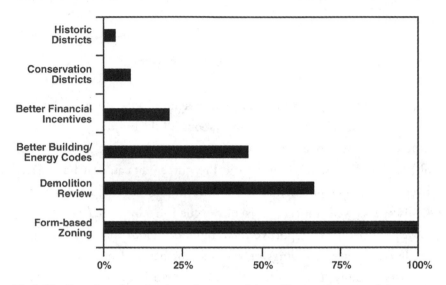

Tools like form-based zoning have the potential to affect much more of the existing building fabric than designating historic or conservation districts. (© National Trust for Historic Preservation)

by no means mutually exclusive. To take an example from the federal realm, most people would agree that one of our government's most fundamental tasks is ensuring food safety: nobody wants dangerous or even spoiled food on supermarket shelves. But they may also wonder why, currently, more than fifteen different federal agencies are involved in this critical oversight role, often with overlapping jurisdictions.[31]

In the case of historic buildings, inasmuch as possible without compromising safety, it makes sense to streamline permitting and approval processes so that opportunities for adaptive reuse aren't compromised by endless red tape. One solution is creating preapproved solutions for typical building conversions in older neighborhoods, such as warehouse to restaurant and one-family to multifamily houses. Ensuring that separate municipal departments, such as planning, building safety, and fire safety, are all working together—and have the necessary resources and staffing capacity to inspect and approve projects in a timely fashion— also can help jump-start urban revitalization.[32]

Step 3: Ensure That Old and New Construction Are Compatible

"Old buildings were a necessary ingredient of city diversity back in the 1920s and 1890s," wrote Jane Jacobs. "Old buildings will still be a necessity when today's new buildings are the old ones." And it's true: although older buildings are a critical resource that can only be replaced over time, new construction has a part to play in the thriving urban landscape as well. Indeed, as Jacobs argued in *Death and Life* and the *Older, Smaller, Better* report verified, neighborhoods that thrive are generally ones where buildings of various vintages and new construction coexist amicably. That is often the job of historic preservation: to help us manage change in our environment and ensure that the best of the past and present are working together to forge a more vibrant future.[33]

There are many preservation zoning tools, traditional and otherwise, that can help bring about this necessary balance of old and new. As noted above, even the very first historic district, in Charleston, was created more to ensure that new construction was compatible with the existing fabric than to prevent any new construction at all.

More recently, in towns ranging from Indianapolis to Boulder to Boise, cities have also adopted what are called conservation overlay districts to safeguard the look and feel of neighborhoods that may have a harder time qualifying as a historic district. In Dallas, for example, conservation overlays have helped protect the character of neighborhoods in East Dallas and Oak Cliff, which have a distinctive ambience worth protecting. Like traditional historic districts and form-based zoning, these overlays help ensure that infill construction and renovations are respectful to traditional historic norms.[34]

When at all possible, we want to keep older buildings working along-side new construction on behalf of the community. Demolition should always be the last resort: when a building is gone, it is not coming back, and all its rich historic potential cannot be replaced. Besides, as we've seen and I discuss further in chapter 4, older buildings are often remark-ably flexible, and if the zoning and code regime in a city sufficiently allows for it, they can be converted to any number of important new uses.

At the same time, there are usually plenty of places to add creative and compatible new construction between, near, and even above older structures. That is especially true given the vehicular turn of urban plan-ning in the last century: many towns have massive parking lots, aban-doned or dilapidated "greyfields," and even underused roads that can be reclaimed. The enormous distances between buildings that the motor-ized life afforded also allow for dynamic infill opportunities.[35]

Historic and conservation district ordinances may help ensure that the exteriors of new buildings are compatible with their older neigh-bors, but architects and developers would do well to have their new creations follow the overall design lessons of older buildings as well. Often, these structures are old for a reason: they have withstood the test of time. And, as both Jacobs and the futuristic-looking, increasingly creaky modernist buildings of the mid-twentieth century in many cities remind us, today's brand-new buildings are tomorrow's quaint historic fabric, so they should be designed and built with flexibility and longev-ity in mind.

"The unit of analysis isn't the building," argued architect Frank Duffy in Stewart Brand's *How Buildings Learn*, "it's the use of the build-ing through time." Usually, a good building will outlast its creators and then some, and over the decades or even centuries, it will likely fulfill a variety of uses over its long life. So, to keep a building a vibrant and well-trafficked place over generations, one should plan for this adaptability in the preliminary design. For example, Brand noted, "pouring concrete on the ground for an instant foundation ('slab-on-grade') is maladaptive—pipes are foolishly buried, and there is no basement space for storage, expansion, and maintenance and services access." Flexible interior spaces, which can be rearranged for a diversity of uses over time without extensive reconstruction, are another way to help a new building become long-lived. "Thinking about buildings in this time-laden way is very practical," argued Duffy. "It means you invent building forms which are very adaptive."[36]

When it comes to adaptive architecture, the wisdom of time is instructive. "The 'specious old box' is old," wrote Brand, citing a complaint Frank Lloyd Wright once made of older buildings, "because it is profoundly adaptive." Occasionally over the years, Brand pointed out, there will be a fad in architecture that aims to throw out all the old rules and begin again with a sleek, futuristic new look. In the 1850s, it was octagon-shaped homes; in the 1970s, it was geodesic domes, popularized by inventor, scientist, architect, and general jack-of-all-trades Buckminster Fuller. After a few years of heroic striving, however, the people living and working in these visionary edifices generally discover there were good reasons things were done in the old manner. "What's good about 90-degree walls," noted author and green building advocate Lloyd Kahn, after one-too-many experiences in a geodesic dome, "they don't catch dust, rain doesn't sit on them, easy to add to; gravity, not tension, holds them in place. It's easy to build in counters, shelves, arrange furniture, bathtubs, beds. *We* are 90 degrees to the earth."[37]

One will note that, generally, we are not living or working in octagons or geodesic domes in the present day. That is not to say new building shouldn't try new things or simply follow age-old rules of construction as they have been handed down. But as with urban planning in general, it is helpful to approach new construction with an eye to, and a healthy respect for, the surrounding urban landscape. As I will discuss more in chapter 7 on the environmental impact of older fabric, there are very good reasons many old buildings are built the way they are.

Step 4: Make Streets for People First

It may seem like something out of a *Twilight Zone* alternate future now, but at the dawn of the twentieth century, virtually every city in the United States with more than 10,000 people boasted its own street-car system. In Boston and San Francisco, Kansas City and Detroit, Orlando, New Haven, and Cincinnati—all across the country—urban life moved and grew at the pace of the "trolley." We all know how this story pans out. In 1910, there had been one car for every 265 people in the United States. By 1928, the ratio was one in six and falling. By 1931, there were twenty times more cars on the road than two decades earlier. Today, it is one car for every two people, and more than five out of six of us drive to work.[38]

"The right to have access to every building in the city by private motorcar, in an age when everyone possesses such a vehicle," warned Lewis Mumford, "is actually the right to destroy the city." Of course, that's exactly what happened. With cars in ascendance, trolleys lost their luster and were soon phased out in city after city. Soon, roads were widened to accommodate faster driving. Pedestrians were shunted to the sidewalk, and new laws against jay-walking were passed to keep them there. The distance between places elongated, making it harder to walk anywhere regardless. Buildings and entire neighborhoods were demolished to make room for ever more highways, byways, throughways, and, above all, parking lots—a great asphalt sea stretching from coast to coast.[39]

Many attribute the decline of streetcars in the United States to an organized conspiracy by car, oil, and rubber interests; namely, car companies bought up many of the existing rail lines and dismantled them to make room for buses instead, all while road- and highway-building projects received enormous government subsidies. "A civilization completely dependent on cars, as ours is now, was not inevitable," argued James Howard Kunstler. "The automobile, a private mode of transport, was heavily subsidized with tax dollars early on, while the nation's streetcar systems, a public mode of transport, had to operate as private companies, received no public funds, and were saddled with onerous regulations that made their survival economically implausible." In his 2008 book *Fighting Traffic: The Dawn of the Motor Age in the Twentieth Century*, historian Peter Norton unearthed an often neglected chronicle of urban residents contesting the sudden explosion of cars in their midst.[40]

At the same time, once cars became affordable enough for the average family, it's hard to discount the passionate love affair the American public felt for this new technology. As even Kunstler conceded, "there was nothing like it before in history: a machine that promised liberation from the daily bondage of place." "The automobile stands unique as the most extravagant piece of machinery ever devised for the pleasure of man," effused one smitten banker in the *Atlantic Monthly* in 1925. Millions more felt the same. As such, author David Owen is almost certainly correct in arguing, in his book *Green Metropolis*, that "there was no public force in the United States, in those days, that could have held back the death of the streetcar, even if anyone had the will to try."[41]

In any event, we all know how the universal adoption of cars, to the exclusion of all other forms of transportation, has transformed our urban landscape today, and often not for the better. This is especially true given that, for decades, traffic planners have been in the grip of the same sort of myopia that afflicted the master builders of Jacobs's time: they have let their abstract theories of automobile transportation overrun what the overwhelming evidence on the ground is telling us. (In her 2004 book *Dark Age Ahead*, Jacobs herself excoriated traffic engineers as an "incurious profession" that "pulls its conclusions about the meaning of evidence out of thin air—sheer guesswork.")[42]

Perhaps the most damning deficiency of current traffic policies is their inability to grapple with the phenomenon of induced demand, whereby more roads result in more people choosing to drive, which results in more gridlock. We have known that induced demand is a problem for decades, going back to the days of Robert Moses. When Moses built his great New York highways system, he purposefully precluded both present and future opportunities for mass transit. For example, he refused to include mass transit rights-of-way in his highway projects, even when they were already paid for, and constructed overpasses that would always be too low to accommodate buses. As one former aide put it, Moses believed "the early twentieth century was the age of the automobile as the nineteenth century was the age of rail," and as such, "mass transit was always a bottomless pit . . . a social good, but a financial loser."[43]

The irony of Moses's city of throughways is that it was ultimately self-defeating. In a given hour, a rail line can move 40,000 people, whereas a lane of highway can only handle 2,500 cars. Between 1930 and 1950, during the first wave of Moses's highway-building, the number of commuters to New York rose by 19 percent, but while the rate of rail commuters actually fell, the number of drivers soared 321 percent. So, despite all the extra asphalt Moses encircled around New York, the roads remained completely gridlocked. It was an increasingly unpopular annoyance for drivers, but Moses himself scarcely noticed—he barely knew how to drive and used a chauffeur.[44]

Fast-forward to today, and we find overwhelming evidence that constant attempts to beat congestion by building even more highways is a Sisyphean task. In 1998, the Surface Transportation Policy Project looked at seventy cities and found that "metro areas that invested heavily in road capacity expansion fared no better in easing congestion than metro areas that did not." The only difference between the two is that those cities that had built more roads had effectively wasted an extra $22 billion to achieve the same result. Six years later, another metastudy compiled the results of previous road use reviews and concluded that "on average, a 10 percent increase in lane miles induces an immediate 4 percent increase in vehicle miles traveled, which climbs to 10 percent—the entire new capacity—in a few years."[45]

"In every case," noted Danish urban designer Jan Gehl, "attempts to relieve traffic pressure by building roads and parking garages have generated more traffic and more congestion," yet despite the increasing preponderance of evidence attesting to this fact, we keep building more roads, and widening others, to accommodate this extra gridlock. "Induced demand," in Jeff Speck's words, "is the great intellectual black hole in city planning, the one professional certainty that everyone thoughtful seems to acknowledge, yet almost no one is willing to act upon. It's as if, despite all our advances, this one (unfortunately central) aspect of how we make our cities has been entrusted to the Flat Earth Society." That is why Speck's number one piece of advice to mayors and municipal leaders whenever asked is: "Stop letting your traffic engineer design your city!"[46]

Even more troubling are the dangers these prevailing theories pose to walkers and drivers both. To accommodate more, quicker, and presumably safer traffic, cities have been expanding the width of road lanes over the years, from 8 to 10 to the current standard of 12 feet. The problem is that we know beyond a shadow of a doubt that these wider streets mean more traffic fatalities. To take just one example, one study of nearly two hundred intersections in Tokyo and Toronto found lanes wider than 10.5 feet saw markedly more crashes and at higher speeds. That is because drivers "feel" safer in these 12-foot lanes and thus drive faster, making it less likely they will be able to stop before hitting another car—or a pedestrian, who now has to traverse an ever-longer distance across this faster thoroughfare to get where he or she is going. This pedestrian is also much more likely not to survive this encounter: A person hit by a car going 30 miles per hour is between seven and nine times more likely to die than one hit by a vehicle going 20 miles per hour.[47]

As noted earlier, the hegemony of cars also extracts considerable health, environmental, and economic costs for families. And, on top of everything else, wider thoroughfares even have a psychic effect on the residents and visitors of a city. A 1971–1972 study in San Francisco found that the more traffic goes by on a given street, the less likely the street is to have any sort of functioning street life or community. People who lived on heavy-traffic roads and were forced to contend with all the noise, pollution, and havoc these roads produce had half as many acquaintances and a third fewer friends on the block than those who lived on quieter streets. They even had a harder time picturing what their road looked like. "No amount of triangulation," wrote Charles Montgomery in *Happy City*, "can account for the corrupting influence that high-velocity transport has on the psychology of public space. . . . Automobiles ha[ve] the power to turn a neighborhood street into a non-place."[48]

The good news is that the converse is true as well. Reclaiming city streets from highways and making them more amenable to pedestrian use can help neighborhoods to reacquire their old activity and thrive once again. When New York City got rid of Robert Moses's beloved West Side Highway in the 1990s, naysayers argued that demolishing America's first-ever elevated highway would result in a traffic cataclysm—even though, when the highway was briefly put out of commission in 1973 due to a trucking accident, no such catastrophe occurred. Instead, about half the traffic using the bridge simply switched to other transit options. Meanwhile, historic neighborhoods along the west of Manhattan, such as Chelsea, Tribeca, and West Midtown, flourished. "It became a gold coast, so to speak," said New York's former traffic commissioner. Toppling the West Side Highway "added air and light and made it easier to get across the street and developed a sense of connection."[49]

New York's experience is not unique. In 2002–2003, Milwaukee removed the Park East Freeway that had split the downtown off from surrounding neighborhoods; by 2006, the land values in the area—now a park and enhanced riverfront—had increased by 180 percent, with no additional traffic issues to speak of. In Portland, Oregon, the city removed the Harbor Drive that ran along the waterfront in 1974. Since then, property values have tripled—exceeding the city's growth rate by 7 percent—and crime has dropped by two-thirds since 1990 (compared to a roughly one-sixth decline citywide). In San Francisco, the removal of the Embarcadero Freeway after it was damaged in the 1989 Loma Prieta earthquake has helped make Hayes Valley one of the Bay Area's hottest neighborhoods. Condo prices along the new Octavia Boulevard jumped from 66 percent to 91 percent of the city average after the highway's demolition.[50]

Today, the same story is unfolding in cities across the United States. In New Haven, Connecticut, neighborhoods once separated by Route 34 and left to fend for themselves are being stitched back together to the rest of the city by the Capitol Crossing project. In Washington, D.C., developers began an extensive restoration project of several acres of land near Union Station above I-395. "Through Capitol Crossing," longtime District of Columbia delegate Eleanor Holmes Norton said at the project's groundbreaking, "we are going to get three city blocks back that were lost to us for 395 when it split the downtown from us. And this time, we're getting city blocks for all kinds of amenities for pedestrians, for cyclists, and even for cars on 395."[51]

As anyone from the Boston area can relate, these extensive reclamation projects don't always go completely smoothly. Bostonians—particularly residents of the North End and Fort Point—are now enjoying the benefits of easier travel, safer streets, and the Rose Fitzgerald Kennedy Greenway, but the so-called Big Dig that submerged Interstate 93 beneath the city was the poster child for cost overruns and questionable construction deals for many years (in part because engineers and city officials unwisely prevaricated about the expected costs at the start).[52]

Similarly, Seattle is currently in the midst of what one observer has memorably deemed an "unbelievable transportation megaproject fustercluck" in its attempt to replace the Alaskan Way Viaduct, an elevated two-lane highway along the city's waterfront, with a deep underground tunnel—even though urban planners, residents, and the law of induced demand all argued that the tunnel was at best unnecessary and at worst an outright terrible idea given the nearby Puget Sound. For two years, from December 2013 to December 2015, that project was on hold while construction workers sheepishly attempted to fish "Bertha," the world's largest broken drill bit, out of what would be the widest deep-bore tunnel in history.[53]

These cautionary tales aside, reclaiming urban spaces from the highways that sliced and diced them in the twentieth century is proving in more places than not to be an exciting and rewarding revitalization strategy, for drivers and residents both. Indeed, some cities are even experimenting with banning car traffic altogether. Perhaps most notably, Mayor Michael Bloomberg made headlines in 2009 when he closed off New York City's iconic Times Square—the most visited tourist destination in New York State, seeing nearly a half million people a day—to vehicular traffic. It used to be, noted Montgomery, that "if you wanted to get run over, Times Square was one of the best places in the city for it." With the cars gone, however, suddenly the teeming crowds could fan out from the crowded sidewalks and fill the space again. Despite Bloomberg's successor's consternation about topless buskers who set up shop in the enlivened pedestrian district, the experiment, by almost any measure, was a resounding success. Before, "90 percent of the [Square's] users were being squished into just over 10 percent of the area," the heads of Gehl Architects noted in a 2015 op-ed. "After the changes, the rate of injuries went down (for pedestrians, but even more so for motorists), traffic flow in Midtown improved, and local businesses thrived—a fact reflected in steeply rising values of rental space." New York has since converted other avenues and areas around the city to the carless life as well.[54]

New York notwithstanding, not all cities in the United States—indeed, very few—have the pedestrian wherewithal to close off entire neighborhoods to car traffic without hurting local businesses. (Indeed, many attempts at "pedestrian malls" in the 1960s, '70s, and '80s ultimately resulted in failure.) At the very least, we can work to make our streets safer for other uses. Since coming together in 2005, the National Complete Streets coalition, created and led by Barbara McCann, has been pushing municipalities all over the United States to install wider sidewalks and medians, more crossing opportunities, bus and bike lanes, and other reforms that help allow for more expansive use of roads. "The fundamental philosophy behind the Complete Streets movement," McCann wrote in her book on the subject, "can seem painfully obvious: roads should be safe for everyone traveling along them. But the history, political standing, habits, and orientation of the transportation industry in the United States have made it extraordinarily difficult for any policy movement to shift the way transportation projects are planned and built."[55]

McCann is right. There are, however, plenty of steps cities can take to mitigate the overwhelming supremacy of automobiles that will improve the livability and liveliness of neighborhoods. In places like Boston, Miami, Seattle, and San Jose, municipalities have opted to close high-trafficked streets on certain days or weekends, sometimes on an experimental basis. Denver, Washington, D.C., Philadelphia, Boston, and other cities have also invested heavily in streetcar, light rail, or bike-share networks in recent years that give tourists and residents a chance to get around without bringing their car to the party.[56]

Anything that can help ensure a more diverse mix of transportation options will benefit neighborhoods. So too will adjustments that slow down the pace of life on the street and encourage more walking. In

1995, for example, Philadelphia passed a law allowing for more side-walk café seating, an ordinance that has clearly helped generate more dollars, visitors, and vibrancy for many of the city's blocks today.[57]

Cities can also spur growth by making some changes to what is often one of the biggest obstacles to their growth: parking. According to professor and parking expert Richard Willson in *Parking Reform Made Easy*, there are between 820 million and 840 million parking spaces in the United States. That amounts to nearly three and a half parking spaces for every car. Another estimate suggests that parking takes up roughly 3,590 square miles of land, more land than Delaware and Rhode Island combined.[58]

Why is parking everywhere? For one, cities have been subsidizing its true cost, which—once you factor in construction, maintenance, and a litany of health, environmental, energy, opportunity, and other costs—"exceeds the value of all cars and may even exceed the value of all roads," according to Donald Shoup, author of *The High Cost of Free Parking*. Shoup calculates the typical parking space to cost about $4,000. Some of these associated costs are heavier than a simple dollar figure suggests. According to a 2010 study cited by Willson, because of "the impact of parking in the lifecycle performance of various types of private vehicles[,] . . . parking adds between 6 and 23 grams of carbon dioxide equivalent per passenger kilometer traveled." (I will talk more about the grim calculus of carbon on our future in chapter 7.)[59]

These surprisingly heavy burdens are ultimately passed on to households. "When we shop in a store, eat in a restaurant, or see a movie, we pay for parking indirectly, because its cost is included," wrote Shoup. "If cities required restaurants to offer a free dessert with each dinner, the price of every dinner would soon increase to include the cost of dessert." Cities often further create disincentives by routinely making street parking so much cheaper than garage parking. As a result, according to one study, about a third of all urban congestion is caused by people circling for a cheaper curbside parking spot rather than biting the bullet and opting for a garage.[60]

Perhaps most problematic for historic preservation purposes is that city laws often mandate that each building include a given number of parking spaces, even when the buildings in question were constructed before the automobile era. Much of San Francisco mandates one parking space per residential unit, for example. Along certain parts of Wilshire Boulevard in Los Angeles, city law mandates two and a half parking spaces for every unit! As Willson noted, another part of the same Los Angeles boulevard demands twenty-two parking spaces for every 1,000 square feet of restaurant space, meaning that the parking lot surrounding many LA eateries is seven times bigger than the restaurant itself.[61]

This unfortunately leads to the catch-22 situation known as Pensacola parking syndrome—a moniker coined by Jeff Speck and his fellow new urbanist colleagues Andres Duany and Elizabeth Plater-Zyberk in their book *Suburban Nation*—whereby cities tear down so many historic buildings to satisfy their mandated parking requirements that they end up creating a beleaguered downtown where nobody goes or parks anymore. Donald Shoup has told a similar story about Buffalo, where seemingly half the city was rooted out to make room for parking. "If our master plan is to demolish all of downtown, then we're only halfway there," deadpanned one Buffalo resident. "If you look very closely, there are still some buildings that are standing in the way of parking progress."[62]

Even when parking demands don't result in the demolition of historic fabric, they still enable what Speck rightly calls "parking-induced commercial stasis," such that older buildings cannot be creatively or adaptively reused because of stringent parking requirements. These blown opportunity costs can metastasize to cause real problems across a city. To take just one example, the one-space-per-unit parking requirement mandated in much of San Francisco increases affordable housing costs by 20 percent, and getting rid of it would, by Shoup's math, make it more feasible for 24 percent more residents to buy their own homes. Meanwhile, at any particular moment, according to a 2010 study, 500 million parking spaces across the country are sitting empty.[63]

"Every architect and developer knows that minimum parking requirements are often the real limit to urban density," argued Willson. In fact, he wrote, these requirements also "subsidize cars, increase vehicle travel, encourage sprawl, worsen air pollution, raise housing costs, degrade urban design, preclude walkability, and exclude poor people."[64]

The good news is this problem can be fixed. In its 1999 adaptive reuse ordinance, Los Angeles waived parking requirements for older buildings in its historic downtown, greatly facilitating—according to Shoup and many others—the reuse of dozens of older structures for residential use. In its analysis of Baltimore, Philadelphia, and other cities, the Partnership for Building Reuse has similarly advocated for eliminating onerous parking requirements for older buildings. "Ample, easy parking is the hallmark of the dispersed city," noted Montgomery. "It is also a killer of street life." In fact, just as with the heavy traffic streets, urban residents are less likely to know anyone in their community if the shops around them have parking lots. Conversely, fewer asphalt dead zones means more foot traffic and more business.[65]

With that in mind, another reform to make street life more pedestrian-friendly and vigorous is—you guessed it—simply allowing the power and potential of older building fabric to work its magic. Over the years, Jan Gehl's observational "Public Space, Public Life" surveys have found that the pace of street life is both slower and more vibrant on what the Green Lab's *Older, Smaller, Better* study would call "high-character" streets, those defined by many small buildings and mixed uses. In the Radiant Cities defined by skyscrapers and highways, Gehl wrote in *Life Between Buildings*, "one sees buildings and cars, but few people, if any, because pedestrian traffic is more or less impossible . . . [and] with great distances between buildings, there is nothing much to experience outdoors." On streets with smaller, lower, and closer buildings, however, "it is possible to see buildings, people coming and going, and people stopping in outdoor areas. . . . This city is a living city."[66]

To test Gehl's theories, Charles Montgomery in *Happy City* asked volunteers to walk around New York City, continuously evaluating their happiness as they moved. He found that people, when traversing Lower Manhattan, were almost invariably most depressed as they walked by "a nearly unbroken swath of smoked glass for much of an entire city block" on East Houston Street—a.k.a. the site of a new and monolithic Whole Foods Market. His walkers "felt much better," though, Montgomery reports, "once they got to a grittier but lively stretch of shops and restaurants just a block east on Houston."[67]

As he pointed out, this is not just an aesthetic issue; it has very serious ramifications on our health and well-being. "Seniors who live among long stretches of dead frontage," Montgomery wrote, "have actually been found to age more quickly than those who live on blocks with plenty of doors, windows, porch stoops, and destinations. Because supersize architecture and blank stretches push their daily destinations beyond walking distance, they get weaker and slower, they socialize less outside the home, and they volunteer less."[68]

This argument echoes a heartbreaking observation by Dr. Richard Jackson, former Centers for Disease Control and Prevention researcher and coauthor of the 2011 book *Making Healthy Places*. One sweltering summer day in 1999, as Jackson was driving along the seven-lane Buford Highway in Atlanta, he saw an old woman on the side of the road dragging two heavy shopping bags as well as she could behind her. If she had expired from heat exhaustion or been hit by a truck, he realized, her cause of death would never have been linked to "lack of sidewalks and transit, poor urban planning, and failed political leadership," yet that is what had brought her to that unhappy and desolate stretch of highway, risking her life just to get the weekly groceries.[69]

As Enrique Peñalosa, the mayor of Bogotá, Colombia, who made his city an early adopter of automobile mitigation, told the United Nations in 2006, "A city can be friendly to people or it can be friendly to cars, but it can't be both." At the very least, we can try to move the balance in favor of the former. Recent polls have shown that Americans—and especially the large, diverse millennial generation—want to see more alternatives to driving in their communities, and they support additional funding for public transportation by wide margins. As I will discuss more in chapter 7, all environmental evidence suggests that our current car-centric landscape and lifestyle will only grow increasingly more untenable as the years go by. This is a critical chance for us to go back, to the future.[70]

Step 5: Invest in Main Street

As I discussed in chapter 2, older, smaller building fabric is a tremendous economic engine for cities. If the *Older, Smaller, Better* findings didn't persuade you, consider the research done by architect and developer Joseph Minicozzi, who has been working on the renovation of downtown Asheville, North Carolina. Minicozzi compared the economic performance of a renovated six-story, former J. C. Penney building in the heart of Asheville's Main Street corridor against the local Wal-Mart, sitting (as Wal-Marts generally do) well outside the traditional city. But—and here's the rub—he compared economic performance per acre of land used. After all, he pointed out, we evaluate the economic performance of a car by examining its miles per gallon, not how many gallons the car's tank actually holds.[71]

When compared in this fashion, there's no contest. The J. C. Penney building—now a mixed-use retail, business, and residential facility—created seventy-four jobs per acre against Wal-Mart's six. And although Wal-Mart paid only $50,800 in retail and property taxes to the city per acre, the J. C. Penney building paid nearly seven times that—$330,000 per acre—just in property tax. The local mall, also built outside the tra-

ditional downtown, only brought in $8,000 per acre. In sum, the build-
ing on Main Street created far more jobs and produced a much larger
economic return per acre than buildings outside downtown.[72]

Minicozzi attempted the same analysis in other cities—Sarasota, Florida; Billings, Montana; Petaluma, California—and got much the same
result. "Even low-rise, mixed-use buildings of two or three stories—
the kind you see on an old-style, small-town main street," summed up
Charles Montgomery of Minicozzi's findings, "bring in ten times the
revenue per acre as that of an average big-box development."[73]

Indeed, exurban big-box stores sometimes even cost cities more than
they bring in due to the need to run out and maintain roads, electricity,
water, and other services to them. As Minicozzi pointed out, however,
because property taxes don't usually factor in the value of land used,
"we've created tax breaks to construct disposable buildings, and there's
nothing smart about that kind of growth. . . . We simply cannot afford
how the current system creates incentives for suburban sprawl. . . . Let's
all do the math so we can make some positive changes in the system
because, in the end, downtown pays."[74]

Downtown does pay, and cities would do well to invest in (or reinvest
in) their traditional downtown shopping districts. Many of these critical
commercial corridors were left moribund by the shopping mall boom of
the 1970s and '80s, but they have been making an amazing comeback
in recent decades.

We have seen it firsthand for years now at the National Main Street
Center, which began in 1980 as a program of the National Trust for
Historic Preservation and is now a full-fledged subsidiary, and it has
been something special. In effect, even before the Green Lab conducted
its own research on the value of older, smaller fabric, the National Main
Street Center helped more than 2,000 communities preserve and revitalize their traditional downtowns and commercial districts. The center has done this by bringing volunteers, stakeholders, and community

leaders together and offering an organizing framework that embraces a town's unique historic resources and leverages them on behalf of economic prosperity.[75]

In 1977, three years before establishing the Main Street Center, the National Trust first undertook a demonstration project in three small cities—Galesburg, Illinois; Madison, Indiana; and Hot Springs, South Dakota—to figure out how to best help downtowns revitalize in the face of the then-burgeoning mall movement. After compiling an analysis of each downtown's distinct assets and needs—data drive decisions!—and figuring out which commercial buildings were ripe for revitalization, the National Trust hired a full-time program manager for each city to bring people together, coordinate efforts, and promote both the short-term and long-term benefits of investing in the historic downtown.[76]

The strategy worked. Almost immediately, six new businesses moved back to downtown Madison, Hot Springs saw seven new companies and a 25 percent jump in sales tax revenues, and Galesburg saw thirty new businesses open their doors and an occupancy rate along the Main Street corridor of 95 percent. All three towns enjoyed a number of restored historic buildings that were working once again for the community, and it was all accomplished with an amazing return on investment: for every dollar spent managing the local Main Streets, an additional $11 was invested by private businesses, eager to take advantage of the opportunities the older buildings in downtown provided.[77]

Soon thereafter, in 1980, the National Trust officially launched the National Main Street Center and expanded the demonstration project to six states—Colorado, Georgia, Massachusetts, North Carolina, Pennsylvania, and Texas—each of which suggested five initial towns to make up their Main Street Network. This time, the National Trust hired state coordinators and encouraged the five communities in each state to hire their own staff, since local advocates would know who the best movers and shakers were.[78]

Three years later, the results were again heartening. Twenty-eight of the thirty original towns either created or expanded their downtown advocacy organizations. The same number set up incentives, such as low-interest loan pools, that would help spur renovations to the historic downtown. As a result, more than 650 façades were fixed up and nearly 600 buildings renovated, thanks to a total investment of $64 million. (An additional $84 million helped support sixty new buildings.) Most important, these thirty downtowns saw more than 1,000 new businesses, and fewer than half that many business failures, along their traditional commercial corridors. Many of the Main Street Network towns had also developed an advocacy infrastructure to build on this strong foundation and encourage more developers and businesses to come back to the old, now revitalized downtown.[79]

The lessons learned from these early Main Streets were clear. Perhaps most obvious was that the older and historic buildings that line Main Street had real economic value. To keep these important assets in use and economically viable, there needed to be a comprehensive focus on, and understanding of, the forces that help make a downtown vibrant. And so, during these early years, what's known as the Main Street Approach took shape. Its hallmark is a comprehensive, grassroots-based framework that not only helps generate new investment, jobs, and building rehabilitations, but rekindles community optimism about the future and pride of place.

With a growing confidence we were on the right track, Main Street began reaching out to more states and communities in 1984 and developing user-friendly materials for more places to follow the same process. By 1990, Main Street was up and running in thirty-one states and more than six hundred towns and cities. Through further demonstration projects, we also honed specific tools for both historic neighborhoods of major cities and the Main Street corridors of very small towns, those numbering fewer than five thousand people. In addition, we created a membership program and annual national conference to further connect the developers, city leaders, and community advocates across the country who were leading the way in reshaping downtowns.[80]

As of 2015, the locally based programs that are now known collectively as Main Street America had reinvested $61.7 billion in historic corridors all over the United States (Table 3.1). They have helped generate nearly 530,000 net new jobs and more than 120,500 net new businesses, and have resulted in the renovation of more than 250,000 historic buildings. In addition, for every $1 Main Street spent in 2014, $26 was invested by public and private sources in rehabs and adaptive use projects.[81]

In 2014, after several decades of experience under its belt, the National Main Street Center further refined its methodology, building on the foundations of the original framework and updating it to reflect new trends and realities facing commercial districts in the twenty-first century. Through intensive conversations with local stakeholders, the center first tries to develop a strong understanding of both the community's goals and expectations for its historic downtown and the market realities and opportunities on the ground. It then works with these local leaders and stakeholders to come up with a few community transformation strategies that will help achieve these goals. These strategies should

Table 3.1 Cumulative Reinvestment Statistics (since 1980) Showing Main Street Impact

$61.7 billion reinvested
120,510 net new businesses
528,557 new jobs
251,838 building rehabs

Source: Main Street America, "National Main Street Center," http://www.preservationnation.org/main-street/.

have outcomes that can be quantifiably measured, such as the number of jobs or businesses created.[82]

These strategies are then implemented across four major areas: economic vitality, design, promotion, and organization. In practice, this "Four-Point Approach," as it is known, means using historic assets to forge a strong foundation for business opportunities and long-term economic growth, in part by emphasizing the Jacobsian ideals of mixed use, density, pedestrian friendliness, and downtown housing. It means capitalizing on the distinctive features that make a particular Main Street unique and historic, and encouraging art, music, events, and other creative uses of the public space that will inspire more visitors and foot traffic. It means highlighting the local downtown as a center of active communal and commercial life, and celebrating the rich history of that particular place. And it means bringing together all the many people in a neighborhood who have a vested interest in the downtown's continued success, and helping them work together toward a brighter future.[83]

This "Four-Point" system works, and has been working for decades. The proof is in the many stretches of historic Main Streets that have once again become thriving hubs of activity. Every year, the National Main Street Center selects a handful of Main Street America communities to be honored as Great American Main Streets, places where it has all come together, and where public and private partners have committed to economic revitalization through the power and potential of historic buildings.

To take one of innumerable examples, Main Street honored Manassas, Virginia, in 2003. Fifteen years earlier, like too many important Civil War battlefields, the Manassas community was threatened by encroaching suburban sprawl, including even a possible Disney park. (The story of that fight, and the National Trust's part in it, is well told in my predecessor's 1997 book, *Changing Places*.) But business owners, city leaders, and government officials came together as Historic Manassas.

They renovated the 1914 train depot and made it a state visitor center. The old candy factory, boarded up for twenty-five years, became an arts center. The opera house became a gourmet food store. The county courthouse became offices for the clerk of the court. By 2003, fifty-four buildings had been renovated, 350 jobs had been created, and $12 million in private investment had been put to good use to make Manassas once again a well-trafficked crossroads.[84]

Two years later, Main Street honored a city on the other side of the Washington, D.C. beltway, Frederick, Maryland. A vibrant and prosperous city going way back, Frederick took a number of hits in the late twentieth century. Retail anchors moved to shopping malls, and a new interstate highway took jobs and dollars away. The 1976 Carroll Creek flood drowned nearly 100 acres of the downtown and caused $25 million in damages, compounding all the other financial problems.[85]

Here again, however, the Frederick community came together on a plan that focused on economic improvement through historic revitalization. The city implemented a $54 million flood-control project that tamed Carroll Creek while creating pedestrian walkways. The county government moved its courthouse to downtown Frederick to encourage movement back to the city. The community converted its historic opera house, dime store, and 1895 mill into performing arts spaces and arts education facilities. The 1923 Francis Scott Key Hotel, through the use of state and federal historic rehab tax credits—a critical tool I will discuss in the next section—was converted into office space, retail, a theater, and upper-floor housing.[86]

Today, Frederick is once again in full bloom. Nearly all its 2,500 historic properties have been renovated for contemporary and mixed use. People from all over the area come to the first Saturday gallery walks and annual outdoor festival. It is one of the fastest-growing communities in Maryland and is a great place to spend a weekend.[87]

This story isn't just about the East Coast. On the other side of the

United States, the small town of Rawlins, Wyoming—population 9,200—was honored by the National Main Street Center in 2015. First founded in 1867, Rawlins had by the end of the twentieth century moved rather far afield from its railroad boom days. "In 1997, you could have shot a cannon down Cedar Street and not hit anybody," quipped Pam Thayer, the local Main Street executive director. The downtown neighborhood was then experiencing vacancy rates as high as 60 percent—unless you count pigeons, which by then had completely taken over the abandoned hotel along the Main Street strip.[88]

Here again, the community went to work reactivating the historic fabric downtown. The local Main Street group fashioned a façade easement program to spur renovation and facilitate the redevelopment of historic storefronts, which benefited eighty businesses and helped restore sixty-five properties. Local artists painted eye-catching murals, which Main Street, Rawlins businesses, and the local museum helped promote. The Rawlins city council passed zoning changes that allowed for more housing downtown and invested in $1 million of streetscaping that included adding two enormous metal hawks, which now serve as a gate to the area. The pigeons have been relocated also; thanks to a $1.8 million renovation, the old hotel is now an entrepreneur center, offering classes, conference rooms, and office space for businesses and innovators.[89]

In total, the Rawlins downtown has seen two hundred new jobs and twenty-eight new businesses. The vacancy rate has dropped to 10 percent. The community has come together to contribute more than 28,000 volunteer hours. And $8.5 million has been reinvested in Rawlins's future. For every dollar Main Street spent, Rawlins's downtown saw $9.56 in returns. Railroad or no, Rawlins is back in a big way.[90]

You can see the pattern. (If not, there are dozens of other impressive success stories available on the National Main Street Center's website.) In city after city, when communities put the historic resources of their old downtowns to work, jobs and prosperity soon follow. That is true even in our largest cities. In Washington, D.C., for example, the revitalization of the H Street corridor as well as other emerging neighborhoods like Shaw has been spearheaded by local Main Street America programs and partners.

Step 6: Take Advantage of Historic Tax Credits

By now, I hope I have convinced you of the tremendous economic and civic opportunities that come with reusing the older buildings in our midst. You may be wondering, however, how to encourage the reinvestment needed to get historic neighborhoods back on their feet. What financial aid and assets are out there to help spur redevelopment in your own city or town?

With that in mind, let's talk about the federal historic tax credit, one of our most powerful preservation tools at present. This tax credit, equal to 20 percent of qualifying rehabilitation costs, is made available to income-producing buildings deemed "certified historic structures" by the National Park Service and the State Historic Preservation Office of record. Developers have the ability to transfer this 20 percent credit to investors in exchange for equity, which helps lower the amount of debt needed to finance a given project. This move in turn draws additional private capital to that project because it is now a less risky and more secure investment.[91]

The historic tax credit was originally conceived of and designed in the 1970s, after bicentennial celebrations in the United States inspired additional interest in the nation's historic building stock. It was never intended to carry the entire freight of a given rehab; rather, it is a tool to help leverage private dollars toward important historic rehabilitation projects, and thus drive both preservation and economic development through adaptive building reuse. First tested in 1978, the federal credit was made a permanent feature of the tax code by President Ronald

Reagan in 1981. Since then, it has been not only one of the largest investments the federal government makes to preserve America's historic properties, but the largest community reinvestment program in the United States.[92]

It has also been a remarkable success story. Through 2014, the tax credit has created 2.5 million jobs, leveraged $117 billion in private investment, resulted in more than 260,000 renovated housing units, and transformed more than 40,000 unused or underused buildings for new and productive uses. Table 3.2 details some of these results.

In addition, every $1 invested as a historic tax credit generates at least $4 of private-sector investment. "Our historic tax credits," Reagan could proudly and correctly claim by 1984, "have made the preservation of older buildings not only a matter of respect for beauty and history, but of course for economic good sense."[93]

What's more, on top of all the other good they do revitalizing our cities, these federal tax credits are a revenue generator for the US Treasury. Since 1981, $22.6 billion in tax credits has generated more than $28.6 billion in federal tax revenue associated with historic rehabilitation

Table 3.2 The Impact of Federal Historic Tax Credits, 1977–2014

Buildings adaptively reused	40,384
Total historic tax credits generated	$22.6 billion
Total historic tax credit–financed investment	$117.6 billion
Total direct and indirect/induced jobs	2.5 million
Total income generated	$98.6 billion
Total federal tax revenue generated	$28.6 billion
Rehabilitated housing units	261,342

Source: *Annual Report on the Economic Impact of Federal Historic Tax Credit for FY 2014*; courtesy National Park Service and the Rutgers University Center for Urban Policy Research, https://www.nps.gov/tps/tax-incentives/taxdocs/economic-impact-2014.pdf.

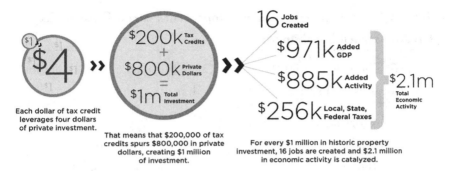

How the historic tax credit leverages private investment. (© National Trust for Historic Preservation)

projects (Table 3.3). Put another way, the US Treasury has made an extra twenty-five cents on every dollar invested.[94]

Even better, 75 percent of the economic benefits of these projects stay on the ground, in state and local communities. That is because developers generally buy materials close to the project site and hire local workers. In addition, because historic rehabs often require more skilled labor than new construction, they often need more workers at higher wages. These workers tend to spend these higher wages in the local community, at nearby shops and restaurants, thus creating a multiplier effect that further lifts all economic boats.[95]

From 2001 to 2013, for example, Maryland partook of $240 million in federal credits to complete nearly 400 rehabs, create nearly 20,000 jobs, and generate more than $753 million in household income. Georgia leveraged $76 million in federal credits to spur nearly 350 projects, create more than 7,000 jobs, and generate more than a quarter million dollars in household income. The same story holds true across the United States, including places in dire need of rebuilding investment. In Detroit, for example, developers and entrepreneurs took advantage of the federal historic tax credit to leverage roughly $681 million in private investment and complete fifty-seven historic rehab projects between

Table 3.3 The National Economic Impacts of Federal Historic Tax Credit–Assisted Rehabilitation

$117.6 billion cumulative (fiscal year 1978–2014) historic rehabilitation expenditures (adjusted for inflation) result in:

Jobs (person-years, in thousands)	2,493.0
Income	$98.6 billion
Output	$271.4 billion
GDP	$134.1 billion
Taxes	$39.3 billion
Federal	$28.6 billion
State	$5.4 billion
Local	$5.3 billion

$4.8 billion annual (fiscal year 2014) historic expenditures result in:

Jobs (person-years, in thousands)	78.0
Income	$3.4 billion
Output	$9.1 billion
GDP	$4.6 billion
Taxes	$1.2 billion
Federal	$0.8 billion
State	$0.2 billion
Local	$0.2 billion

Source: *Annual Report on the Economic Impact of Federal Historic Tax Credit for FY 2014*; courtesy National Park Service and the Rutgers University Center for Urban Policy Research, https://www.nps.gov/tps/tax-incentives/taxdocs/economic-impact-2014.pdf.

National Economic and Tax Impacts of Federal HTC-related Activity
FY 1978 through FY 2014 (HTC Investment: $117.6 billion in 2014 dollars)

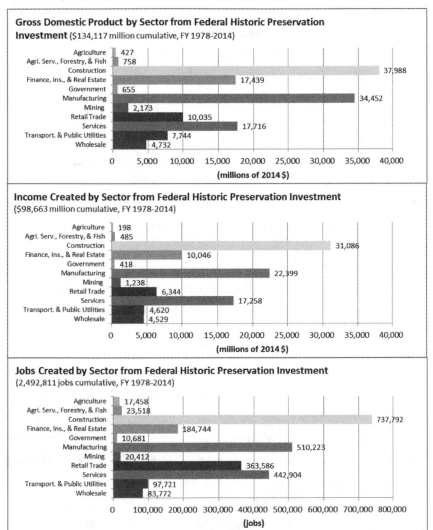

The national economic and tax Impacts of federal historic tax credit–related activity. (*Annual Report on the Economic Impact of Federal Historic Tax Credit for FY 2014*; courtesy National Park Service and the Rutgers University Center for Urban Policy Research, https://www.nps.gov/tps/tax-incentives/taxdocs/economic-impact-2014.pdf.)

2004 and 2014. These projects created more than 9,000 jobs and introduced new life into some of the city's most struggling neighborhoods.[96]

Seeing strong and consistent economic returns roll in, Maryland,
New Mexico, and Colorado moved to augment these gains by creating
their own state historic tax credits in the late 1980s and early 1990s.
Since then, thirty-one other states have followed suit to further encourage both private and federal investment in their historic neighborhoods.
Even places that don't have a state income tax, like Texas, have created
a program that works for them, and these have also resulted in positive
dividends. States with high-performing tax credit programs generally
bring between $3 million and $7 million in federal credits a year back
to those states. After Kansas passed its own state credit, for example, the
number of federal credit projects a year jumped from 2.4, on average, to
68—quite a jump.[97]

Each $1 of state tax credit also leverages an additional $4. Put another
way $200,000 in state tax credits creates $1 million in investment. In
addition, one-third of the state's money comes back when the building
goes into service, before the credits are even awarded. Another Maryland study found that every $1 of tax credit generates $8.53 in total
economic output, including $3.30 of wages, which is again a massive
return on investment. Even cities have gotten in on the act. In 1996,
Baltimore passed its own Historic Restoration and Rehabilitation Tax
Credit, which has helped finance more than two thousand rehabs and
$700 million in investment across Baltimore's eighty historic districts.[98]

In sum, historic tax credits now have a substantial positive record
going back decades. They are a proven vehicle for enhancing investment, promoting economic growth, revitalizing neighborhoods, and
enlarging state and federal tax coffers.

To encourage their further use, and help worthy projects navigate
the sometimes complicated financial transactions involved, the National
Trust created another subsidiary, the for-profit National Trust Commu-

nity Investment Corporation (NTCIC), in 2000. NTCIC partners with major banks, insurance companies, manufacturers, and other corporations to make equity investments and loans to projects that qualify for historic tax credits (as well as credits that are often "twinned" with them, such as new market, low-income housing, and even solar credits). We will look at some of their projects in more depth in chapter 4, but they range from affordable housing to community arts spaces to educational institutions. From 2000 to 2015, NTCIC managed to raise $964.4 million in capital for 120 tax credit transactions with more than $3.6 billion in total development costs—and more than 40 percent of their projects have been for nonprofits. If you want to learn more about how to bring historic tax credits to your community, NTCIC—along with your local state historic preservation office—is a great place to start.[99]

Despite their proven impact on community revitalization and economic vitality, historic tax credits have actually come under threat in some legislatures around the United States, not the least the US Congress. In 2012, for example, and after $42.3 million in state credits had been approved, Michigan repealed its own historic tax credit in a move that met the very definition of penny-wise and pound-foolish. The federal credit has also been threatened in recent years by tax reform efforts on Capitol Hill. In 2014, House Ways and Means chairman Dave Camp (R-MI)—following the unwise example set by legislators in his home state—proposed a sweeping tax overhaul that eliminated the historic tax credit, even though, again, it is a net positive for the US Treasury.[100]

Obviously, repeal is the wrong direction. If anything, the sixteen states that are currently missing out on these tremendous benefits should pass (or, in Michigan's case, restore) their state credits. And with some tweaks, the federal credit could be an even greater job creation and economic development engine, and generate even more high-impact community benefits.

To take just one example, after Hurricane Katrina, city and state leaders in Louisiana successfully lobbied Congress for a temporary increase in the federal credit from 20 percent to 26 percent to encourage rebuilding efforts in New Orleans and neighboring areas that were designated disaster areas. In April 2014, seven US senators put forward similar legislation (which did not pass) that would extend this 6 percent increase to historic buildings in federally declared disaster zones in 2012 and 2013, places that had suffered from Hurricane Sandy, extreme flooding in the South, dangerous wildfires in the West, and devastating winter storms in the Northeast and Northwest.[101]

These ideas are both excellent, but natural disasters need not be the only time the hardest hit areas receive tax incentives to rebuild. From Detroit on down the line, many of America's legacy cities were severely impacted by the Great Recession or have been facing financial crises in their own right. By now, a temporary increase in the federal credit is a proven and effective approach to kick-starting rebuilding and helping more cities take advantage of their underutilized historic fabric. All the data and all our experience suggest that investing in historic tax credits brings enormous financial, economic, and community returns. We need only the will and leadership to make it happen.

Step 7: Find and Support Other Funding Methods

The historic tax credit may be America's flagship preservation investment program, but—as the payroll tax break that helped San Francisco's Mid-Market flourish again attests—there are other creative ways cities and developers can help finance valuable revitalization projects. Some are tax credits that are already helping particular cities or states revive their historic fabric and could possibly be used in other municipalities if given the chance. Others involve innovative financing mechanisms like revolving funds and program-related investment (PRI) loans. Any or all of them might make the difference between a city that merely survives and a city that thrives.

Not surprisingly, older cities that have extensive historic fabric have often been leading the way in offering innovative supports for investment and redevelopment. Baltimore, already home to its own citywide historic tax credit since 1996, also offers a number of other strong financial incentives to encourage building rehabilitation. In 2013, Mayor Stephanie Rawlings-Blake introduced and passed a fifteen-year tax abatement on increased assessed values to encourage the creation of more multiunit housing in downtown areas, through both adaptive reuse and infill projects. The following year, the mayor signed a ten-year property tax credit to further promote downtown housing. Coupled with the Maryland Sustainable Communities Tax Credit—a.k.a. the state historic tax credit—both of these initiatives are helping Baltimore redeploy its considerable historic building stock to meet today's needs.[102]

Pennsylvania's historic tax credit is fairly new, but Philadelphia has surged ahead of its state in coming up with new investment mechanisms. Since 1997, the City of Brotherly Love has offered a number of city property tax abatements that have sparked investment, particularly in Center City and nearby neighborhoods. Nearly sixteen thousand properties have benefited, including more than six thousand rehabs, although this latter number dropped off dramatically after the city expanded this tax relief to new projects as well as improvements. Philadelphia also offers a homestead exemption of $30,000 to owners who live in their properties, further encouraging people to live and work downtown.[103]

Joining the roster of preservation leaders is Phoenix, which has passed a number of redevelopment incentives in recent years, among them support for low-income historic housing, exterior rehabilitation assistance, an adaptive reuse ordinance based on the Los Angeles model, and the repurposing of historic warehouses in a downtown warehouse overlay district. Some of this support comes in the form of faster approvals and relief from otherwise onerous regulations. In Boulder, meanwhile, the city offers a sales tax waiver on construction materials for restoring local landmarked properties, provided that 30 percent of the value of those materials will be used for the building's exterior.[104]

Under the leadership of Mayor Byron Brown, Buffalo too has been packaging a number of financial and other incentives to redevelop the city. "Being able to reuse the legacy buildings that we have in this community is critical," he argued. "We believe that if we can restore . . . more of these structures, not only can we make the economy of Buffalo more vibrant but we can also preserve our great architectural heritage, which people come from all over the world to see."[105]

At the state level, South Carolina Governor Nikki Haley signed into law what one local expert calls "the most powerful incentive for neighborhood revitalization that South Carolina has ever seen" in 2013. The Abandoned Buildings Revitalization Act (ABRA) provides a state income tax credit of up to 25 percent for renovating any income-producing building that has been at least two-thirds vacant for five years or more. (So as not to encourage bad behavior, developers who owned the properties before they went vacant are disqualified from benefiting.) ABRA passed in part because of a strong coalition of support that included the Palmetto Trust for Historic Preservation, community groups, and fire and police departments across the state, who were eager to see dilapidated structures that could be fire hazards or trouble spots restored to positive use. The beauty of ABRA is that it applies to all vacant buildings, not just designated landmarks, allowing for much more expansive restoration to South Carolina's historic fabric.[106]

South Carolina is also one of several states that offer business investment tax credits to encourage companies and financial institutions to support community development. Donations made to certified nonprofit organizations called community development corporations (CDCs) that have shown a demonstrable interest in undertaking specific revitalization projects in South Carolina receive a 33 percent credit against state tax liabilities. In Massachusetts, a similar credit goes up to 50 percent. Indiana has created a tax credit that applies to older buildings in certain designated community revitalization enhancement districts. And New Jersey's Neighborhood Revitalization Tax Credit, established in 2002, now goes up to 100 percent, provided that the nonprofit is using at least 60 percent of the funds for housing and economic development.[107]

There are even more funding streams out there. As noted in the last section, low-income housing, energy efficiency, new markets, and other types of tax incentives that are not strictly related to preservation can often be used, alongside historic tax credits, to make refurbishing older buildings more affordable than ever. Some cities, such as San Antonio, and states are successfully leveraging federal Community Development Block Grants toward historic renovation. Communities can also take advantage of tested tools like business improvement and tax increment financing districts, business development assistance, and façade improvement programs to further galvanize downtown redevelopment.[108]

Creative real estate financing mechanisms provide another avenue for funding rehabilitation efforts at scale. For example, preservation revolving funds are pools of money that are used to support renovation efforts, after which, once a given project is completed, all profits and surplus are returned to fund the next wave of work.[109]

As with so many other innovative preservation initiatives, from the local historic district to ABRA, South Carolina led the way: the Historic Charleston Foundation set up the first preservation revolving fund in 1957, to great success. Proceeds from this fund were used to purchase and renovate sixty dilapidated homes in the neighborhood of Ansonborough, which were then sold on the open market with restrictive covenants attached. Profits from the sales went back into the revolving fund to finance more real estate acquisitions. In this manner, nearly one hundred buildings in Ansonborough were renovated between 1959 and

1976, by the foundation, the buyers, or neighbors inspired by the revitalization happening all around them.[110]

In the late 1970s, Preservation North Carolina, under the leadership of J. Myrick Howard, launched the first statewide preservation revolving fund, to similar success. Today, there are more than sixty preservation revolving funds in use across the country, in places like Galveston, Knoxville, Fort Worth, Boston, and New Orleans. In the fall of 2014, the Savannah College of Art and Design studied the impact of twenty of these funds and found that, taken together, they had generated more than $3.1 million in property tax revenue and saved nearly five million square feet of usable space.[111]

More recently, and often to supplement revolving funds, enterprising preservation-minded groups have been using PRIs (program-related investments) to finance their work. Essentially, PRIs are loans made to a nonprofit organization by a foundation—for example, the 1772 Foundation, Knight Foundation, or Kresge Foundation—at below-market rates. Along with making more funds available to worthwhile causes that accord with a foundation's particular goals, PRIs allow organizations to expect their money back eventually with a small rate of return, and include other tax incentives that make it in a foundation's interest to offer support.[112]

To see how revolving funds, PRIs, and other creative financing methods can be woven together to achieve a striking turnaround for a community, consider the good work of the Historic Macon Foundation (HMF) in revitalizing the Beall's Hill neighborhood in Macon, Georgia. Josh Rogers, the executive director of HMF, was looking for new tools to help this thirty-two-block National Register district near Mercer University, which had fallen on hard times. After talking with preservation colleagues in Providence, who had achieved considerable success with program-related investments, Rogers decided to bring PRIs home to Macon, and they fast became part of a powerful suite of tools that is transforming this historic neighborhood for the better.[113]

In 2007, Historic Macon raised a $700,000 grant from the Knight Foundation, which was used to build and rehab twenty-two houses in Beall's Hill. That was a major coup in and of itself, and double the number of homes HMF had promised in its proposal to the Knight Foundation. That persuaded the foundation to step up in a much bigger way in 2014, with $3 million in grants and a program-related investment. (HMF's current executive director, Ethiel Garlington, wryly labeled this investment a "groan"—both a grant and a loan. Roughly half this "groan" will eventually need to be repaid at 1% interest.)[114]

This investment doubled the size of Historic Macon's existing revolving fund, allowing it to rehab an additional one hundred homes over the next five to seven years. According to Garlington, that is half the time it would have taken had HMF had to pay market rates to borrow the money.[115]

Then, guided by its fantastic program officer in Macon, Beverly Blake, the Knight Foundation went a step further and combined the loan with other community-building investments. Included was a $185,000 low-interest façade loan fund, financed in part by a Knight Neighborhood Challenge Grant, which helps Macon homeowners make capital improvements. By 2014, that fund had made forty-five loans totaling $350,000, with twenty-five loans of roughly $185,000 already returned. The default rate on these loans has been zero, and Historic Macon has made 2 percent interest on the transactions.[116]

Thanks to the local utility, Georgia Power, offering rebates of up to $2,200 for energy-efficiency programs, Historic Macon could also offer energy-efficiency loans to residents. In addition, HMF helped Mercer University secure a Knight Foundation matching grant that provided down-payment assistance to faculty and staff buying homes in Beall's Hill. Finally, the county invested in roads, sidewalks, lighting, and other infrastructure improvements, further helping revitalize the entire neighborhood.[117]

In total, an investment of roughly $5.8 million is transforming nearly five hundred homes. Garlington and his wife bought a house in the neighborhood too and have applied for façade and energy-efficiency loans; they find it incredibly satisfying to see the neighborhood regaining shape around them. As evidence that the rehab is working, total property tax revenue in the area had increased by nearly $1 million by the end of 2014, much of it from rehabbing abandoned houses and building on empty land. Indeed, Historic Macon never displaces current landowners by acquiring occupied houses. It also counters displacement in other ways too, such as recruiting low-income homeowners and advocating for property tax freezes.[118]

Organizations like Historic Macon are not just demonstrating that history, sustainability, fairness, and economic vitality can all go hand-in-hand. They are showing the rest of us that by taking advantage of innovative financing and maintaining a commitment to getting it right, entire neighborhoods and even cities can see their fortunes transformed. If they can do it in Macon, we can do it all over the United States.

Step 8: Try New Things

The creative synergy at Beall's Hill attests to two important lessons. First, a historic revitalization project done correctly anywhere can be a model for us to reproduce everywhere. Second, achieving real success in historic revitalization often requires embracing innovative new tools.

To unlock the full powers of the past for economic growth and urban regeneration, we must look to the future and try new things. Communities should not be afraid to use their older neighborhoods as real-world experimental laboratories to test out policies, flexible zoning and codes, financial incentives, and other innovative ideas that might further encourage revitalization. They should also assess the impact of these new ideas on older building stock, as well as the well-being of the families who live, work, and play there.

I have talked about a number of novel policy and financial tools over

the course of this chapter, and there are many more out the
2015, San Antonio's Office of Historic Preservation launched
buildings registration program to assess what empty structures exist
in the city, determine which have the most potential to serve the community, and protect them from being demolished by neglect. With the
help of the Green Lab, Seattle also recently enacted an outcome-based
energy code that better accords with the inherent energy efficiency of
older buildings, something I will discuss more in chapter 7.[119]

In July 2016, University of Massachusetts historians Max Page and
Marla Miller released a timely book of essays entitled *Bending the Future:
Fifty Ideas for the Next Fifty Years of Preservation*. It includes dozens of
innovative ideas and policies from across the spectrum of preservation
and urban revitalization, many of which could very well be replicable at
scale. To take just one example, Tom Mayes, the deputy general counsel
at the National Trust and a scholar who has written extensively on why
old places matter, floated the idea of a "building reuse ordinance" that
would establish a streamlined and coordinated set of rules for adaptive
reuse projects and in effect make building reuse the default option. By
putting the burden of proof on those who want to tear down a building
rather than on those who want to adapt it, Mayes's ordinance would
help ensure that demolition becomes what—particularly in this day and
age—it should be: the tool of last resort.[120]

Another promising frontier is twenty-first-century information
technology, such as GIS mapping, 3D-modeling, crowdsourcing, and
digitized surveys, all of which are opening new avenues of inquiry and
experimentation for cities. With issues like accelerating climate change
being the mother of invention, we are also getting better at moving and
waterproofing buildings, and even raising them up, without harming
the original structures. That too might play a part in refurbishing historic fabric and helping it breathe new life into communities.

The important thing is to apply the Jacobsian method of scientific testing and rigorous urban observation: try new things, develop metrics of accountability, see what works, and share your results, positive and negative, with others in the community. As Jaime Lerner, architect and former mayor of Curitiba, Brazil, put it, "the idea that action should only be taken after all the answers and the resources have been found is a sure recipe of paralysis. The planning of a city is a process that allows for corrections."[121]

Lerner is the author of a 2014 book entitled *Urban Acupuncture: Celebrating the Pinpricks of Change That Enrich City Life* and one of the original proponents of a burgeoning do-it-yourself movement that is now sometimes known as "tactical urbanism". In a book by that name, *Tactical Urbanism: Short-term Action for Long-term Change*, coauthors Mike Lydon and Anthony Garcia detailed a number of innovative, small-scale, temporary interventions that cities, or really anyone, could take to improve their local environment.[122]

Perhaps the most well known is Park(ing) Day, in which urban residents are encouraged to convert one of their city's ubiquitous parking spaces for a day into a tiny 9- by 18-foot garden, "parklet," or playground. Another is Build a Better Block, which originated in the Oak Cliff section of Dallas in 2010 and involves spending forty-eight hours revamping one single block, perhaps by creating more green space, painting in additional crosswalks or bike lanes, or opening up a temporary art exhibit. "For every one of these tactics that's in here," conceded Lydon, "you probably have several failed versions. But when you hit a nerve at the right time with the right group of people and you have enough people watching, you can really help transition these things into larger initiatives."[123]

These same sorts of "tactical" interventions can help act as a springboard for the strategic revitalization of historic neighborhoods. Indeed, they are exactly the sorts of promotions that Main Streets America has long advocated for to generate more interest in historic downtowns. In the summer of 2015, for example, Main Street volunteers in Bartow, Florida, sent out a call to artists, encouraging them to create a new piece using a mobile app called AppArt, which lets them take a photograph and then edit it in various creative ways. The fifteen winning submissions were then printed out and installed in ten empty buildings along Bartow's Main Street. This turned what had been a string of vacant structures into an impromptu art gallery and brought both foot traffic to the downtown and additional interest in the buildings. The pop-up art show proved so popular that it is slated to become a regular feature in Bartow, with new art contests held every few months.[124]

In the fall of 2014, as part of the campaign to save Cincinnati's iconic Union Terminal, the National Trust undertook a similar experiment by opening a pop-up shop and "Yes on 8" campaign center in a storefront in Fountain Square. (Proposition 8 was the ballot measure providing for a small sales tax increase to fund renovations to the terminal. It ultimately passed with 61% of the vote.) The temporary base on Walnut Street gave the National Trust a high-profile spot to get the message out about Union Terminal, and to make the case for the many virtues of historic preservation in general. Similar pop-up shops have and can be opened in vacant or underutilized storefronts all over the United States, giving vendors a chance to test their business models and make a little money, building owners an opportunity to see if there is a demand for their site, and neighborhoods to show they can draw more people. Add a few food trucks, a street musician, and some community art, and suddenly you can have a thriving corner almost anywhere.[125]

Pop-ups—or parklets or surveys or bike shares or streetcars or anything else discussed in this chapter—shouldn't be thought of as any kind of silver bullet. Very rarely does one single intervention completely transform a historic neighborhood from dismal to dynamic. Over time, however, applying these many ideas—and being unafraid to attempt new ways of spurring investment and creating community engagement—will pay enormous dividends. The most important thing is not to get discouraged.

Step 9: Be Okay with Starting Small

Envisioning and then realizing a more promising future for a city, or even one urban neighborhood, is a daunting task. It's easy to get despondent at countless points along the way. Remember, though, that Rome wasn't rehabilitated in a day. Take the positive steps you can, and then next month or next year make some more. Over time, the street in question will, one hopes, experience a snowball effect: regenerating one building spills over to its neighbors, then to a city block, and then to an entire neighborhood.

As proof that this strategy of patience works, consider Denver, a city I know well as a Loveland native and a graduate of the University of Colorado Boulder. Today, the Mile High City is a national leader in almost every way that counts. It is one of the fastest-growing cities in the United States, with a surging young population and some of the strongest economic growth in the country. Its population grew at a 1.5 percent clip between 2004 and 2014, double the national growth rate. It has seen more than 100,000 out-of-state residents move there since 2010, one of the highest rates in the United States, even higher than destination cities like Seattle and Washington, D.C. From 2011 to 2015, Denver saw 3,200 new businesses and more than 165,000 new jobs, pushing the unemployment rate down to an enviable 4.1 percent. And each year—in part because of its proximity to the Rockies and the Great Plains, but also thanks to its pedestrian-, bike-, and rail-friendly urban landscape—Denver rivals places like Washington, D.C., San Francisco, and Minneapolis–St. Paul for the title of America's Fittest City.[126]

How has Denver become such an urban powerhouse? There are a number of reasons, of course. To be sure, as with New York City, Denver enjoys some distinct geographic advantages. If Denver didn't exist, another great city would likely have formed in the exact same spot between the Plains and the Rockies. I would also submit, however, that the Mile High City is flourishing today because municipal leaders there "got" historic preservation as a tool for urban renewal much earlier than most. For decades now, long before others figured it out, Denver has been using its historic building stock to revitalize the city.

It all started with humble beginnings in one small neighborhood, Larimer Square, and through the committed efforts of one remarkable woman, Denver developer and preservationist Dana Crawford. Simply put, in the words of historian Judy Mattivi Morley, Crawford "showed that historic preservation could be profitable. By developing old buildings, Crawford used historic preservation to revitalize Denver's central business district and, in the process, defined a civic identity for Denver."[127]

In the mid-1960s, when Crawford began her work, Larimer Square was a notoriously down-on-its-heels Skid Row: to give his carefree spirit, Dean Moriarty, in *On the Road* some dramatic heft, Jack Kerouac made him "the son of a wino, one of the most tottering bums of Larimer Street," who begged and grifted "in front of Larimer alleys . . . among the broken bottles." "The word was that Larimer Street was just evil," Crawford later recalled. "There were schlocky bars on the street and . . . drunks lying on the sidewalk."[128]

True to the time, the original proposal to turn Larimer Square and its environs around, as conceived by the Denver Urban Renewal Authority, was a massive 117-acre project called Skyline that threatened to raze thirty blocks of the historic downtown. Dana Crawford had another vision for Larimer Square. "Downtown Denver was pretty much intact from its Victorian boom days and it reminded me a lot of Boston," said Crawford. So, even as Jane Jacobs was going toe-to-toe with Robert Moses for the future of Lower Manhattan, Crawford—inspired by Boston and the Gaslight Square neighborhood in St. Louis—began a corporation (Larimer Square Associates, or LSA) and, with her friends and neighbors, began buying older buildings in the blighted area, often for little more than the price of the land they sat on. "We think Larimer Square will be here 10 years from now," she told the *Christian Science Monitor*, "and paying both cultural and financial dividends to the city and to the investors."[129]

By 1965, LSA had acquired fifteen of eighteen buildings on the 1400 block of Larimer, enough to begin realizing Crawford's goal of a flourishing historic neighborhood in downtown Denver. That year, displaying a fearlessness she would become known for, Crawford announced a press conference for the mayor to tout the revised plan for Larimer Square—and then invited the mayor. Presented with a fait accompli, Mayor Thomas Currigan endorsed the new plan. "Before the turn of the century, Denver was a gay and boisterous city, and its spirit was typified by Larimer Street," he said at the presser. "Recapturing that spirit of youthful Denver in this fashion and at the same time preserving some of our historic buildings is a marvelous concept. In addition, this plan, when it comes to fruition, will help stabilize the lower downtown area, improve the tax base, and become a source of pride for all Coloradoans."[130]

At this point, Crawford went to work. Downplaying the area's seedier history in favor of a colorful mining boom past, she embarked on a press offensive to sell the potential of Larimer Square to all comers. She then renovated LSA's historic buildings in keeping with the older time frame she wanted the overall neighborhood to invoke, encouraged commercial tenants that fit the same historic theme, and obtained a historic designation for Larimer Square—Denver's first historic district—to stave off any further demolition ideas from the Urban Renewal Authority. Meanwhile, the city added benches, trees, and wider sidewalks to encourage pedestrians to the area.[131]

It was not always an easy lift. "I spent a great deal of time sitting at the

Urban Renewal Authority office fighting the fight," Crawford recalls. "At times, I can barely talk about it, it was such a hard fight. . . . Everyone said no one would ever live downtown. The bankers and business people said this was a ridiculous conversation." Twenty years later, however, when Crawford sold LSA's stake in Larimer Square, the neighborhood was in full flourish and was a powerful example of what could be accomplished in other parts of the city. "Crawford's fusion of preservation and development," wrote Morley, "had a tremendous impact on Denver's city planning policy. . . . By the mid-1980s, Denver's city government, planners, and business leaders accepted historic preservation as a powerful development strategy." "We really learned from Dana the whole importance of historic preservation," one developer later recalled, "not only what it could do for the community, but, frankly, what it could do for business."[132]

Now fully on board, the city of Denver set its sights on the revitalization of an adjacent neighborhood, the twenty-three-block warehouse district of Lower Downtown. To that effect, under the leadership of Mayor Federico Peña, the city put together a Downtown Area Plan in 1985 that included strong preservation guidelines and a moratorium on the demolition of historic buildings. It then created the Lower Downtown Historic District in 1988, and, two years later, Colorado became only the third state in the United States to pass a state historic tax credit.[133]

As any Denver resident can tell you, Lower Downtown—or LoDo, as it was rebranded and is now known—followed much the same path to success as Larimer Square. Today, it is considered the heart of the city, with the lowest commercial vacancy rates around. The neighborhood also afforded enormous opportunities for enterprising entrepreneurs who thought in the long term. Before he was Denver's mayor and later governor of Colorado, John Hickenlooper and three friends opened the Wynkoop Brewery in 1988, the same year the LoDo Historic District was formed. They bought space in Denver's historic Mercantile Building that year for $6 per square foot. A decade later, it was already worth 100 times that.[134]

Although others had now taken the lead on what she started back in Larimer Square, Crawford continued to play a role in LoDo's redevelopment as well, helping redevelop properties such as the Oxford Hotel and the Ice House—once a dairy warehouse, now a design center. And she is still pushing the envelope. Working with a group of partners, she also helped revamp Denver's nearby Union Station, originally built between 1881 and 1914. In the late 1940s, Union Station saw more than fifty trains a day, but that had dwindled down to two by the beginning of this century. As a result, even as much of LoDo became an active and thriving urban destination, the area around the Union Station stayed comparatively quiet. So Crawford helped assemble a public-private partnership that reimagined the station as the centerpiece of an inter-modal transit hub, capable of handling trains, commuter rail, and buses. Through a $40 million restoration project—financed in part by $8.1 million of federal historic tax credits—the station itself became the 112-room Crawford Hotel. Instead of sitting dark all day, it is surrounded by shops and restaurants.[135]

The preservation-minded spirit of Larimer and LoDo is now at work all over Denver, in neighborhoods like Capitol Hill, Uptown, Highland, and River North. Indeed, the same rules of growth are applying here as across the rest of the United States. A preliminary *Older, Smaller, Better* analysis by the Green Lab found that areas in Denver with older, smaller buildings and mixed-vintage blocks have more millennial residents, more small businesses, and more new businesses than other areas of the city. In addition, 42 percent of the jobs in areas of the city that are mostly prewar buildings are small business jobs, compared to 28 percent citywide.[136]

All across Denver, older buildings are breathing new life into their environment. Take the Stanley Aviation building in Aurora, on the edge of Stapleton. The facility, with its bright red "Stanley Aviation" sign, was a well-known area landmark in the 1960s, '70s, and '80s, seen by visitors going into the city from the airport. It looked like the facility would be demolished, but it was recently acquired by Flightline Ventures, which has proposed a $15 million rehabilitation instead. The proposed Stanley Marketplace, modeled after a similar overhaul of the Ferry Building in San Francisco, will include shops, dining, groceries, and offices.[137]

Another example is the remarkable Highlands' Garden Village. A mixed-use neighborhood of more than three hundred homes and 75,000 square feet of commercial space in Denver's West Highlands neighborhood, it was called "the best development in America" by the former director of the Congress for New Urbanism. Highlands' Garden Village was built by developer (and former National Trust trustee) Jonathan Rose on the grounds of an old amusement park that closed in 1995, and it has embraced all the steps outlined in this chapter, including the adaptive reuse of historic buildings, to create a dense, affordable, and sustainable mixed-use community where residents live, work, and play without ever getting in a car. The centerpiece of the Garden Village is the old Elitch Theatre, which is now a performing arts and community center that binds the neighborhood together.[138]

While Denver's future looks bright today, it is important to remember that the city's trajectory could have been very different if the historic downtown had been demolished as originally planned. Its success is in part because, as Jennifer Bradley of the Brookings Metropolitan Policy Program observed, Denver in the 1980s chose to "experiment in doing business in new ways." The city's resurgence came in "a thousand different steps," concurs Tami Door, president of the Denver Downtown Partnership, a coalition of more than seven hundred businesses in the city. "Nothing you see in downtown Denver is an accident. There isn't a tree or public space that wasn't thought about methodically." Denver happened, Door argues, because the city kept trying new things to lever-age their historic assets. "You don't know what's going to work until you try."[139]

Denver is by no means resting on its laurels. Door spends the bulk of her time envisioning ways to keep the city's downtown thriving, from promoting events, to recruiting businesses and entrepreneurs, to fight-ing for expanded parks and transit options. From virtually nothing, the city now has 122 miles of light rail and commuter rail built or under construction, with seven light rail lines converging downtown and three commuter rail lines meeting at Union Station. "Together," remarked Jay Walljasper of the McKnight Foundation, "this marks the most ambi-tious new transit system built in America since the Washington subway in the 1970s."[140]

Important civic projects like these are being funded in some novel ways. Since 1990, Colorado has had a state historical fund, financed through taxes on gambling, that makes grants ranging from a few hun-dred dollars to more than $200,000 to preservation projects that benefit local communities. In 2014, to finance more improvements and for the fifth time since 1990, Denver offered $500 "minibonds" to Colorado residents who wanted to invest in the future of the region. They sold out within an hour, raising $12 million in sixty minutes.[141]

In addition, in the summer of 2015, Colorado significantly expanded and improved its twenty-five-year-old historic state tax credit. The state now offers a 20 percent credit for the rehabilitation of historic owner-occupied homes and a 20 to 30 percent credit for historic buildings used for commercial purposes. Since it first passed its own credit in 1990, more than $800 million has been invested in tax credit–related projects in Colorado, and more than a thousand historic buildings have been successfully restored and rehabilitated.[142]

In sum, city and community leaders in Denver have been putting into practice all the steps outlined in this chapter to create huge opportunities for urban growth. By unleashing the tremendous potential of older buildings and neighborhoods to transform their city for the better, they have fashioned, as one observer put it, "a twenty-first-century city built on the foundations of its frontier past." Their experience proves that, rather than demolishing historic fabric, we should harness it to grow our economy and meet the needs of citizens in the twenty-first century.[143]

Of course, there is one more critically important step to getting this urban regeneration right. This tenth step is probably intuitive in a lot of ways, and yet is still so important that I'm giving it its own chapter:

Historic buildings should play a necessary role in the life of the community.

CHAPTER 4

Buildings Reborn: Keeping Historic Properties in Active Use

Designing a dream city is easy; rebuilding a living one takes imagination.

    —Jane Jacobs[1]

Precisely because they are old, the older buildings all around us are ripe for reinvention. These structures have already withstood the test of time, so they have likely already shown themselves effective at fulfilling a particular need for the community. For the reasons discussed in chapter 3, these "specious old boxes" are often especially well suited for adaptation to a new use or uses. Finally, and just as important, old buildings have inherent and unmistakable character, the type of character that only time can convey. Because they give us a sense of history and connect us to earlier generations of city life, people like them and like being around them.

When making the case for older buildings as a key to urban vitality, Jane Jacobs pointed to this endless capacity for reinvention. "Among the most admirable and enjoyable sights to be found along the sidewalks of big cities are the ingenious adaptations of old quarters to new uses," she wrote in 1961. "The town-house parlor that becomes a craft-man's showroom, the stable that becomes a house, the basement that becomes an immigrants' club, the garage or brewery that becomes a theater, the beauty parlor that becomes the ground floor of a duplex, the warehouse that becomes a factory for Chinese food, the dancing school that becomes a pamphlet printer's, the cobbler's that becomes a church[,] . . . the butcher shop that becomes a restaurant: these are the kind of minor changes forever occurring where city districts have vitality and are responsive to human needs."[2]

Although rehabs can sometimes be a tricky enterprise, "the fact is that obsolete buildings are fun to convert and a delight to use once they're converted," Stewart Brand argued similarly three decades later. "Wouldn't you rather go to school in a former firehouse, have dinner in a converted brick kiln, do your office work in a restored mansion?" For the majority of Americans, by all available metrics, the answer is yes. In city after city, the hot new restaurant, nightclub, or bar is frequently in a converted structure of some kind. Both the condos drawing young tenants and the affordable housing meeting the needs of seniors are often historic rehabs that offer all contemporary amenities while retaining the old distinctive quirks. The offices of innovative start-ups once saw garment workers, machinists, barbers, or distillers ply their respective trades within the same four walls. "A building being reconfigured for a foreign new use is filled with novel opportunities," said Brand.[3]

Often, people tend to think that these sorts of innovative and adaptive reuse projects aren't really the bailiwick of historic preservation—that those who call themselves preservationists would rather take these old buildings, throw a few plaques on the front, and bottle them up like, well, preserves. But in fact, adaptive reuse is the very warp and woof of preservation, and has been central to our mission for at least a half century.

As Lady Bird Johnson wrote in her foreword to the 1966 *With Heritage So Rich* report: "In its best sense preservation does not mean merely the setting aside of thousands of buildings as museum pieces. It means retaining the culturally valuable structures as useful objects, a home in which human beings live, a building in the service of some commercial or community purpose." Mike Buhler, executive director of San Francisco Heritage, agrees. "One of the central tenets of historic preservation," he has said, "is that historic buildings must have an active use, and must be valued by people, in order to survive and thrive."[4]

Preservation is not just about keeping old buildings around. It is about keeping them alive, in active use, and relevant to the needs of the families and the cities that surround them. We do not honor the historic buildings in our midst, nor those who once inhabited them, by trapping these structures in amber or sequestering them away behind velvet ropes. We do it by working to see that they continue to play a vibrant role at the heart of the community.

And, although there are many excellent exceptions across the country that belie the rule, that can't always mean turning them into museums.

Beyond House Museums

In the earliest days of preservation, often the go-to answer for reviving a historic building was reconverting it into a house museum. In fact, one of the foundational narratives of the American preservation movement is the story of how the nation's first-ever house museum came to be.

In 1853, traveling home by boat from Philadelphia after visiting her doctor, a South Carolina woman named Ann Pamela Cunningham was awoken late one night just as the ship was passing Mount Vernon, the palatial estate of America's first president. She despaired at what she saw. "I was painfully distressed at the ruin and desolation of the home of Washington," she wrote to her daughter, "and the thought passed through my mind: Why was it that the women of his country did not try to keep it in repair, if the men could not do it? It does seem such a blot on our country!"[5]

At the time, the men in Congress and on both sides of the Potomac were lurching toward the "irrepressible conflict," and had neither the time nor much of an inclination to worry about the state of George Washington's old home. So Cunningham founded the Mount Vernon Ladies Association and began raising funds to purchase the plantation. She galvanized women from both the North and South to invest in her restoration plan, proving that, even during the darkest of times, Americans of wildly different political outlooks could come together to protect a cultural resource whose value they shared. By 1859, Cunningham had made a down payment on the home—the current owner, George Washington's great-grandnephew, was inspired by Cunningham's resolve—and had begun restoration work.[6]

That work was soon derailed by the Civil War. In 1866, however, and although in failing health, Cunningham returned to Mount Vernon to continue the rehabilitation. Over the next eight years, even as the country remained bitterly divided over Reconstruction, Cunningham worked to bring women together behind Mount Vernon and laid the groundwork for the enormously successful house museum it is today. "Ladies, the Home of Washington is in your charge," she declared in 1874 as she stepped down, only a year before her death. "See to it that you keep it the Home of Washington. Let no irreverent hand change it; no vandal hands desecrate it with the fingers of progress!"[7]

Score one for Cunningham. Today, Mount Vernon is the most popular and visited historic estate in the United States, teeming with life, scholarship, interpretation, and roughly one million visitors a year. In the years since Mount Vernon was saved, and in part because it was the only vehicle people knew of at the time to save an important building, a vast tide of house museums emerged. In communities all over the country, people enshrined the homes of local, state, and national heroes, from Paul Revere, to Louisa May Alcott, to Alex Haley, to James K. Polk. Fans of the fourteenth president, for example, can visit Franklin Pierce's childhood home in Hillsborough, New Hampshire, and then venture on to Pierce Manse, his adult home, in Concord after lunch.[8]

Many of these house museums make for wonderful day trips. I have spent many a crisp fall afternoon tromping among the preserved 1850 log cabins of Pryor Hollow at Land Between the Lakes in Tennessee, buying freshly ground cornmeal at the Colvin Run Mill in Great Falls, Virginia, and admiring the painstaking detail of the Gamble House in Pasadena, California. The National Trust also proudly owns or is affiliated with a portfolio of twenty-seven historic sites around the United States. Among them are Filoli house and gardens in Woodside, California; the Shadows on the Teche, in New Iberia, Louisiana; Philip Johnson's Glass House in New Canaan, Connecticut; and Drayton Hall, outside of Charleston, South Carolina.[9]

Ann Pamela Cunningham's resurrection and restoration of George Washington's estate established and forever legitimized the house museum model for historic buildings. But, for all Mount Vernon's many charms, it is also in many ways a beguiling exception. After all—and with all due respect to Maryland's John Hanson, president under the Articles of Confederation (who has his own museum in Williamsfield, Ohio)—there's only one first president of the United States. At best count, however, there are roughly fifteen thousand house museums in the United States today.[10]

Put another way, there are more house museums in the United States than McDonald's restaurants. There are two house museums for every CVS pharmacy and three for every Wal-Mart. If they were evenly distributed, there would be five of them in every single county in the country.[11]

To be sure, this astounding proliferation speaks to both Americans' deep interest in our own history and our profound desire to see older

HISTORIC HOUSE MUSEUMS

15,000
nationwide

 = 1,000

5 per county

There are fifteen thousand house museums in the United States. (© National Trust for Historic Preservation)

buildings continue playing a role in our communities. Sadly, though, many of these house museums are not thriving: often, these places are barely scraping by, deferring critical maintenance, and cutting programming and staff. More than half see fewer than five thousand visitors a year. "There's a disconnect between the impulse of wanting to save an old house," noted professional preservationist Vince Michael, "and the economic reality of running a house museum." That disconnect has made many otherwise worthwhile historic enterprises simply unsustainable. In 2002, the average house museum incurred a cost of $40 per attendee, but only took in $8 per person. No amount of creativity in the gift shop is likely to bridge that $32 gap.[12]

In 2007, Donna Ann Harris, a preservation consultant and former state Main Street coordinator, wrote a book entitled *New Solutions for*

House Museums that gets to the heart of the dilemma many of these museums are facing. "The initial motivation of preservationists who saved the building," she noted, "was to retain the structure as part of the historic fabric of the community. In most cases, the initial group who saved the site chose a museum use by instinct or by default with little understanding of the harsh realities of the costs, skills, and experience needed to actually run a museum."[13]

But "museum use," Harris correctly pointed out, "is not necessarily the best conclusion for every hard-won preservation battle." Indeed, cordoning older buildings behind a plaque and some ropes can contribute to them remaining sterile, shut off, and, soon, in need of ever more support. Instead of trying to squeeze more from the house museum stone, we should channel our energy into the original impulse—the desire to see these places continue to thrive.[14]

Often, that can involve returning a house museum to its original function. For example, the boyhood home of Robert E. Lee in Alexandria, Virginia, was once a house museum, but it was attracting fewer and fewer visitors and faced clear and mounting restoration needs. So, after much deliberation, the nonprofit foundation that owned the home decided its best option was to return the house to use as a private residence. The nonprofit sold the house in 2000, precipitating an uproar among Civil War enthusiasts. But the new buyers—longtime preservationists Ann and Mark Kington—undertook a meticulous two-year restoration, and today the house is in much better shape than before.[15]

Returning a historic home to the private market is by no means a silver bullet for securing its future. In 2007, for example, Colonial Williamsburg sold the historic Carter's Grove plantation on the James River to a tech entrepreneur, with attached easements to protect the future of the property. After the financial crisis eroded the purchaser's fortunes, however, Colonial Williamsburg ended up buying back the property at auction in 2014. (It resold the plantation that fall to Samuel Mencoff, a preservation-minded Chicago investment firm executive who is committed to a sensitive restoration.) Nonetheless, similar arrangements, such as Historic New England's successful preservation easement program, have helped return many historic houses to their original residential use. Other tools, such as the revolving fund programs discussed in chapter 3, have also helped save thousands of other historic homes, like the Fisher-Kahn house (designed by venerable architect Louis Kahn) in Hatboro, Pennsylvania.[16]

The outright transfer or sale of historic house museums is still a contentious tool in the preservation world and is often fraught with legal, ethical, financial and public relations issues. (One former museum director even dubbed it "the Final Solution for house museums.") If the ultimate goal is saving places that matter, though, transfers and sales can be very effective—provided there are accompanying easements to protect the future of the homes in question.[17]

Places Revived

That being said, in the twenty-first century, returning a historic building to its former use is far from the only potential outcome. Notwithstanding Ann Pamela Cunningham's admonitions about "the fingers of progress," preservation has evolved since the antebellum era. Today, there are many good options for keeping older and historic buildings alive, options that retain what makes them special while keeping them engaged in the life of the community. They are literally happening all around us.

Performance, Art, and Event Spaces

Consider the Todd Bolender Center for Dance and Creativity in Kansas City, Missouri. This 52,000-square-foot facility began life as a coal plant in 1914 and closed in the 1970s. Today, though, what was once a boxy, inelegant power plant is now the remarkable new home of the Kansas

City Ballet. "We're now creating a new source of power—dance energy," said the company's executive director of the former Power House, and it is working: season attendance nearly doubled in their first year in the renovated dance complex, and student enrollment rose 70 percent in three years.[18]

Or look at the Park Avenue Armory, in the heart of New York City. Once a jewel of Gotham's Gilded Age, the armory first opened on New York's Upper East Side in 1881 to honor and house the National Guard's Seventh Regiment, the first volunteer militia to answer Lincoln's call in 1861. This Silk Stocking Brigade, as it was known, included famous New York family names like Harriman, Van Rensselaer, Livingston, and Roosevelt—the pinnacles of city society.[19]

As such, no expense was spared. The armory features the 55,000-square-foot Wade Thompson drill hall—one of the largest unobstructed spaces of its kind in the city—and a suite of rooms that the city's Landmarks Commission has called "the single most important collection of 19th century interiors to survive intact in one building." Each of them was appointed by a leading artist, architect, or designer of the time, people like Louis Comfort Tiffany, Stanford White, and the cabinet-makers Pottier and Stymus.[20]

Despite this embarrassment of riches, this remarkable armory was left poorly maintained for much of the second half of the twentieth century and fell into disrepair—that is until 2006, when members of the local Upper East Side community gathered together and formed the not-for-profit Park Avenue Armory Conservancy to save the building. They signed a ninety-nine-year lease with the state of New York and, in less than a decade, completely revitalized the structure—and not just by restoring the beautiful rooms and updating the amenities. They have restored the armory's central place in the life of the Upper East Side.

Today, the Park Avenue Armory is an unconventional arts space and one of the New York art world's creative hot spots. It has hosted groundbreaking visual installations, music, theater, and dance, including the New York Philharmonic and the Merce Cunningham Dance Company. For six weeks, the famous Royal Shakespeare Company even rebuilt a replica of its theater in the drill hall. This type of active-use enriches buildings and communities alike.

A similar story is unfolding nearby at the Williamsburgh Savings Bank. Built between 1870 and 1875, the Williamsburgh Bank was once the headquarters of one of Brooklyn's wealthiest and most influential financial institutions, an early manifestation of the Beaux Arts style, and, again according to the city Landmarks Commission, "one of the most monumental public spaces that survives in New York City from the post-Civil War era." It too had fallen into disrepair, until two investors, Juan Figueroa and Carlos Perez San Martin, saw it as an opportunity to revitalize the entire neighborhood around Broadway and Driggs Avenue. They bought the bank building from HSBC in 2010 and invested $24 million in repairs, including restoring the murals that adorn the interior of the bank's distinctive dome and reattaching its original circular skylight (which had been languishing in the basement for seventy-five years).[21]

Today, the bank is now Weylin B. Seymour's (thus maintaining the WSB monogram on the doorknobs and light fixtures throughout the building), a breathtaking performance, wedding, and events space that has been drawing rave reviews. "It's just the most beautiful venue any of us had ever seen," said the publisher of VICE Media after holding the company's office party there, "really inspirational and epic." It is also helping anchor similar revitalization efforts around the Williamsburgh neighborhood.[22]

In no small part because they were designed as monumental spaces in a city that's often at a premium for them, many other nineteenth- and early twentieth-century banks in and around New York City have been similarly converted into arts, performance, and event halls. The

magisterial Bowery Savings Bank, built on Grand Street in 1895 by
McKim, Mead, & White, is now a premium events and performance
venue called Capitale. The large Bowery branch on East 42nd, which
dates to 1923 and was deemed "a castle in the clouds brought to earth"
by *Architectural Forum* in 1928, now fulfills the same function in East
Midtown, as does the former Greenwich Savings Bank at Broadway and
36th. Another Williamsburgh Bank branch in Brooklyn is now Skylight
One Hanson (a.k.a. the street address), where events and weddings can
take place beneath its 63-foot ceilings and grand 40-foot windows.[23]

Not surprisingly, old theaters are extraordinarily well suited to serve
as twenty-first-century performance spaces too. When it first opened its
doors in 1929, the Kings Theatre on Brooklyn's Flatbush Avenue, for
example, was once one of the most beautiful cinemas in the country.
Indeed, it was one of the Loews Corporation's five "Wonder Theatres"
built in and around New York City, and designed by notable architects
of the time to go above and beyond the usual cinema experience. After
closing in 1977, however, the more than 3,000-seat venue sat vacant
and deteriorating for decades. Now, thanks to a $95 million renovation
spearheaded by the ACE Theatrical Group and the city of New York,
and through ample use of historic tax credits, the theater reopened in
February 2015 as a modern performing arts center. Hundreds of perfor-
mances and special events are planned, and it is already generating buzz
in and for the neighborhood. "It's going to revitalize Flatbush Avenue,"
said Brooklyn's borough president of the new arrival.[24]

On the other side of the country, the Fox Oakland Theater—built as
a state-of-the-art, cinema palace in 1928—is following much the same
path forward. The *San Francisco Chronicle* once marveled at the "different, novel, and mystical" theater, and applauded "its spaciousness,
luxurious appointments, and beautiful designs." After the Fox closed in
1966 and was the victim of arson in 1973, however, it gained another
nickname: "the largest outdoor urinal in the world." Then, the Fox only

barely escaped demolition. Today, after recent renovations, the Fox in Oakland is a 3,800-seat commercial theater and performing arts magnet school. Other "Fabulous Fox" theaters, built just before the Great Depression made "luxurious appointments" an increasing rarity, are now multipurpose performance halls and concert venues in Atlanta and Detroit.[25]

When it opened in 1910—two decades before Harlem's Apollo Theater became an African American institution—the Howard Theatre in the Shaw neighborhood of Washington, D.C., was known as "the largest colored theatre in the world" and one of the jewels of "Black Broadway." Over the years, it hosted Ella Fitzgerald, Nat King Cole, Duke Ellington, Marvin Gaye, Aretha Franklin, and the Supremes. In 1970, however, two years after rioting that devastated the surrounding U Street corridor, the Howard closed its doors and fell into disrepair. Then, in 2012, the reborn and refurbished Howard Theatre—now with museum and gift shop—reopened, helping bring further life back to the already revitalizing neighborhood. Today, it is once again a Washington, D.C., institution, where residents come together to see national acts take the stage.[26]

Back in the five boroughs, the new chapter for Flatbush's Kings Theatre is helping supporters of another former Loew's Wonder Theatre, the Jersey in Jersey City's Journal Square, make the case that it too should be an arts space and cultural center. (Although the other three Wonder Theatres are now primarily used as churches, the United Palace Theater on 175th Street still regularly hosts concerts, community events, and classes.)[27]

If a theater can be a church, a church can be a theater. In Cambridge, Massachusetts, the Jose Mateo Ballet Theatre, with the enthusiastic support of the local congregation, now trains and performs in the Old Cambridge Baptist Church, an American Gothic Revival building built before the Civil War. "The Sanctuary Theatre . . . provides an almost religious experience," said *Boston* magazine in 2011 of the unconventional hall. "The seats are so close that you can see every slash of muscle, hear each clack of a pointe shoe, and practically feel the performer's exhalations."[28]

Dancers of the Jose Mateo Ballet Theatre practice in the Old Cambridge Baptist Church. (Photo by Warren Jagger Photography)

Schools and Former Schools

In Baltimore, the old Crown Cork and Seal bottling cap factory in the neighborhood of Station North has experienced a similar creative rebirth. Originally built in 1915 and converted to a garment factory in the 1950s, the four-story, 120,000-square-foot machine shop closed its doors in 1985 and was such an archetypal example of dilapidated industrial blight that scenes from HBO's *The Wire* were filmed there. In 2013, however, after a nearly $27 million renovation, the old factory became the new home of the Baltimore Design School, a public middle and high school dedicated to training and inspiring future artists, architects, and fashion and video game designers.[29]

"The bones of the building were really great and we have a really high ceiling height," said architect Steve Ziger of the design school. "Since . . . natural light was such an important component of the original design, we really celebrated that with the new windows and it brings incredible light into the classrooms and throughout the building." Although studio spaces, labs, a media center, and other needed educational resources were added, Ziger and his colleagues used the machine shop innards of the factory to foreground the endless adaptability of older buildings and inspire students to use the space as their ideas and creations demand. "The concept for the building was pretty much just a blank canvas for them to transform," said Ziger, "and we built in the infrastructure for them to use their imaginations in transforming the building."[30]

That same pedagogical philosophy—harnessing the creative energy of reuse projects to inspire young artists and builders—is also on full display farther down the Atlantic Coast. The Hostess City of Savannah, Georgia, with its traditional grid layout, hauntingly beautiful buildings and parks, and Spanish moss-laden oak trees, has long been one of the nation's leaders in traditional historic preservation. That's why it remains a much-beloved southern destination that sees thirteen million visitors a year and counting. Savannah, however, is also now a leader in preservation through adaptive reuse, thanks to the committed efforts of the Savannah College of Art and Design (SCAD) and the vision of its president and cofounder, Paula Wallace.[31]

A former kindergarten teacher and interior designer, Wallace helped form SCAD in 1978 and has steered it to great success ever since. Under her leadership, the college has doubled in size; expanded to Atlanta, Hong Kong, and Lacoste, France; embraced new technologies; and been named one of Kaplan's "25 Cutting-Edge Schools with an Eye Toward the Future." One of the keys to the institution's success has been Wallace's innovative embrace of adaptive reuse projects around the city to make up the campus.[32]

Today, SCAD includes among its lecture halls and dormitories former nineteenth-century homes and twentieth-century hotels, reused factories and pharmacies, nunneries and synagogues, restaurants and diners, and elementary schools and car dealerships. The university library was once the Maass Brothers Department Store. From 1887 to roughly 1980, the classrooms that make up Habersham Hall housed Savannah's police department and jail. The school's art museum, designed by a SCAD alumnus, is also the oldest surviving antebellum train depot in the United States. Of its 110 buildings on four campuses around the world, SCAD had built only eight new structures from scratch—the other 102 are all adaptive reuse projects.[33]

This reuse is entirely intentional. "SCAD's adaptive reuse of historic buildings," Wallace said, "allows students to experience the varied purposes a building has had over the decades. Historic structures have quality materials and workmanship, interesting details, and a sense of connection with the past that new buildings do not have." In fact, Paula Wallace has overseen the adaptive reuse and design of every SCAD structure. "When students are surrounded by sustainability and thoughtful design on such a macro level," she said, "they absorb that ethos. When they come to SCAD, they see quite vividly how the transformation of one property can launch the rebirth of whole blocks, whole neighborhoods, a whole world." In Savannah, that's exactly what has happened. "The rise of SCAD definitely coincides with the revitalization downtown," said one SCAD board member and longtime resident of the city. Thanks to SCAD's efforts, formerly "worthless property is now priceless."[34]

Older buildings being an endlessly convertible resource, the line of regeneration runs the other way as well. Just as warehouses, hotels, and department stores can become educational buildings, former schools can readily serve other functions. In Portland, Oregon, the century-old John D. Kennedy Elementary School (named after the Oregonian who donated the land in 1915) is now a quirky destination hotel run by the McMenamins chain; its classrooms and gymnasium are now bedrooms, a movie theater, pool, and brewery. ("Just wait until the principal hears about this!" deadpans the hotel's website.) Over in New York's East Harlem, the 1898-built Public School 109 on East 99th Street, after closing its doors in 1995, has been reborn as the El Barrio Artspace Lofts, an affordable housing complex and a vibrant center of community engagement and creativity. This rehab, driven by a local nonprofit arts advocacy organization, now holds eighty-nine units of affordable live/work housing for artists and their families, as well as 13,000 square feet of space for arts organizations.[35]

Indeed, former schools are often especially good candidates for innovative reuse for two reasons: they have already served an important purpose for the families who live around them, and every city or neighborhood usually has them. The same logic applies to other common community buildings that are everywhere but that may be looking for a new purpose.

Along with housing the Jose Mateo Ballet Theatre in Cambridge, historic churches have been converted into award-winning restaurants in Norfolk, Syracuse, Madison, and Naples. Former places of worship also serve as much-needed housing in Boston and Erie, Pennsylvania; as retail outlets in Cincinnati and Brattleboro, Vermont; and as lofts, offices, and condos in Philadelphia. Two other community cornerstones in cities across the United States—post offices and libraries—have also found new life as hotels, restaurants, office complexes, and retail centers, from the Jessie Ball duPont community center in Jacksonville, Florida, to the Restoration Hardware retail store in Greenwich, Connecticut.[36]

Community Services

There are always important needs in a neighborhood that an older structure can help fulfill. For example, thanks to a community investment of $50 million and federal historic tax credits, a former 255,000-square-foot Michigan Bell building on Detroit's west side, originally built in 1929, was recently reconverted into 155 one-bedroom apartments for formerly homeless individuals. The now-refurbished Neighborhood Service Organization (NSO) Bell Building features a gym, chapel, library, and computer room, and offers mental health and addiction treatment, financial literacy and nutrition classes, and a health care clinic. "The building allows me to have a whole new sense of independence," said one former marine who found a home in the building. "I thank God every day for this place," said another resident now taking classes and working on her high school equivalency there. "It's a blessing for me—a roof over my head where I have the opportunity to achieve."[37]

In East Baltimore, an immigrant named John Frederick Wiessner built a remarkable eleven-story, 30,000-square-foot brewery in 1887 to house his family business. Notwithstanding the Prohibition years, the Wiessner Brewery—later the American Brewery—was a fixture in Baltimore's Broadway East until it closed its doors in 1973. Over the next four decades, as crime rates soared and half the population moved out of the increasingly depressed neighborhood, the building sat forlorn, abandoned, and often vandalized. But in 2008, after another extensive renovation financed in part through state and federal tax credits, the Maryland organization Humanim reopened the American Brewery as its new home and hub for social, mental health, and disability services and workforce development in the area.[38]

"It's a monumental and historic opportunity for our community," said one local pastor at the opening. "In these times of high unemployment, and the disinvestment and dilapidation we see here, the project brings us hope." That's exactly what Humanim's CEO, Henry Posko, was hoping to achieve. "The building stood as a symbol of the disinvestment of the neighborhood," he said, "and if it were to come back, what were the possibilities?" Humanim took extra pains to restore the original paint colors, and it retained the large grain silo, beer vats, and other distinctive elements of the beautiful brewery. Within its first year, the brewery was serving thirteen hundred low-income Baltimoreans, and forty local residents had been hired to work there.[39]

Over on Chicago's Near West Side, and with an investment of $22 million, architects and antipoverty advocates worked together to convert the blighted Viceroy Hotel into housing for the homeless with the eighty-nine-unit Harvest Commons Apartments. Along with restoring the 1930 hotel's interior to its original art deco look, the Heartland Alliance and Landon Bone Baker Architects added a community garden, chicken coop, and café to help residents learn how to grow and sell their own food. "To actually see that this building wasn't just demolished and torn down," said Jeff Bone, who worked on the project, "but was restored to its original former glory—it's really meaningful for the neighborhood. I was talking to the security guard and he said, 'You know, this building is like [Rip Van Winkle]—it was asleep for all these years and now it's awake.'"[40]

The Viceroy Hotel is not alone. Given their layout, historic hotels have proved particularly adaptable to filling affordable housing needs all over the country. For example, the Dunbar Hotel in South Los Angeles was once an upscale destination after its opening in 1928, especially for African Americans who were routinely discriminated against at other hotels. The Dunbar hosted the first conference of the National Association for the Advancement of Colored People (NAACP)—W. E. B. Du Bois called the hotel "a jewel done with loving hands . . . a beautiful inn with soul"—and luminaries like Duke Ellington, Louis Armstrong, and Ray Charles regularly played there. By the end of the twentieth century, however, time had taken its toll on the Dunbar. That held true until 2013, when it reopened as eighty-three units of affordable senior housing, with rents ranging from $437 to $875 a month. In the Boyle Heights community of East Los Angeles, another historic hotel—the 1889 Boyle Hotel—reopened in 2012 as fifty-one affordable housing units, with rents going from $330 for a studio to $975 for a three-bedroom apartment. The California Hotel (1929) and the San Pablo Hotel (1920) in Oakland, recently rehabbed by the East Bay Asian Local Development Corporation, are other examples of this promising historic hotel–to–affordable housing trend.[41]

Not every one of these transformative reuse projects requires millions in investment. Yet another beautiful and community-minded adaptive evolution of a property has taken place at Ottinger Hall in Salt Lake City, Utah. First built in 1899 by the Veteran Volunteer Fireman Association, Ottinger Hall (after Utah's first fire chief, George Ottinger) served as a meetinghouse and museum for nearly a century. When that use was no longer feasible and the building became vacant, the city of Salt Lake sought out the local Rotary Club. Together, these partners invested $150,000 into rehabilitation and converted the site into a youth center. Through a city-sponsored initiative called YouthCity, Ottinger Hall now houses an afterschool program for neighborhood kids aged nine to thirteen, one that includes stop-motion videos, guitar lessons, cooking classes, and career exploration tours. "It's a community amenity with a tremendous history," said Janet Wolf, the city's director of youth services. "It was called the old fire station, but what it really was is a gathering place, a social hall. The fact that we can bring it back to the idea that it's a gathering place and a place to be social is wonderful."[42]

Mixed-Use and Retail Space

One of the best ways to make old buildings social and gathering places again is to convert them into mixed-use spaces so that they are experiencing visitors at all times of the day and for different reasons. Here again, creative rehab projects all over the United States are illustrating what is possible with existing building stock.

Six hundred and sixty feet long and capped by an iconic 275-foot clock tower modeled after Spain's Seville Cathedral, the Ferry Building along San Francisco's waterfront was constructed in 1898 to be the gateway to the city, and so it was. The second-busiest transit terminal in the world in its heyday, it saw fifty thousand souls a day arrive by ferry or depart by train or trolley. Then the automobile completely transformed transportation patterns into and out of the city, and the car-friendly Golden Gate Bridge soon took the Ferry Building's place as the symbol of San Francisco. The building itself ended up being lodged behind the Embarcadero Freeway, cut off from the rest of the city.[43]

After the 1989 Loma Prieta earthquake led to the Embarcadero's removal, however, the city rediscovered some of the historic building's original magic. "When [the highway] was taken down," said Jane Connors, a senior property manager of the company that manages the complex today, "it connected the Ferry Building all along Market Street and up to Twin Peaks. There was suddenly this new interest in the building, and you started to see what San Francisco was meant to be." Beginning in 1998, the city and private partners embarked on a two-year, $110 million renovation, painstakingly restoring tiles and cornices, adding photos that tell the history of the building and the area, and converting the interior to modern use. Today, the Ferry Building is once again a San Francisco destination, with restaurants, retail, office space, a farmers' market, and renewed crowds, and is helping revitalize even more of the city's waterfront.[44]

In Nashville, Tennessee, the same song is playing at the longtime home of the Acme Stock and Poultry Company, a few blocks from the Ryman Auditorium, the former (and now winter) home of the *Grand Ole Opry*. (It too is a story of reuse—Ryman Auditorium began its days as the Union Gospel Tabernacle.) When Acme bought the three-floor, 7,000-square-foot edifice in 1943, it had already been around for fifty years and had played home to a number of different businesses, including makers of drugs, baking powder, soda, and buggies. For the next fifty years, even as Nashville became better known for its music than its agriculture, the Acme Feed and Seed served as a way station and impromptu community center for farmers, selling bulk feed and pet food until the day it closed in 1999.[45]

Thirteen years later, Tom Morales, a local businessman with fond memories of the old Feed and Seed, bought the abandoned storefront and aimed to have it restored to its former glory. "Our whole perspective was to save an iconic landmark and make it appear not to have changed at all," he said. "It was the Home Depot of the time, but with a whole social setting. Part of our business plan was to revive that community." After an investment of roughly $6.5 million, Morales and his partners reopened the Feed and Seed in 2014 as a performance space, bar, restaurant, and community center, catering to both tourists and locals with yoga classes, concerts, and trivia nights. He even added an in-house radio station to help local, unknown, and underappreciated acts to get their music out. As a result, the Feed and Seed building, in its 126th year, is now pulsing with life again.[46]

Nashville has its country music, and Milwaukee has its beer. For 150 years, the twenty-six historic buildings that made up the Pabst Brewery on the west edge of downtown were a Milwaukee fixture. When the storied brewery shut down in 1996, six once-vital city blocks quickly went dark. Local preservationists pushed hard to save the old Pabst complex, and in 2006, the brewery was purchased by the late developer and philanthropist Joseph J. Zilber. He wanted to make the next great Milwaukee neighborhood, with an emphasis on sustainability and historic preservation.[47]

Today, that vision is becoming a reality. As Kaid Benfield of Place-Makers put it, "Milwaukee's newest trendy neighborhood is likely to become one of its best, and almost certainly its greenest." The brewery now includes an apartment complex, office building, the Cardinal Stitch University School of Education and Leadership, and the University of Wisconsin–Milwaukee's School of Public Health. One of the complex's most historic buildings is now the Brewhouse Inn and Suites, with ninety individualized and charming rooms, and Jackson's Blue Ribbon Pub. Six projects in the complex, including the Brewhouse, benefited from state historic tax credits, which in turn have spurred development of neighboring Pabst buildings as well. These once vacant and underperforming buildings are back on the property tax rolls—the assessed value of the Brewhouse has risen 907 percent—and the neighborhood is lively once again. Perhaps best of all for Milwaukee's beer enthusiasts, the revitalized area helped lure Pabst back to the city. In the summer of 2015, Pabst opened a microbrewery and test kitchen in the first floor of its former offices (which, as it happened, began life as a church).[48]

In the Southeast, meanwhile, the city of Atlanta's largest-ever adaptive reuse project—at 1.1 million square feet—is taking shape at the Ponce Market on the east side of Midtown. The market began life in 1926 as the Sears-Roebuck distribution center and flourished in the years when the Sears catalog was everyone's Amazon. Sears closed the shop in 1986 and sold the distribution center to the city, however, after which—give or take a few weeks during the 1996 Olympics—it remained mostly shuttered. By 2010, the city was paying $600,000 a year to maintain a complex that was 90 percent vacant.[49]

In June 2011, Jamestown Properties purchased the site and, with the help of $35 million in state and federal historic tax credits, began converting it into a mixed-use hub of residential, commercial, and retail outlets, including twenty-three vendors and restaurants and the eponymous market for local buyers and sellers to come together. The developers are even planning to add a small amusement park to the roof. "One of the things that's happened over the past couple of decades in this country is the overwhelming majority of the development that has occurred has led to a lack of authenticity," said Jim Irwin, a senior developer on the project. "This plague of sameness has really stripped away a lot of what is special and authentic about places. I think there's a real curiosity about history, about the things that have a sense of permanence and place. . . . We want people, when they walk through the building, to really experience what it has been like for the past 90 years."[50]

With that in mind, Jamestown maintained the boxcar and trestle that run along the side of the complex and has renovated the giant water tank on the premises for continued use. As the building was just coming to life in 2015, signs looked very promising for the market. "If you look at the median age of many of the companies" moving in, said Irwin, the owners "are in the low 30's. And what they have said is that a building like this is a huge differentiator for them. . . . It's a place that has character and it's not just the next big glass high rise. So all of those [historic elements of the center] really create a culture and create a community, which is really at the heart of what we're trying to do."[51]

The pattern is clear: restoring older buildings to active, mixed-use space is breathing new life into both these structures and the communities that surround them. So, at the National Trust, we are revamping how we run our twenty-seven historic sites to take advantage of this synergy.

For example, the Cooper-Molera Adobe in Monterey, California, was first occupied by Captain John Rogers Cooper and his wife, Encarnacion Vallejo de Cooper, in 1827. Owned by the National Trust and operated as a house museum by California State Parks since 1972, the Cooper-Molera Adobe helps tell the complex and diverse history of the origins of modern California. The site was also identified in 1962 as a critical anchor to a more cohesive downtown Monterey. But due to low visitation revenues and state budget challenges, the adobe was open by appointment only, and the benefits it could provide the rest of the downtown district were being lost.[52]

At the same time, the Cooper-Molera Adobe cried out for adaptive reuse. Over the years before it became a house museum, the 2.5-acre property with six historic structures had been used for everything from a dance school to a beauty salon, and from a tavern to a meeting place for the Boys Club of Monterey (although not at the same time!). That is why, after much discussion and collaboration with the local community, the National Trust developed a "shared-use" model for the site. It includes both tours and exhibits in the adobe residences that offer an interpretation of 1800s California life along with commercial, community-oriented uses, such as performance and event space in the distinctive redwood barns, a restaurant in the site's historic adobe commercial warehouse, and a retail store in the building that has stood on the corner of Munras Avenue and Polk Street for more than a century. We are also working to make the gardens and orchards a community resource as well as a historic one. In the shared-use model, these many uses strengthen and enliven one another while generating multiple revenue streams to support the property's preservation and interpretation.[53]

Ultimately, while ensuring that its historic character is maintained and significance is communicated, the National Trust wants to see Cooper-Molera play a more dynamic role in the revitalization of downtown Monterey's National Historic Landmark district. We see this type of creative solution as a useful model for other historic sites across the United States. Now, rather than simply being a mostly shuttered relic of a bygone day, the Cooper-Molera Adobe will be open to more people. Its story will be more broadly told, and its history will be imprinted on a new generation, who will be responsible for its care long after we're gone.[54]

And House Museums Too!

Of course, we should not completely do away with house museums or convert them all into new uses. Many of these museums tell valuable stories and convey important facets of American history. If a city or community does decide to make a museum of a historic property, however, we should work hard to see that the property is meeting the needs of local residents and reflecting the energy and diversity of its environment.

Consider the path of Brucemore, a 26-acre nineteenth-century estate in Cedar Rapids, Iowa, that came to the National Trust in 1981. Because the local leadership and supporters have never been content with the status quo, Brucemore is in many ways an exercise in the ongoing process of rediscovery. The staff and volunteers there continually work to add new interpretative exhibits about various facets of the estate and the larger Cedar Rapids community. They have also opened their doors to concerts, plays, and other community events. Now visitors come to this former private residence not just to learn about the three families who lived there since the 1880s. They also come to take in plays like *South Pacific* or *As You Like It*, enjoy Cabaret on the Courtyard shows, tour the gardens and flower shop, or build a scarecrow to celebrate the harvest.[55]

Over the years, Brucemore's leadership has kept two principles firmly in mind. First, always think about the audiences who might never visit a static house museum. Second, to cement Brucemore as an anchor in the community, maintain the vigorous involvement of as many local stakeholders as possible.

The National Trust has been inspired to take the same approach at President Lincoln's Cottage in Washington, D.C., where the president and his family spent one-fourth of his presidency and where he wrote much of the Emancipation Proclamation. When the cottage opened to the public in 2008, we wanted to craft an experience that kept the site relevant to the needs of the community today, while emphasizing Lincoln's ideas and momentous achievements at the cottage. So, rather than simply showcasing the president's brilliance and courage, the cottage holds events and exhibits that apply his writings and ideas to the modern fight against human trafficking throughout the world. It holds an annual Students Opposing Slavery summit, which brings thirty-five students from six countries to the cottage to develop ways they can be active in ending modern slavery. And we are constantly developing new tools for interpreting the cottage, such as using tablets to offer a more responsive, customized, and resource-rich tour for visitors.[56]

So far, this approach has been a huge success. In 2015, for example, a class from Baltimore's Cross Country Elementary/Middle School had scheduled a field trip to visit President Lincoln's Cottage, but it had to be canceled due to the civil unrest following the death of Freddie Gray while in police custody. So cottage staff worked with Cross Country to reschedule the trip and customize a program for the class. "The job you did of getting the students to see beyond the myth of Lincoln and start understanding the man and the stress he bore during the war was outstanding," the teacher wrote afterward. "Many of our students . . . said they were enlightened by the discussion in which you helped them connect the turbulence surrounding the Freddie Gray situation to similar disturbances and unrest during the Lincoln administration. They began to see History as a fluid continuum of which they are a part, and in which they play a real role—rather than a static thing already dead and gone and without relevance for them."[57]

Ultimately, powerful testimonials like that are why we work to create museums in the first place, and they also demonstrate why this model should be allowed to evolve. These students saw why what happened during the Civil War a century and a half ago was directly relevant to their lives today, and felt the power of history to illuminate our past, present, and future all at once. Their experience shows that the house museum model can still accomplish amazing things, if the site is well suited to it and if the volunteers and staff on hand work to provide dynamic content and resources that speak to visitors.

House museums are no longer our only model, and often there are better paths forward to seeing that older buildings are helping their communities grow, develop, and thrive. As my predecessor Richard Moe well put it in 2000, "Preservation is more than just saving buildings, a house museum here and there. It's about creating and enhancing environments that support, inform, and enrich the lives of all Americans." So it is.[58]

Go Forth and Revive

We could go on for another hundred pages on this topic. I'm sure you know of older buildings in your city that have found new life through adaptive reuse and are now the "it" bar, restaurant, or event space, or are helping fulfill an important community need.

Ultimately, there is no limit to how and which buildings can be rejuvenated in this fashion. In her book and on her website *Big Box Reuse*, author and writer Julia Christensen traces in detail how abandoned big-box stores—former Wal-Marts, K-Marts, Targets, and the like—have become day care centers, charter schools, churches, and housing all over the United States. Similarly, the fun website Used to Be a Pizza Hut tracks all the myriad reuses of those distinctively red-roofed pizzerias, once in strip malls all over the country. Although many are still restaurants, former Pizza Huts have also found new uses as inns, churches, offices, and even morgues and funeral homes.[59]

As with so much preservation work, really exciting things can happen when this preservation through adaptive reuse is taken to scale. After being battered by Hurricane Katrina in 2005, many of the neighborhoods in one of the country's most historic cities were in desperate need of revitalization. But New Orleans has always had a keen sense of history, and although there is much hard work ahead, the city has found a path to the future by restoring its treasured past.

Downtown, the twenty-three-story Hibernia Tower has been a signature of the Crescent City's skyline since 1921. After the Hibernia National Bank was bought out by Capital One in 2005, however, the tower became a mixed-use complex of retail, office space, and 175 mixed-income residential units. It was almost immediately 100 percent occupied after the conversion.[60]

In the French Quarter, the beloved 1927 Saenger Theater was devastated by Katrina and saw its basement flooded by 20 feet of water. After an eight-year restoration project in which exquisite care was taken to preserve all the theater's historic features, it reopened in 2013—first act: Jerry Seinfeld—and is expected to draw 350,000 visitors a year, boosting local businesses in and around Canal Street.[61]

In Central City, a working-class residential neighborhood made up first of European immigrants and later African Americans, a 1910 Italian Renaissance Revival–style elementary school that was closed in 2002 and almost burned down in 2008 has reopened as the Myrtle Banks Building, named after the school's longtime principal and an early civil rights leader in New Orleans. The school now includes office and community space and a grocery store, and opened its doors with a museum exhibit on the history of the neighborhood and the civil rights movement in the Crescent City. It is helping make Oretha Castle Haley Boulevard—once a thriving and inclusive retail area in the middle of the twentieth century—an equally dynamic neighborhood today.[62]

In these places and many more, New Orleans and cities across the

United States are redefining, reinterpreting, and reconceptualizing their old and historic places to meet the needs of the twenty-first century. And for good reason: these buildings are often what make each neighborhood distinctive and beloved. "Each city has its own history, its own points of reference," wrote Jaime Lerner, former mayor of Curitiba, Brazil, "the places that belong to the city's collective memory and that are vital to its identity—the intangible bond that forges a sense of belonging. It might be a particular factory, an old tram station, or one of those bygone general stores. . . . There is nothing that flatters a neighborhood—indeed, an entire community—more than the revival of such 'lost' spaces."[63]

To fully unleash the power of a city's historic fabric, don't leave these community and economic engines dormant. Find these lost spaces, reawaken them, and let them breathe life into our communities anew.

CHAPTER 5

Our Diverse History: Toward More Inclusive History and Communities

History is no longer a spotlight. We are turning up the stagelights to show the entire cast.
    —David McCullough[1]

Up to this point, I have talked about many of the critical ways old and historic buildings improve our cities: their significant economic impact; their contributions to urban character and distinctiveness; how they draw residents, tourists, and crowds to places; and how they can be endlessly adapted to meet the needs of families today. This historic fabric also enriches our environment for other reasons—reasons that, as Tom Mayes eloquently noted in his "Why Old Places Matter" series of essays, are no less important for being difficult to quantify. "Old places," argued Mayes, "are deeply beneficial to people because of the way they give us a sense of continuity, identity, and belonging, because they inspire us with awe, beauty, and sacredness, because they tell us about history, ancestry, and learning, and because they foster healthy, sustainable communities."[2]

"Identity, self-esteem, the feeling of belonging," Jaime Lerner argued similarly in *Urban Acupuncture*, "everything is related to the reference points a person has in relation to his city." As novelist Wendell Berry put it, "If you don't know where you are, you don't know who you are." Indeed, place's connection to our sense of identity runs even further than our present location. "To know who you are," wrote Carson McCullers in *The Heart Is a Lonely Hunter*, "you have to have a place to come from."[3]

Simply put, older places tell our story—the story of a city, a community, and a nation across time. They reflect who we are and how we arrived there. They can imbue us with self-knowledge, understanding, and, sometimes, pride. They can make our cities more welcome and inclusive places, with a strong community foundation. They can bring us together, help us learn from our mistakes, and inspire us to be better toward one another.

These powers of place to inform identity and create community are particularly important in the United States. Americans are bound together not by blood or common ancestry but by a commitment to the same democratic ideals and the democratic story we tell ourselves. So we have to ensure that all Americans can see themselves in it. This holds especially true as the United States grows ever more ethnically and racially diverse. In 2010, according to the US Census Bureau, we reached an important milestone: fewer than half of the nation's three-year-olds were white. By 2018, it is estimated the same will be true of Americans under age eighteen, and by 2043, the United States will be a majority-minority nation.[4]

Because cities have been the crucible of the American melting pot for centuries, there's a certain elegance to Americans simultaneously becoming a more urban and diverse people. We need to make sure, though, that existing communities of color continue to play a thriving role in our cities' future and that they aren't being pushed out by this boom in urban redevelopment. I will discuss this critical issue more in chapter 6.

Now more than ever, we also should work to see that the old places, landmarks, and focal points in our cities and communities reflect diverse peoples and stories. Our American landscape needs to tell the full American story.

Tinner Hill and Other Tales

With that in mind, let me tell you a story about my own community of Falls Church, Virginia. As president of the National Trust, I have the opportunity to visit the grand opening of historic places all over the United States—it's one of the great perks of my job! But in the winter of 2015, I had the chance to attend the dedication of a small historic monument that was particularly special to me because it told the story of *my* town, where I have lived for twenty years with my husband and raised my children.

The commemoration in question was for the Tinner Hill Historic Site in Falls Church, Virginia. There, a century ago, Falls Church residents met to organize and protest against the proposed segregation of the town. In January 1915, the all-white town council—taking advantage of a statewide law passed three years earlier—had adopted an ordinance forcing all black residents to live in one tiny quadrant of Falls Church, even if their property was elsewhere in the city. Henceforth, it would be illegal for "any person to sell or rent land or dwellings to the negro race." In essence, this ordinance meant that one-third of Falls Church's residents would have to live in 5 percent of the town's space. It also meant that more than one hundred African Americans would be forcibly relocated from their homes and from neighborhoods that they and their families had lived in for more than a century, since even before the American Revolution.[5]

So, under the leadership of Dr. E. B. Henderson, outraged black citizens convened in the home of Joseph and Mary Tinner (who also lived outside the new designated area) to take action. They decided to form the Colored Citizens Protection League to stand against the new segregation law, and they appealed to the national offices of the NAACP for aid. They also started a letter-writing campaign and supported a suit to prevent the town from forcing families to move. And they won. Two years later, in a landmark case, the US Supreme Court found laws like Falls Church's ordinance unconstitutional, and so it was never enforced, even though amazingly it remained on the books until the 1990s.[6]

It may not seem like it today, with highways and the Metro connecting it firmly to Washington, D.C., but in 1915, Falls Church was a rural, agricultural community of fewer than fourteen hundred people. The families that were being discriminated against there were in many ways on their own. They chose to take enormous risks to stand up for their rights, and for basic justice, in Falls Church. Together, they laid the foundation for what became the first rural chapter of the NAACP.[7]

This inspiring story is one that should be told. It reminds us that the struggle for justice, civil rights, and the fundamental values in the Bill of Rights—a struggle that continues to this day—took place not just in cities like Selma and Montgomery, but in communities all across the United States. It helps us recognize that the progress that's been made on these critical issues only happened because Americans of a different time took huge risks, right where they lived, to secure social justice and equality. And it shows us that to achieve the progress we still have to make, we all have to raise our voices against bigotry and injustice, whenever we see it in our communities.

You won't find Tinner Hill in many history books, but it is such an important story for Falls Church. It lives on today through the tremendous efforts of Edwin Henderson, a descendant of the original Dr. Henderson, and his wife, Nikki Graves Henderson. They have worked tirelessly to see that this story has a place on the city's landscape so that it can be remembered by future generations. They formed the Tinner Hill Heritage Foundation and, working with Virginia preservationists and the local community, helped the Tinner Hill Historic Site find a home.

Over in Seattle, in the heart of the city's *Nihonmachi*, or Japantown, another important story is embodied in the six-story Panama Hotel, at the corner of Sixth and Main. Built in 1910 and designed by Seattle's first Japanese architect, Sabro Ozasa, the Panama was once a gathering and welcoming place for thousands of Japanese immigrants as they arrived in the United States to make a new home. Today, the hotel is one of the few surviving and truly authentic remnants of the thriving Nisei community in Washington before the war, and stepping through its doors is like taking a time machine to the Seattle of a century ago. In the basement, the hotel features a *sento*, or traditional Japanese-style public bath house. Once there were hundreds of such bath houses in the United States. Today, there are only two; the other, in Walnut Grove, California, has been completely refurbished as part of a functioning spa, but the Panama's *sento* is untouched and retains all its original integrity.[8]

The Panama didn't garner its most important, and melancholy, historic feature until 1942, though, when the forced internment of 110,000 Japanese Americans began after Pearl Harbor. Because each person was only allowed to take two suitcases to the internment camps and had only a little over a week to prepare for incarceration, many families left the rest of their belongings at a place they knew and trusted—the basement of the hotel. Trunks and boxes piled up there, containing everyday items—furniture, old records, family photos, formal wear—all remnants of lives torn asunder. "Stepping into [the hotel's] cellar," noted one writer, "is a little like entering Miss Havisham's room in Dickens's *Great Expectations*, a place where time stopped, in the Panama's case at a moment when one immigrant group straddled two cultures." In fact, because items that might seem "too" Japanese would arouse suspicion from American authorities, some of the possessions left at the hotel include kimonos, Japanese books and newspapers, and traditional objects such as drums.[9]

The owner of the Panama Hotel from 1938 to 1985, Takashi Hori, was himself sent to the Minidoka Relocation Center in Idaho with his family; he leased the Panama during his internment. After the war, Hori tried to return the trunks and other personal effects at the hotel to their original owners. Japanese Americans had been urged by the War Relocation Authority to give up their ethnic neighborhoods and assimilate into the larger American populace, however, and many families never came back to Seattle for the possessions they had been forced to leave behind. "Others," said Hori, "no longer wanted them and asked me to get rid of them." Instead, they are still there, a museum of artifacts from that time.[10]

When Hori retired, he sold the building and hotel business to Jan Johnson, who has continued to maintain and operate the hotel ever since. She rehabilitated the retail spaces, established a tea shop, worked to share the hotel's stories with countless groups of students of all ages, and made sure the legacy of this special, even sacred, place was honored. "It's important for people to know what went on here," she said, and many agree. "This story has everything to do with civil rights," argued Toshiko Hasegawa, president of the Seattle chapter of the Japanese American Citizens League and the grandson of internees. More than just an old hotel, the Panama today is a place that teaches us about the immigrant experience and reminds us of the troubling frailty of civil liberties, even in the United States.[11]

The Silences in Our Story

Unfortunately, in the early days of historic preservation, beloved historic places like Tinner Hill and the Panama Hotel—as well as the Maravilla Handball Court I described in the introduction—would likely not have ranked very high in a list of places that should be saved, unless someone like John Adams or John Hancock had happened to visit, sleep, or play handball there. Then, historic preservation often followed the same methodological approach, and held the same conscious and unconscious biases and oversights, as American historians in general. For decades, whether in textbooks or house museums, we all too often specialized in top-down history that primarily, if not solely, focused on the great deeds of white men.

Former secretary of the interior Ken Salazar, who can trace his family roots to the days of New Spain, has often talked about his confusion as a child when his teachers said that American history "began" in Jamestown. He knew quite well that his own ancestors had been living in the foothills of the Rocky Mountains of New Mexico for at least five hundred years! "The history of Latinos in the U.S. goes way back before the founding of Jamestown or Plymouth Rock," he has said. "Our history is rooted in the American landscape." That is not to say that the stories of English colonial settlement aren't hugely important, but they only represent one facet of the United States. As they "define America," Salazar said, "so do the Indian Pueblos and burial mounds, Ebenezer Baptist Church, Fort Monroe, Nuestra Señora de la Paz, Stonewall Inn, and Angel Island."[12]

In other words, not all our tales began on the *Mayflower*. Many American families run through Ellis Island, the Middle Passage, the Mariel boatlift, and the Bering Strait, but these other stories were too often downplayed or even ignored in the old telling of our history. The same goes for women's contributions. It used to be that when you picked up a textbook, the only women in its pages were First Ladies and maybe a handful of outliers: Susan B. Anthony or Jane Addams or Amelia Earhart or Sacajawea. Otherwise, the contributions of millions of American women were completely overlooked from the American story.

These silences had repercussions on our historic landscape. For decades, many voices were just not represented within the traditional boundaries of preservation. So the mansions of Founding Fathers, wealthy plantation owners, and famous industrialists have been maintained, while the cabins that housed enslaved persons and the tenements of ordinary workers have been left to ruin. We have worked to preserve many of our western forts, but only recently have we told the stories there of the societies and cultures, often Native American or Hispanic, that were displaced in their wake. Great men have been venerated, the vast majority of them rightfully so, while the stories of pioneering women have been consigned to footnotes at best.

In many of his writings and sermons, one of America's greatest civil rights leaders, Martin Luther King Jr., lamented the distortive effect this narrow vision of history had on our understanding of ourselves as a people. "Before the Pilgrim fathers landed at Plymouth, we were here," he reminded parishioners at Washington, D.C.'s National Cathedral in his final Sunday sermon in 1968. "Before Jefferson etched across the pages of history the majestic words of the Declaration of Independence, we were here. Before the beautiful words of the 'Star Spangled Banner' were written, we were here."[13]

In his final 1967 book, *Where Do We Go from Here—Chaos or Community?*, King deplored "America's penchant for ignoring the Negro, making him invisible and making his contributions insignificant." He told the stories of overlooked African Americans like Dr. Charles Drew, who first separated and stored blood plasma, and Crispus Attucks, the first man to die in the American Revolution, and he wrote of how he wept for the black children "denied a knowledge of their heritage" and the white children "who, through daily miseducation, are taught that the Negro is an irrelevant entity in American society." What all should realize, King argued, is that "the wealth of cultural and technological progress in the United States is a result of the commonwealth of inpouring contributions."[14]

In his most famous speech—the "I Have a Dream" address on the steps of the Lincoln Memorial in 1963—King worked hard to bring about that realization in the American people and to weave a new national narrative that would give the country a more inclusive sense of itself. More than just a call to arms on behalf of justice and civil rights, this remarkable speech is a founding statement of a new, broader American history, and one that relies very heavily on the power of place to make its case.

Like Lincoln at Gettysburg, King began by rooting the opening chapter of the story in the Declaration of Independence. For although the US Constitution had deemed African Americans "three-fifths of a person," the Declaration of Independence instead begins with a simple, foundational truth: "We hold these truths to be self-evident, that all men are created equal." These words, he said, were a "promissory note"—a "promise that *all* men, yes, black men as well as white men, would be guaranteed the 'unalienable rights' of 'Life, liberty, and the pursuit of Happiness.'" By reframing the American story in this way, Harvard professor Henry Louis Gates has noted, King "made freedom—'at last'— the ideal by which we measure progress in our country."[15]

King also very purposefully invokes other resonant aspects of our history in his address. He quotes the refrain of "My Country, 'Tis of Thee," a song white and black Americans both held dear. "Sweet land of liberty . . . let freedom ring!" Then, after telling us of his dream, he wields the poetry of place to cement the foundation of his more expansive American story. He talks of the "red hills of Georgia" and the "mighty mountains of New York," Stone Mountain in Georgia and Lookout Mountain in Tennessee.[16]

They were, he argued, American ideals we should live up to and American places we should all do right by. We were not yet living up to the moral of our American story. By invoking a creed and history we all cherish, and places we all love, King hoped to bring all Americans together, as one country and one people—in his words, to "transform the jangling discords of our nation into one symphony of brotherhood."[17]

Speaking of the power of place to bring people together, it is interesting to note in passing how King's speech both relied on and enhanced the power of the Lincoln Memorial. When it was dedicated in 1922, the memorial had mainly been envisioned—by white Americans—as a place to bury the hatchet of the Civil War at last. But to African Americans, Lincoln the Great Emancipator was much more important than Lincoln the Savior of the Union. And within a few years, the memorial had already become a potent symbol of the struggle for civil rights.[18]

In 1939, Marian Anderson gave a concert on the very steps King would speak from twenty-four years later. When the Daughters of the American Revolution refused to let her perform at their nearby hall, she sang at the Lincoln Memorial instead, beginning with a powerful rendition of "My Country, 'Tis of Thee." That concert had a powerful effect on a ten-year-old boy in Atlanta, and five years later, fifteen-year-old Martin Luther King Jr. won a speechwriting contest for an address that referenced Anderson's concert. Speaking there himself in 1963, King helped reshape and broaden the national meaning of the Lincoln Memorial, much in the same way he worked to reframe and broaden the American story. The place became more than just a site to reflect on the Civil War. It was a sacred monument to justice and equality—and to the America we should be, an America where all citizens can live in freedom and dignity.[19]

King understood a crucial fact: our history is the story we use to explain ourselves and define our community, so we have to get it right. If our national story excludes more people than it lets in, we will never know equality, justice, or peace. So we need a vision of the United States that values and recognizes the contribution of all our people. "Preservation of one's own culture," as another remarkable civil rights leader, Cesar Chavez, put it, "does not require contempt or disrespect for other cultures." Rather, "we need to help students and parents cherish and preserve the ethnic and cultural diversity that nourishes and strengthens this community and this nation."[20]

King and Chavez are, of course, right about the need for an inclusive history, and that story must be reflected in our landscape—in the places we honor, the landmarks we name, and the memorials we consecrate. Although it is hugely important, this isn't just about fairness to all the families and descendants of the many who have been overlooked. As any historian today will attest, telling the American story in such a top-down and one-sided fashion often obscured our understanding of it. For example, we were taught for generations that slavery in the United States ended mainly because Lincoln issued the Emancipation Proclamation on January 1, 1863, followed by the ratification of the Thirteenth Amendment in December 1865. These events are both critical political acts, to be sure. But we now also know—by looking at history through a wider and more appropriate lens—that Lincoln's hand had in part been forced by enslaved persons in the South voting with their feet to end the "peculiar institution" in the United States as soon as Union troops entered the field. Thousands of these self-emancipated slaves ended up at Fort Monroe in Hampton, Virginia, and that site now does an exemplary job of highlighting this important story.[21]

Looking at history more broadly not only illuminates the past but our present and our future. It is impossible to understand the very real struggles we still grapple with as a nation with the old, top-down blinders on. We cannot understand the current debates about immigration without looking to how the same story played out in 1840 and 1880 and 1920. We cannot understand what's happening today in cities like Ferguson unless we know about the struggles in Selma, Montgomery, Atlanta, and hundreds of other American cities to see justice and equal rights triumph.

Thankfully, our broadening understanding of our past accelerated in exciting ways in the 1970s, when a new generation of historians came of age. Informed by the civil rights movement and the "people power" of the 1960s, they worked to restore the stories and struggles of the many

Americans who had been overlooked by the traditional, top-down history of years past. With the lives of congressmen and politicians already well recorded, these scholars instead studied the day-to-day social and cultural life of our communities across time. Through their efforts, we rediscovered that women led the boycotts that fomented the American Revolution, formed the backbone of the antislavery cause, and powered the productive engine that helped the United States win World War II. We began to better understand the long struggles against racism that communities of color had fought in the United States, well before *Brown v. Board of Education.* We saw all the ways ordinary men and women drove the policy debates that changed the nation.

Historic preservation began to follow suit. Because traditional preservationists had often been slow to help in the past, many communities who believed their stories had not been told, and the places they cared about had not received the attention they deserve, had been working on their own to restore neighborhoods and beloved places. Now, the preservation movement joined the fight.

Led by Fred Williamson of Rhode Island and Elizabeth Lyon of Georgia, state historic preservation offices across the United States started working to ensure that more diverse stories and places were being saved and more Americans represented. In California, a state at the vanguard of the demographic trends toward diversity, the Office of Historic Preservation published in 1988 a comprehensive and then-groundbreaking survey of ethnic historic sites called *Five Views.* Although "most surveys record architecturally distinguished or widely known buildings," it argued, "ethnic properties are often modest structures or important because of people or events less familiar to many." The report reflected nearly a decade of work by experts and preservationists, and focused on the largest five minority groups in California as of the end of the nineteenth century: Native Americans, African Americans, Mexican, Japanese, and Chinese Americans. (Since then, California has built on this foundation to include other minority groups, such as LGBTQ Americans.)[22]

In New York City, traditional preservationists allied with local community leaders in two back-to-back high-profile cases in 1989 and 1991: to save the Audubon Ballroom in Washington Heights, where Malcolm X had been assassinated, and an African burial ground unearthed just north of City Hall. "A shared vision came to motivate our work," preservationist Ned Kaufman wrote in 1996, "a vision of a city whose buildings and spaces proudly display the history of its people, and whose people cherish their historical and cultural sites and use them to understand their past and chart their future."[23]

Today, we are closer to that vision than ever before, but let's be clear: we still have a lot of work to do. When I became president of the National Trust in 2010, I learned that only 8 percent of the 87,000 listings on the National Register of Historic Places, and only 3 percent of our 2,500 National Landmarks, represent women and racially and ethnically diverse places. Now, these numbers are by the National Park Service's own accounting, and to its credit, the Park Service has been working extremely hard to address this shortfall in a number of ways and has made some impressive strides. Also, these statistics should be higher when one takes into account the layers of history at many historic places (more on that in a moment).[24]

Still, these meager percentages underscore the significant amount of work we still have to do, in all our communities, to get this right and tell America's full story. Especially when you consider that we will soon be a majority-minority nation, and women are more than 50 percent of the population already! Until we do—until our urban landscape reflects all the contours of our past—too many Americans are being disenfranchised from our history, and our cities are neither as welcoming nor as livable as they should be.

So how can we work to capture a fuller record of our past and see more diverse places saved and stories honored in our communities? There are a number of ways forward. You might have guessed what the first and most obvious step is.

Step 1: Save More Diverse Places

We all recognize that the undercount of diverse historic sites is a problem that needs remedy. Now that the scope of historic preservation has expanded, we can use the tools we have honed over the past few decades to see that more formerly overlooked places are getting their due.

Most recently, the National Trust has been working to accomplish this goal through our National Treasures, our signature initiative since 2010. This revolving portfolio of more than eighty and counting threatened historic places of national significance includes buildings, neighborhoods, communities, landscapes, engineering landmarks, and even ships. We choose these National Treasures very carefully, based on their importance to the communities in which they reside, the stories they tell about our American past, and the ways we can work to make a positive difference in protecting them and keeping them thriving. We have also worked hard to ensure that nearly half those treasures tell diverse stories.

Among them are places like Joe Frazier's gym, a modest, three-story brick building in Philadelphia where the gold medal winner at the 1964 Olympics and later heavyweight champion of the world trained. Another is the Palace of the Governors in New Mexico, seat of the old Spanish government and the oldest public building in the United States. Other treasures include the Great Bend of the Gila, a crossroads of human activity for thousands of years, long before Europeans ventured to this continent; Hinchliffe Stadium in Paterson, New Jersey, one of the three remaining stadiums of the Negro League; the Antiguo Acueducto del Rio Piedras in San Juan, one of the last remaining Spanish-period aqueducts remaining on US soil; and Seattle's Panama Hotel, whose story I recounted earlier.[25]

Some of the treasures are entire communities—places like the historic Hispanic neighborhoods along the 710 freeway in California, including El Sereno, the oldest community in Los Angeles; the Little Havana neighborhood of Miami; and the Sweet Auburn District in Atlanta, once known as the "richest Negro street in the world," where Martin Luther King Jr. was born and raised, where he led his congregation at Ebenezer Baptist Church, and where, today, he and Coretta Scott King are buried. Others are historic resources that reside in many cities and are under threat of disuse or demolition, such as America's historic post offices or Texas's remarkable courthouses.[26]

One such National Treasure we have been working to draw attention to, even well before this program existed, is America's one thousand remaining Rosenwald Schools. The result of a collaboration between the Tuskegee Institute's Booker T. Washington and Julius Rosenwald, the president of Sears, Roebuck, Rosenwald Schools were the center of the African American education system in the days before *Brown v. Board of Education.*

In effect, the schools were the result of one of the first formal challenge grants. Beginning in 1912, Washington and Rosenwald offered African American communities who wished to build a school an architectural plan and a portion of the funding and encouraged local residents to provide the balance. And they did. All across the South, even in the face of systematic discrimination and grinding poverty, families gave whatever they could to see these schools constructed—to see that the children of their community could get an education and make more of themselves. In total, more than 5,300 buildings were constructed in fifteen states. By 1928, four years before the program concluded, one in every five rural schools for black students in the South was a Rosenwald School, and together they served one-third of the region's black schoolchildren. (Congressman John Lewis of Georgia, one of the most esteemed heroes of the civil rights movement and today a national figure

The PeeDee Rosenwald School (built in 1922–1923) in Marion County, South Carolina, circa 1935. (Courtesy South Carolina Department of Archives and History)

of conscience, spent his early years in a Rosenwald School, as did the grandmother of Attorney General Loretta Lynch.)[27]

These schools reflect the endurance and resolve of the many African American communities who stood up and stood together against oppression and worked to create educational opportunities in the face of Jim Crow. They are a feature of many of our cities that should be remembered. Today, thanks to dedicated volunteers in towns all over the South, they are finding new life—as community, health, and day care centers, offices and restaurants, and schools once more.[28]

As the Rosenwald Schools demonstrate, saving more diverse places in our community helps give important stories from our past a greater airing. For instance, Madam C. J. Walker isn't a household name today like some of her contemporaries in the early twentieth-century business world, such as Henry Ford and J. P. Morgan. But Walker—the first free-born person in her family—was in fact the first self-made female millionaire in the United States. Born only two years after the close of the

Civil War, her story is in essence the rags-to-riches American dream, one that is all the more remarkable and inspiring because she thrived when the glass ceiling for African American women in the business world was more like impenetrable marble.[29]

The hair and beauty products business that Walker founded ultimately employed more than 23,000 sales agents, and her thirty-four-room mansion in Irvington, New York, called Villa Lewaro—one of our National Treasures—stands as a testament to her remarkable success and belief in hard work and perseverance. Today, Villa Lewaro sits proudly alongside the similarly preserved Hudson Valley mansions of well-to-do families like the Rockefellers, Roosevelts, and Vanderbilts.[30]

Even as Walker was building her business, one of those Vanderbilts, Gertrude Vanderbilt Whitney, was rebelling against her high-society upbringing to create a world all her own. Whitney aspired to become a sculptor and arts patron, and she used her wealth to buy a studio in Greenwich Village's MacDougal Alley in New York City. This purchase, she reminisced later, prompted "a chorus of horror-stricken voices, a knowing lifting of the eyebrows or a twist of the mouth that is equally expressive" from those who thought a woman's place was definitely not the art world.[31]

But she had the last laugh. Whitney encouraged American artists at a time when more established art institutions considered them provincial. While many collectors balked at the daring new trends coming into vogue then, she gave these budding artists a platform. Today, the Whitney Museum is one of the foremost twentieth-century art collections in the United States, and the Whitney Studio—another National Treasure—remains a haven for artists within the New York Studio School campus.[32]

In 1914, as Whitney's studio was gaining acclaim in New York, a mother in Baltimore died suddenly from a cerebral hemorrhage, and her three-year-old daughter was sent to live with her aunt and grandparents in a modest home in Durham, North Carolina. That house is also one of our National Treasures, and that young girl, Anna Pauline (Pauli) Murray, would grow up to become a novelist, a poet, a civil rights activist, one of the most brilliant and influential legal minds of the twentieth century, a cofounder of the National Organization for Women, an LGBTQ pioneer, and even an Episcopal saint![33]

Blocked from the University of North Carolina for being black and rejected from Harvard Law School for being a woman—despite having won a Rosenwald fellowship to attend—Pauli Murray graduated from Howard and the University of California, Berkeley instead and embarked on a legal career. Her 1951 book *States' Laws on Race and Color* was deemed the bible of civil rights law by no less than Thurgood Marshall. In the early 1960s, however, while a counselor to men like Martin Luther King Jr. and A. Philip Randolph, she balked at "the blatant disparity between the major role which Negro women have played and are playing in the crucial grass-roots level of our struggle and the minor role of leadership they have been assigned in the national policy-making decisions." She would go on to cofound the National Organization for Women and in 1977 became the first African American woman to become an Episcopal priest.[34]

Walker, Whitney, Murray—all these fascinating women defied the conventions of their day to achieve unprecedented success, and their stories, like countless others, should be part of the history we honor and preserve. Making their homes National Treasures is a good first step, but we also need to bring more sites representing racial and ethnic diversity into our formal preservation designations, like the National Register and the National Landmarks list.

Doing that correctly will involve more scholarship and comprehensive surveys, like the *Five Views* study in California, that take into account a broader view of history. To take another example, the National Park Service recently completed an extensive theme study of American Latino

History to ensure that important places in that part of our story are being protected. Additional needed research is under way all over the United States and is being made simpler through the same communications technologies that have facilitated surveys in Los Angeles, Detroit, and elsewhere. Moving forward will also require listening to communities about the stories that matter to them so that unsung heroes like Joseph and Mary Tinner and Michi Nishiyama can get their due.[35]

Step 2: Tell the Full Story at Existing Sites

Along with saving new places, we also need to expand the canvas at traditional historic sites so that they reflect the stories of all the Americans who helped shape them. Often in the past—too often—many otherwise extraordinarily rich historic places, either by oversight or willful ignorance, didn't tell that full story.

Perhaps the most notorious example of this tendency is the United States Capitol. When the brand-new, underground Capitol Visitor Center opened its doors in December 2008, its large central area was named, by a bipartisan act of Congress, Emancipation Hall. That is because, up until that point—a full 208 years after the Capitol originally opened—there was no reference at all to slavery on the grounds! Nor was there any reference to the enslaved laborers who actually built much of the building. The grand murals in the Capitol corridors, which depict key moments in American history from Christopher Columbus to the Wright brothers, featured no African Americans. The only people of color, in fact, were American Indians. Even design elements that could obliquely reference slavery or emancipation, like the "liberty cap" on the Statue of Freedom atop the Capitol (which instead became a helmet), were scrubbed by former secretary of war Jefferson Davis, who oversaw the Capitol's construction during the extremely tense 1850s.[36]

It shouldn't be too much to expect a full and accurate portrayal of our nation's history, not to mention one that recognizes our strength in diversity, in the center of our democratic government. The good news is that since the opening of Emancipation Hall, a fuller history is beginning to be presented at the Capitol. Before then, aside from a bust of Martin Luther King Jr. added in 1986, the Statuary Hall and surrounding Capitol environment was a virtual whitewash. In April 2009, however, abolitionist and activist Sojourner Truth became the first African American woman honored with a bust in the building, and in February 2013, a likeness of civil rights pioneer Rosa Parks became the first full-bodied statue of a black woman in the Capitol. Similarly, congresswoman and former presidential candidate Shirley Chisholm received a distinctive portrait in the Capitol in March 2009, and—when Washington, D.C., was granted only one statue to go alongside all the states' two (the proposed second one was of architect Pierre L'Enfant)—abolitionist Frederick Douglass entered Statuary Hall as well in June 2013.[37]

All over the United States, historians, preservationists, and ordinary citizens are giving "established" historic sites a similarly thorough and much-needed review. Take Montpelier, the well-preserved estate of James Madison near Orange, Virginia, which the National Trust owns and which is managed by its costewardship partner, the Montpelier Foundation. Yes, Montpelier was the home of America's fourth president and the remarkable mind who authored our Constitution, and his story remains front and center. But Dolley Madison, a keen political mind and influential figure in her own right, also lived there too. And it was home to the many people who, despite James Madison's eloquent writings on American liberty, were held in bondage there.

In November 2014, thanks to a $3.5 million gift from philanthropist David Rubenstein (part of a larger $10 million commitment to the site), workers at Montpelier began reconstructing the slave cabins on the property that were removed 165 years earlier, so that the full story of the property and its many inhabitants could be better told. "For folks that have been coming to any of these presidential sites," said

Kat Imhoff, the Montpelier Foundation's president, "the fact that we're bringing the complete American story back into the landscape I think is very important. It is challenging, but I also think it's that wonderful tension that we as Americans are embracing. . . . Making the invisible visible is very important to us as a nation, and it will make a stronger American story."[38]

Today, Montpelier's 125,000 visitors a year can learn a great deal about James and Dolley Madison, but they can also learn about Paul Jennings, a slave who was born there and followed the Madisons to the White House. When the British set fire to the White House during the War of 1812, fifteen-year-old Paul helped Dolley Madison save important documents, silver, and even Gilbert Stuart's portrait of George Washington. He served as James Madison's personal manservant until the former president's death in 1837, and later he was able purchase his freedom. In 1848, Jennings helped organize the largest nonviolent attempted slave escape in American history, the so-called Pearl Incident, in which free African Americans chartered a schooner to ferry enslaved family and friends from Virginia to Philadelphia. (The *Pearl* was captured en route.) And, during the Civil War, he wrote *A Colored Man's Reminiscences of James Madison*, a.k.a. the first-ever White House memoir.[39]

Of course, restoring Paul Jennings and the other enslaved persons at Montpelier to the story not only enhances our understanding of all the people who lived and worked in James and Dolley's orbit; it also gives us a richer impression of the Madisons themselves. "It's this dichotomy," said Rubenstein. "You have people who were extraordinarily intelligent, well-informed, educated; they created this incredible country—Jefferson, Washington, Madison—yet they lived with this system of slavery. Jefferson, Washington, and Madison all abhorred slavery, but they didn't do, they couldn't do much about it. We shouldn't deify our Founding Fathers without recognizing that they did participate in a system that had its terrible flaws."[40]

Thanks to another grant from Rubenstein, Jefferson's nearby estate, Monticello, unveiled its renovated slave quarters in May 2015, with one hundred descendants of families that had been enslaved there on hand. "This is probably the most transformational project we've mounted at Monticello in 90 years," said Leslie Greene Bowman, the president of the foundation there. "Our visitors now understand that this wasn't a house separate from the plantation community. It was inextricably linked to it." At Mount Vernon, the slave quarters of George and Martha Washington's estate were similarly rehabilitated in 2010.[41]

The mansions of the Founding Fathers are just the tip of the iceberg. From forts to factories and parks to public squares, many historic places can do a better job of relating the stories of the many diverse people who interacted with them. In fact, seeing beloved historic places embrace this broader vision of diversity, and recalibrate their exhibitions and offerings to reflect a more dynamic past, is one of the most exciting and inspiring frontiers in our field today.

Step 3: Move Beyond Buildings

Preservationists have also begun to think differently about the work we do and the tools we use to accomplish it. In the early days—in part because of the nineteenth-century precedent set by Ann Pamela Cunningham at Mount Vernon, in part because architects were especially well-represented among the cadre of preservationists in the 1950s and '60s, and in part because of the traditionalist biases of American history at that time—there was a long-standing emphasis in historic preservation on saving grand and beautiful buildings. This original "great men and great houses" emphasis was encoded into law with the National Historic Preservation Act. For example, current federal guidelines for buildings to be listed on the National Register of Historic Places stipulate that they must have "integrity," a determination that involves the building's location, design, materials, workmanship, and other factors, and either be at least fifty years old or meet a standard of "exceptional importance."[42]

Those are very high standards to meet, and although standards are important, this high bar tends to limit our perspective of history to architectural significance. There is so much more to our story than that. For many of the places that represent histories we would now characterize as exceptionally important, the physical structures might have changed substantially, particularly if they had been adaptively reused over the years. Sometimes—as in the case of Shockoe Bottom in Richmond, Virginia, once the nation's second-largest slave market—there are no longer any buildings at all.[43]

Now, saving beautiful buildings is hugely important, and it's not something we plan to stop doing anytime soon. But, as abolitionist Wendell Phillips said while trying to save the Old South Meetinghouse in Boston, "They say the Old South is ugly! I should be ashamed to know where it is ugly or handsome. Does a man love his mother because she is handsome?" Not every American of importance grew up or lived in a grand manse. Far from it. Sometimes the places that matter most to us are plain, simple, and unadorned. They won't catch an architect's eye, but they still matter.[44]

The handball court in Maravilla that I talked about in the introduction is one such place. It may look like just a regular blacktop next to a grocery store and would have a hard time passing muster under the traditional rules of preservation, but it is a beloved and even historic center of the community that should be honored. Another is the La Laguna Playground in San Gabriel, California. Known as Dragon Park or Dinosaur Park by the locals and designed by Mexican-born artist Benjamin Dominguez in 1965, the playground is filled with sculptures of whimsical sea creatures that have delighted generations of children and adults. "Dinosaur Park is a creative experience without rival for our children," said San Gabriel resident Senya Lubisich. "You really do feel like you've crossed into another world, you've sort of left a park and gone into a fantasy lagoon. It's really evident in the way that they play." "I do not have a memory of my childhood without La Laguna," said Senya's husband, Eloy Zarate. "I've been going there since I was one, all my life. This place is amazing, it's an experience that transcends. People just stand in awe. I always try to explain to adults: okay you're 30, or you're 40, or 50. Now just imagine for a moment that you are five and you're here in the middle of this."[45]

When the city considered demolishing La Laguna in 2006 to build a more traditional playground in its place, Lubisich and Zarate helped form the Friends of La Laguna to save Dominguez's creation. "It never occurred to [the city] that it was anything other than a playground," Lubisich said, "that it could be art, or that it was unique, or rare in the terms of the experience it afforded." They rounded up more than three thousand signatures from other local residents, applied for grants to protect the playground, and enlisted the aid of preservation groups like the Los Angeles Conservancy and the National Trust. Now, this last commissioned work of an underappreciated Chicano artist is on the local register of historic places, and kids will be able to slide along the La Laguna sea serpent and play among its fanciful dinosaurs and octopuses for years to come.[46]

Recognizing a handball court or a playground as historic resources may challenge the bylaws of traditional preservation, but more and more often, we are finding ways to recognize and affirm such sites and landmarks around us. We are also working harder to dig deeper—to move beyond buildings and help preserve more intangible but no less important historic assets, like heritage, arts, and culture.

Ultimately, we want to celebrate all the ways that places are special to communities and inspire deep emotions and personal connections, even if they aren't always what we would consider capital H-historic. Here again, the excitement in our field is palpable because, even when it comes to buildings, we have room to grow.

The La Laguna Playground in Vincent Lugo Park, San Gabriel, California.
(© National Trust for Historic Preservation)

One of our National Treasures is the Ralph Munro Marine Stadium, a breathtaking, one-of-a-kind modernist venue just outside Miami and the only arena in the United States designed for watching powerboat races. Conceived by twenty-seven-year-old Cuban American architect Hilario Candela, the Miami Marine Stadium began hosting concerts, boat shows, and other national events in 1963, including the filming of the 1967 Elvis Presley film *Clambake* and a memorable 1972 campaign rally where Sammy Davis Jr. endorsed Richard Nixon. After Hurricane Andrew thrashed the stadium in 1992, however, the venue closed and fast became a gallery for Miami graffiti artists. They turned it into a massive canvas and covered nearly every square inch with paint, sometimes multiple times.[47]

So, in 2014, we did something rather extraordinary for the National Trust. As part of our campaign to revive the stadium, we worked with our local partners to host nine celebrated graffiti artists from around the world. Under the watchful eye of professional conservators, they painted murals on the stadium's walls, which were then photographed to be sold as prints to raise money to rehabilitate Miami Marine. We also held an Instagram tour of the graffiti event and had to turn people away. In fact, more than 450 people tried to sign up in the first hour for the forty-five available slots.[48]

Now, we won't be sneaking the international street-art sensation Banksy onto Mount Vernon any time soon, but this event gave us a chance to celebrate the street artists who embraced Miami Marine Stadium for two decades and kept it alive when it was chained up and left to crumble. Their connection to this place is also special and should be recognized.

In the twenty-first century, preservation has to be about more than just maintaining grand, historic homes. The places that all people cherish need to be recognized, protected, and actively thriving. In moving beyond the strictures of the National Register and embracing a broader sense of preservation, we are only following an example set by communities all over the country.

In February 2015, President Barack Obama returned to his old hometown of Chicago to announce the designation of the Pullman Historic District as a National Monument, something the National Trust had been pushing for a long time. In his remarks, he described so well why we should look beyond beautiful buildings and should work to protect the modest places where small actions helped transform the world.

He first explained the importance of Pullman, telling the audience about labor leader A. Philip Randolph and the Pullman Porters, who fought to make Pullman the first company in the United States to recognize a union of black workers and who helped seed the civil rights movement. "Part of what we're preserving here," he said, "is understanding that places that look ordinary are nothing but extraordinary. The places you live are extraordinary, which means you can be extraordinary. You can make something happen, the same way these workers here at Pullman made something happen.[49]

"No matter who you are," Obama concluded, "you stand on the shoulders of giants. You stand on the site of great historic movements. And that means you can initiate great historic movements by your own actions." He's right. History doesn't just happen at the White House or Mount Vernon. It happens all around us, in all our neighborhoods and communities, in everyday deeds of kindness, compassion, justice, and love. These stories should be honored and preserved as well.[50]

Step 4: Ensure That All Voices Are Heard

The best preservation projects can create opportunities for community residents at all income levels to live, work, and play, all the while retaining the local history that ties together current and future generations. To make sure preservation and adaptive reuse is happening in the right way, however, everyone has to have a voice at the table.

A few years ago, the National Trust commissioned a seventeen-hundred-participant research study of the leadership of preservation groups across the United States that found there is considerable room for improvement in this regard. The composition of "preservation leaders" was 93 percent white, 2 percent black, 1 percent Latino, and 2 percent Asian or Pacific Islander. By contrast, according to the US Census at the time, the nation was 72 percent white, 16 percent Hispanic, 13 percent African American, and 5 percent Asian. Nor did these leadership statistics reflect the grassroots energy of young, diverse millennials all over the United States, who don't necessarily think of themselves as preservationists but are working, on their own, to save places they love.[51]

Simply put, when diverse communities are not represented in preservation, important places and stories will be lost. Take the example of Compton's Cafeteria, a former diner in San Francisco's Tenderloin. Many people know the story of the Stonewall Inn in New York City, where, in June 1969, a police raid led to a riot and protest that jump-started the gay rights movements in the United States. A few years before that, however, in August 1966, a very similar incident occurred when police tried to kick transgender women and drag queens out of Compton's in San Francisco. The Compton's protest, according to historian Susan Stryker, was "the transgender community's debut on the stage of American political history. It was the first known instance of collective militant queer resistance to police harassment in United States history." Although we rightfully commemorate the anniversary of Stonewall every year—and the Stonewall Inn was recently named both a New York City landmark and a national monument—the Compton's riot is much less well known, and the building no longer even exists. Only a plaque, installed in 2006, remains to commemorate this important civil rights story.[52]

We don't want to see stories like this neglected or overlooked. (To its credit, the National Park Service embarked on an LGBTQ Heritage Initiative in May 2014 to see more such stories reflected at national sites.) So, along with enhancing our commitment at the National Trust to protecting diverse histories, we set to work on rethinking our diversity initiatives. We wanted to develop concrete benchmarks for diversifying our staff and volunteer leadership, find new ways to reach out to more Americans, and make sure we are hearing what they have to tell us.[53]

One of our newest initiatives is the Hands-On Preservation Experience Crew, or HOPE Crew, a partnership with the Corps Network and the National Park Service. Based in part on the Civilian Conservation Corps, Franklin Roosevelt's favorite and most popular New Deal program, HOPE Crew helps young people in diverse communities receive critical training and experience in preservation skills by giving them the opportunity to rehabilitate historic places in need.

We began HOPE Crew in March 2014 with a project in Shenandoah

National Park, and it has been going strong ever since. In its first year, HOPE Crews worked with local partners and other members of the Corps Network to restore the final resting place of veterans at Raleigh National Cemetery and Little Bighorn Battlefield National Monument. They helped repair historic barns in Michigan, stables in Virginia, adobes in New Mexico, Boy Scout camps in New Jersey, and cabins in Wyoming's Grand Teton National Park. They rehabilitated the log cabin home of Lyndon Johnson's grandfather with the Texas Conservation Corps and reroofed a historic structure at Hyde Park, lifelong home of Franklin Roosevelt, with Conservation Legacy. HOPE Crew members and volunteers helped repaint Hinchliffe Stadium in Paterson, New Jersey, once the home of the New York Black Yankees in the Negro Baseball League. Others, with the help of the Greening Youth Foundation, restored shotgun homes along the Atlanta street where Martin Luther King Jr. was born, and they got the chance to learn firsthand the truth of his maxim: "Everybody can be great, because everybody can serve."[54]

Across twenty projects in its first year, HOPE Crews saw more than one hundred young men and women in twelve states, including several veterans, contribute more than 12,000 hours to serving their communities by restoring historic sites. The program is only growing: 2015 saw fifty HOPE Crew projects, and we expect there will be many more in the years to come.[55]

HOPE Crew has not only helped alleviate the multi-billion-dollar backlog in deferred maintenance at many National Parks sites. It has given young men and women the opportunity to enter a high-need field, obtain education and training in preservation skills that can otherwise be hard to come by, and feel the positive power of transforming a place in their community that matters. "Working on the HOPE Crew," said one young Corps member, "has taught me many new skills and opened my eyes to a number of professions that I would never have

considered pursuing." Others have emphasized the pride they felt in
helping to preserve our national legacy. "It's going to make me feel real
good," another crew leader said of her work, "walking down the street
with my kids and showing them what their mother did and what they
can do when they get older."[56]

We are excited about the possibilities to continue expanding HOPE
Crew so that more young Americans and more historic sites in need can
benefit from a hands-on preservation experience. We are also looking to
broaden preservation's reach in other ways. For example, the National
Trust has been working with the HBCU Internship Program to link
college students attending historically black colleges and universities to
National Park Service sites that focus on the important role African
Americans have played in the development and progress of the United
States. Since 1992, the National Trust Diversity Scholarship Program
has also helped make preservation more inclusive and accessible by providing scholarships to our annual conference. And we have been reaching out to sibling organizations focused on the labor movement, the
Latino and Asian American experience, the women's rights struggle, and
the LGBTQ movement to find other places of meaning.[57]

What we have been hearing at the National Trust is that, for many
diverse communities, the value of historic preservation is less about
architectural integrity than it is about social issues and working to see
that communities have a say in their own future. (I will say more about
one of the most important issues we hear about—affordability and displacement—in chapter 6.)

As such, historic preservation can no longer just be about saving old
places, independent of the men, women, and children who live among
them. We have to see that diverse history is being honored and diverse
stories are being told. And we need to see that the concerns of families
are heard, and their needs met, by adaptive reuse projects and urban
revitalization strategies.

Step 5: Confront Our Difficult History

Fifth and finally, we should work harder to come to terms with the more complex and difficult chapters of our national story through our historic places. It's safe to say that, as a nation, we haven't done the best job of that so far.

Take the example of our National Mall in Washington, D.C., a beautiful, even hallowed American place filled with first-rate museums, monuments, and memorials. A visitor to the Mall can visit the nearby United States Holocaust Memorial Museum, a powerful, necessary reminder of one of the most evil and depraved acts humanity has ever witnessed. If she chooses to walk down Massachusetts or New Jersey Avenue, she can take in the Memorial to the Victims of Communism, which opened in 2006. By Union Station, she can take in the stark sculpture of wheat, added in 2015, that signifies the Holodomor, the man-made famine in Ukraine that saw millions starve to death at the hand of Stalinism.

She'd have to search far and wide, though, for an American Slavery Memorial in Washington, D.C., or a monument to the Native American peoples displaced, imprisoned, and killed by the original European settlers or the germs they inadvertently carried with them. Congress has partially rectified these oversights by adding a National Museum of the American Indian and a National Museum of African-American History and Culture to the Mall, which opened in 2004 and 2016, respectively. Still, when it comes to our own national sins—which also must be confronted and reflected upon—our landscape is too often silent.

It does us no good to pretend that our history has always been pretty. Slavery, the displacement of native peoples, the internment of Japanese Americans during World War II, racist exclusion laws, Jim Crow—they are all a part of the American story as well, with effects and legacies that resonate into the present. We cannot hide our heads from these ugly facets of our narrative. To help us contextualize and come to terms with this difficult past, so that we can forge a more equitable and fair path forward, we need more historic sites properly interpreted all over the United States.

That is why, in Richmond, Virginia, the National Trust has been working to protect Shockoe Bottom from inappropriate development. "Shockoe Bottom might just be the best place in the nation to understand the history of slavery and its ongoing legacy," historian Max Page has argued. "The commerce in human lives 150 years ago still shapes a city today." But for a while, it looked like this downtown area of the former capital of the Confederacy would instead become the home of a new baseball stadium for the Richmond Flying Squirrels, a minor league team in the Giants system.[58]

We agree with the many descendants of enslaved persons in Richmond that such a stadium is not an appropriate use for land where hundreds of thousands of African Americans were held, bought, and sold. As actress Lupita Nyong'o put it in a letter to Richmond Mayor Dwight Jones: "Evidence of America's slave history simply must be preserved, as the legacy of slavery affects all American people. The tactic of the enslaver was to systematically erase all memory of the African's past; let us not repeat this ill by contributing to the erasure of his past in America too." Shockoe Bottom was ground zero for an industry that generated great wealth for the nation by torturing individuals and terrorizing families. We should treat it as a site of conscience, where the public can reflect on past struggles for freedom, seek harmony and reconciliation, and join together to address contemporary legacies of injustice.[59]

This is true not just in Richmond but all over the United States, both North and South. Our history is often complicated, and we have to do a better job of coming to terms with the darker chapters in our story. Historic places and memorials that relate these chapters help us understand ourselves as a nation and a people, even if they do not always paint us, or our ancestors, in the best light. They give us the chance to come together, confront troubling eras in our history, and examine how they continue to inform the America of today. And by showing us the missteps we have made along the way, they help us see more clearly the path forward to real justice, equality, and freedom.

To see how past events continue to resonate in today's struggles, just look at the growing debate in many communities about how best to commemorate the Civil War, and whether the many statues and memorials honoring the Confederate war effort in our public squares are still appropriate. After nine African American churchgoers were murdered by a white supremacist in Charleston, South Carolina, the summer and fall of 2015 saw several states make the long-overdue decision to stop flying the Confederate flag. City councils in Nashville, New Orleans, and other places also voted to remove statues of Robert E. Lee and Nathan Bedford Forrest from public squares. Towns and colleges looked to rename schools, roads, and buildings named after southern slave-holders.[60]

Shouldn't the National Trust and other historic preservationists step in here, some of our members have asked, and help save these "historic" statues and monuments under threat? And if some see Confederate memorials as "heritage" and others see them as "instruments of racial terror," as one columnist put it, how can we ever find a way forward? These debates have opened up a necessary and worthwhile discussion, even in our own preservation community, about the best way to confront what remains, 150 years after Appomattox, the most contentious aspect of our national story.[61]

Clearly, the end of the Civil War held different meanings for white and black southerners at the time. For Confederates, the bloodiest conflict in our history by far ended not just in defeat; in the words of many contemporaries, it was also a "harvest of death." One of every five white southern men of military age died during the war, and many more were wounded. The South's overall mortality rate, including civilians, is estimated to have been worse than that of any nation in the killing fields of

World War I. Such a horrible culling demanded memorialization from those white southerners who survived.[62]

But there was also the Jubilee. During those same four tumultuous years, nearly four million enslaved African Americans across the South won their freedom—often, as noted earlier, by voting with their feet and forcing the Union to embrace a policy of emancipation. After nearly 250 years since the first enslaved Africans arrived in Virginia, the sin of slavery was finally expunged from American life.

The basis of much of today's current dilemma is that grieving white southerners erected hundreds of monuments to honor the valor of fallen leaders and loved ones in the years after the war, but black communities had neither the power nor the means for an equal effort to acknowledge their experience of the war or the end of slavery. As a result, an incomplete and one-sided version of this seminal moment was enshrined in our parks and squares. We are struggling with this deficit of heritage today.

Even more troubling is that this deficit was mostly intentional. As historian David Blight and many others have recounted, the memorial process in the South was soon taken over by advocates of the Lost Cause, who explicitly wanted to vindicate the Confederacy at the bar of history, erase the central issues of slavery and emancipation from the popular understanding of the war, and reaffirm the system of state-sanctioned white supremacy that the war and Reconstruction had sought to dismantle. Put simply, the erection of these Confederate memorials and Jim Crow went hand in hand.[63]

As such, a wave of monument building ensued, and testaments to Confederate valor arose in unlikely places. In Rockville, Maryland—a Union state where nearly three times as many citizens fought for the North—stands a monument "To Our Heroes of Montgomery Co. Maryland That We Through Life May Not Forget To Love The Thin Gray Line." (In 2015, this statue received a new epigram in spray paint: "Black Lives Matter.") In Kentucky, where two and a half times more soldiers fought in Union blue, there are seventy-two Confederate monuments and two Union ones.[64]

The historical project of these sorts of memorials was not lost on African Americans at the time. "As you passed by," said Mamie Garvin Fields, a black educator from Charleston at the turn of the twentieth century, "here was [John C.] Calhoun looking at you in the face and telling you, 'you may not be a slave, but I am back to see you stay in your place. . . .' I believe white people were talking to us about Jim Crow through that statue."[65]

Some statues were even more explicit. Early in the twentieth century, the United Daughters of the Confederacy made an unsightly push to erect memorials to "faithful slaves" in every state of the Union. Thankfully, few of these exist today, although one in Fort Mill, South Carolina, extols "the Faithful Slaves who, loyal to a sacred trust, Toiled for the support of the Army with matchless Devotion, and with sterling fidelity guarded our defenseless homes, women, and children." Another in Harpers Ferry, West Virginia, praises "the character and faithfulness of thousands of negroes" despite "many temptations throughout subsequent years of war."[66]

Many of the Confederate memorials we have among us now are more circumspect, but they still shine a light on this time when Jim Crow and segregation were ascendant in the South. The values of that time are rightfully embarrassing and offensive to us today. When Jaime Lerner, mayor of Curitiba, Brazil, wrote, "I don't like the monuments of people that have no warmth or affection, or who consider themselves above the common people, with phrases intended to defend them," he could be talking about many of the stern Confederate generals on horseback in city after city.[67]

But even if their values are no longer ours, these memorials are important to our understanding of the present and the problems we face in the twenty-first century. "I don't know if I want to forget that, at some point, somebody was crazy enough to have a monument to Nathan Bedford Forrest," noted author and activist Ta-Nehisi Coates. "That's a statement about what society was. That shouldn't be forgotten." We at the National Trust agree that whitewashing this period from our history and public memory is not the answer. If anything, we need more memorials to interpret and explain this time in its full context.[68]

There are creative ways that even the most unregenerate and offensive Confederate memorials can be adapted for this purpose. In Dallas, for example, a "Whites Only" drinking fountain unearthed in the County Records Building in 2003 was turned into a striking piece of public art: pressing the "drink" button now plays a video of police training water hoses on civil rights protestors. Jill Ogline Titus, assistant director of the Civil War Institute at Gettysburg College, suggested how "a monument standing in a town square might be reframed through an evening art installation, projecting images of civil rights protestors marching through the same square." In places like Leesburg, Virginia, and Chapel Hill, North Carolina, citizens have proposed adding contextualizing plaques, or an alternate memorial next to the original one, to create a dialogue.[69]

Ultimately, the continued propriety of specific memorials in the public space is something that must be determined by communities on a case-by-case basis, in a transparent and deliberative manner. If memorials are retained, they should provide an appropriate context about the war and its causes. And if cities choose to substantially modify or even remove offending memorials, it is hoped that these changes will be done in a way that engages with rather than silences the past.

That holds true for the rest of our story as well. The founders of the United States often owned slaves. Andrew Jackson and Franklin Roosevelt, considered among the most important US presidents, presided over Indian removal and Japanese internment, respectively. Woodrow Wilson guided the nation through World War I, but he also restored segregation to the federal government. North, South, East, or West, few of our heroes' hands are clean.

Examining our past without rose-colored glasses can be tough. It can arouse strong emotions. But, as President Lincoln said at the start of that terrible conflict a century and a half ago, "we are not enemies but friends. We must not be enemies. Though passion may have strained, it must not break our bonds of affection." As we reckon with our past and reflect on the mistakes we have made in our communities and as a country, let's try to empathize with our neighbors of different backgrounds and walk a mile in their shoes. Ultimately, we are all Americans, and even the grimmest chapters of our collective story can illuminate our present and inspire us to be better in the future.

In Falls Church, at the Tinner Hill Historic Site I discussed at the beginning of this chapter, there now rests on the site's grounds a beautiful stone sculpture by artist Martha Jackson Jarvis that depicts a West African Adinkra symbol called *Nkyinkym*. It is a symbol of toughness, initiative, dynamism, devotion to service, and resolve—all traits that the families of Tinner Hill exhibited in full measure when they stood up against segregation a century ago. And all traits that we will have to adopt in confronting the many challenging moments in our collective past.[70]

This symbol has its roots in an African expression that translates as "the course of life is full of twisting, ups and downs, and zigzags." Those ups and downs, those zigzags, also represent our national story. It has not always been pretty. We have had to work hard, over centuries, to live up to our democratic ideals, and we are still working at it. Our historic places help illuminate that important, often zigzagging journey we are taking in the United States toward justice, freedom, and equality. They show us that our communities have evolved over the years, and must continue to evolve, to attain these worthy goals. And they remind us of those who, in their own time, carried the beacon forward.[71]

CHAPTER 6

Mitigating the Great Inversion: The Problems of Affordability and Displacement

I woke up this morning, I looked next door.
There was one family living where there once were four.
I got the gentrifi-gentrification blues.
I wonder where my neighbors went, 'cause I know I'll soon be
moving there too.
   — "Gentrification Blues," Judith Levine and Laura Liben[1]

As we have seen, preservation can save important places, enhance
neighborhoods, and turn historic resources into community anchors
that accommodate the ever-changing needs of society—from food markets to clothing stores to cultural centers. A central argument of this
book is that cities and neighborhoods that want to see more residents,
jobs, and investment would do well to take a page from the Preservation
Green Lab's research and work to reemploy their older building fabric to
jump-start urban revitalization. We are seeing it happen over and over
again—in Baltimore, Philadelphia, Detroit, and all across the country.

At the same time, although there are neighborhoods in every city in the United States that are looking for more investment, some places—and increasingly more places—are facing a somewhat different problem. In these cases, rapid revitalization is helping produce neighborhoods that are in danger of being completely hollowed out and drained of character. Chain stores and luxury lofts are quickly crowding out small businesses and affordable housing. Young, white, and comparatively wealthy new arrivals are moving in, and communities of color, who have lived and worked there for decades, feel they are suddenly being pushed out.

Preservation shouldn't be something that happens *to* communities. We have to make sure we're doing it right, and that the quality of life for existing urban residents isn't being diminished by the associated impacts that come when a street, block, or neighborhood begins to improve its fortunes. Affordability, displacement, the rising cost of living, and loss of neighborhood identity are all issues that preservation and revitalization efforts must contend with and, if possible, work to mitigate.

Life on the High Line

Consider the High Line, a breathtaking 1.5-mile-long park that wends from Gansevoort Street to West 34th Street in Manhattan. As its five million visitors a year can attest, the High Line is one of the most intriguing examples around of how a creative preservation project can remake an entire neighborhood.

It began its life in 1934 as an elevated railroad trestle of the New York Central Railroad, so that goods could be moved efficiently along the industry-minded West Side. Today, it is, in critic Paul Goldberger's words, the "Miracle Above Manhattan." "Not since Central Park in 1857," wrote *New York Times* architecture critic Michael Kimmelman, "has a park reshaped New Yorkers' thinking about public space and the city more profoundly. . . . [It shows] how one exceptional design—in this case, a work of landscape architecture—might miraculously alter a whole neighborhood, even a whole city's fortunes."[2]

Yet it came very close to never happening. After the railroad trestle saw its last train in 1980, the elevated tracks were considered a useless relic and even something of a public embarrassment by city officials, who began tearing them down south of Gansevoort. That they continued to exist at all is mainly thanks to two local residents, Robert Hammond and Joshua David—an artist and freelance writer, respectively—who first met in 1999 at a meeting to discuss the future of the trestle. "I saw an article in the *New York Times* saying that the High Line was going to be demolished," Hammond later told Goldberger, "and I wondered if anyone was going to save it. I was in love with the steel structure, the rivets, the ruin."[3]

As it happens, the two most committed preservationists in the room that day were Hammond and David, and they struck up a fast friendship. They asked for a tour of the railroad's remnants and were amazed at the overgrown wilderness they discovered. "When we got up there, we saw a mile and a half of wildflowers. . . . It was another world, right in the middle of Manhattan," Hammond said. "There was a powerful sense of the passing of time. You could see what the High Line was built for, and feel that its moment had slipped away. All the buildings alongside it were brick warehouses and factories with smokestacks and casement windows, like buildings from a Hopper painting."[4]

So the two men went to work, enlisting friends and neighbors to join the Friends of the High Line and making the case that rather than succumbing to demolition, the old tracks could be remade into a unique and amazing elevated public park. After some years of wrestling with the Giuliani administration to prevent the tracks' removal, the two made a key ally in new mayor Michael Bloomberg, who saw the potential of Hammond and David's vision and helped secure financing for it. Then, in 2009, after years of advocacy, fund-raising, and creative design, the first leg of the High Line Park opened to almost instant acclaim. By the time the third and final major section was finished in September 2014, the park was already a New York institution. "If the newest, last stretch of the High Line doesn't make you fall in love with New York all over again," wrote the *Times*' Kimmelman, "I really don't know what to say."[5]

I agree with Kimmelman—the experience of the High Line is magical. It gives us a completely new way of looking at the city. It shows how, through dedication and commitment, local activists with a vision of a better future for their neighborhood can reimagine their community in creative ways. And it illustrates perfectly the often hidden potential of older urban resources to rejuvenate our neighborhoods, if given the opportunity.

Unfortunately, there is also another side to this story.

As *New Yorker* art critic Peter Schjeldahl put it, "The High Line has been to usual gentrification what a bomb is to bottle rockets." Because of the park's popularity, property values more than doubled in the area around the High Line between 2003 and 2011. After West Chelsea was rezoned for luxury development in 2005, the old character of the neighborhood began to change rapidly. Unable to afford the increased rents, businesses that had served the community for decades began to close up shop, and local residents were forced to relocate. "The High Line is a monument to gentrification," argued one writer, "a showcase of what can happen when hip young college graduates invade an impoverished area and repopulate it with art galleries and fancy restaurants." Blogger Jeremiah Moss argued much the same in the *New York Times*. "West Chelsea was a mix of working-class residents and light-industrial businesses," he wrote. "But the High Line is washing all that away." The High Line might be "Disney World on the Hudson," but if trends continued, "gone entirely will be regular New Yorkers, the people who used to call the neighborhood home."[6]

The High Cost of Living

Although the High Line is a particularly stark example of a rapidly changing neighborhood, you can see the same story unfolding in other communities across New York City—in the Lower East Side, in Harlem, in neighborhoods across Brooklyn. Despite the city's strong preservation laws, historic buildings are coming down to make room for luxury residential high-rises throughout the city. Just as often, the welcome revitalization of a historic neighborhood becomes the prelude to the potential mass displacement of existing families and businesses.

Moss, the blogger who called out the displacement that came in the High Line's wake, has been tracking the closing of businesses and local landmarks at his website Vanishing New York. They are everywhere—restaurants, delis, bodegas, music shops. From the punk club CBGB to St. Mark's Bookshop to the Ziegfeld cinema, the face of New York is changing.[7]

One of the most damning recent transformations, from a symbolic perspective, is Jane Jacobs's old townhouse on 555 Hudson Street. Although protected as a historic place, her building—which she and her husband bought in 1947 for $7,000—sold for $3.3 million in 2009 and now holds a real estate office. "Cities need not 'bring back' a middle class and carefully protect it like an artificial growth," Jacobs wrote from that very building. "Cities grow the middle class. But to keep it as it grows, to keep it as a stabilizing force in the form of a self-diversified population, means considering the city's people valuable and worth retaining, right where they are, before they become middle class." Today, though, the average per-capita income in Jacobs's old neighborhood is more than $110,000 a year, and many of the working-class establishments that she once hailed as keys to vibrant urban life have moved on. Instead, expensive retail outlets are increasingly common. In response, guerilla stickers popped up all over Greenwich Village reading "Less Marc Jacobs, More Jane Jacobs," a reference to the high-end fashion franchise.[8]

San Francisco is another white-hot real estate market at the vanguard of this urban transformation. As noted earlier, average rents in New York City and San Francisco hit new heights in 2015, with a one-bedroom apartment commanding more than $3,000 a month, and showed no signs of slowing in 2016. According to Sarah Karlinsky, a senior policy advisor with SPUR (formerly the San Francisco Planning Urban Research Association), the San Francisco region added 480,000 private-sector jobs between 2011 and 2016, but only around 50,000 new housing units, slightly more than 10 percent of what is needed.[9]

Compounding the problem is that what little new construction there is tends to favor the desires of the city's wealthiest citizens over the needs of average residents. As a result, according to one recent study, one-fourth of San Francisco's neighborhoods are at risk of seeing mass displacement by 2030. A similar logic prevails in nearby Los Angeles. A University of California, Los Angeles study of housing patterns there found that "the market is distorted by the large buying power of a wealthy minority, and not enough supply made available at prices that are affordable to those with stagnant incomes."[10]

What's happening in New York, San Francisco, and Los Angeles is also being seen in cities like London and Barcelona: long-thriving neighborhoods are being hollowed out to accommodate the world's richest citizens. "Houses in Mayfair," commented one London observer, "are now bitcoins for oligarchs."[11]

To be fair, several studies have argued that concerns about gentrification—which date back to 1964, when the term was first coined by British sociologist Ruth Glass—are overstating the case. "That gentrification displaces poor people of color by well-off white people is a claim so commonplace that most people accept it as a widespread fact of urban life," one 2015 *Slate* article observed after surveying the recent literature. "It's not. Gentrification of this sort is actually exceedingly rare. The socio-economic status of most neighborhoods is strikingly stable over time."[12]

As evidence, the article pointed to the work of University of Washington economist Jacob Vigdor, who, looking at Boston from 1974 to 1997, found that poorer residents were actually *less* likely to move out of a neighborhood in the midst of gentrification. Another study by Columbia University's Lance Freeman and Frank Braconi found the pattern held in New York too: higher rents meant *fewer* people moved out of an area. "The most plausible interpretation," they wrote, "may be the simplest: As neighborhoods gentrify, they also improve in many ways that may be as appreciated by their disadvantaged residents as by their more affluent ones." Broader follow-up studies by Freeman have supported his initial conclusion. In 2009, he found that, from 1970 to 2000, neighborhoods experiencing gentrification were more racially, socioeconomically, and educationally diverse than neighborhoods that weren't.[13]

Other studies have followed the same pattern. One by the American Housing Survey in 2002 found that only between 4 and 5 percent of relocations in the United States are caused by displacement. Another, conducted by the Federal Reserve Bank of Cleveland in 2013, declared that in 75 percent of America's fifty-five largest cities, fewer than 10 percent of all neighborhoods felt the impact of gentrification between 2000 and 2007. Instead, it was mostly a problem of America's largest and most popular cities, like New York, San Francisco, Washington, D.C., and Seattle.[14]

This news may be somewhat heartening at first, and, as noted at the outset, many cities across the United States would be ecstatic to see more residents and investment. As one developer and community advocate said to me about his work helping revitalize neighborhoods in Baltimore, saying that gentrification is always bad is tantamount to saying that poorer communities must forevermore remain that way.

That does not mean there is no cause for concern, however. Even low rates of displacement are cold comfort to the families that are still being displaced from their homes and communities. Taken together, the population of America's already impacted cities is considerable. And there are troubling signs that the affordability crisis will soon spread to many other places.

Looking at patterns nationwide, the US Census Bureau reported at the end of 2015 that the median rent in the United States was at a twenty-year high—$850 a month, $50 higher than the year before. Fourteen cities around the country saw double-digit growth in rents last year. Another study—this one by Harvard researchers—found that nearly half of households making between $30,000 and $45,000 a year are now paying close to a third of their income on rent. As costs go up, families of more limited means are being pushed out.[15]

Over at *Vanishing New York*, blogger Moss likens the "hyper-gentrification" his city is now experiencing to climate change. "It's like the way people argue about climate change and say, 'Well, the climate's always changed throughout time,'" he wrote. "Yes, it has, but climate change is dramatic, it's overpowering, it's overwhelming, and it's certainly sped up. I think in New York we are seeing change on an unnatural scale." Many residents caught in the grip of this change would agree. Clearly, something is going wrong when entire cities become completely unaffordable to all but the wealthy few, and when businesses that have served communities for generations have to close up shop just because their rent suddenly tripled to make way for another chain store.[16]

The ill omens are not just anecdotal. Some research supports blogger Moss's contention that the dynamics of displacement are changing. A 2005 study by Rutgers University and the University of British Columbia suggested that gentrification since the late 1990s is "of a scale and pace that is unmatched historically." Instead of displacement simply being a "minor phenomenon that affects a few communities," the authors concluded, there appears to be growing "evidence of vast urban restructuring."[17]

In a 2012 book, author and journalist Alan Ehrenhalt described this broad restructuring as "the great inversion." America's cities, he argued, are "gradually coming to resemble a traditional European city—Vienna or Paris in the nineteenth century, or, for that matter, Paris today. The poor and the newcomers are living on the outskirts. The people who live near the center are those, some of them black or Hispanic, but most of them white, who can afford to do so." In sum, "we are witnessing a rearrangement of population across entire metropolitan areas. 'Gentrification' is too small a word for it[;] . . . 'demographic inversion' comes closer to capturing the scope of what is going on."[18]

This inversion has huge ramifications for Americans and their well-being. Because suburbs generally offer fewer social services than metropolitan hubs, families in need will be much less likely to receive assistance once they have been displaced from their original communities. There are fewer transportation options and jobs available in suburban areas as well. Being forced out of one's home also extracts huge psychic and even physical tolls. "Displacement," noted the Centers for Disease Control and Prevention, "has many health implications that contribute to disparities among special populations, including the poor, women, children, the elderly, and members of racial/ethnic minority groups."[19]

Speaking of members of racial and ethnic minority groups, this great inversion is also deeply unfair to communities of color, who embedded deep roots in America's historic urban neighborhoods even as many white residents moved out.

Race and the American City
In chapter 5, I talked about how critical it is that, as a nation, we work harder to confront the more complex and difficult dimensions of our American story. That has to include the ways that systematic and institutionalized racism helped determine the current contours of our urban landscape.

In 2015, *Atlantic* writers like Ta-Nehisi Coates and Alexis Madrigal reemphasized how, for decades, the Federal Housing Authority's patently racist and indefensible practice of "redlining"—cutting off loans to communities of color—robbed African American neighborhoods of investment and economic growth. Although "previously, prejudices were personalized and individualized," historian Kenneth Jackson wrote, surveying the impacts of redlining, the "FHA exhorted segregation and enshrined it as public policy." As Charles Abrams put it in 1955, "The FHA adopted a racial policy that could well have been culled from the Nuremberg laws."[20]

Redlining did not operate in a vacuum. It worked alongside a number of other policies to conspire against the economic success of neighborhoods of color. Years after the families of Tinner Hill helped successfully defeat racial zoning in their community, restrictive covenants barred African Americans from moving into white areas. Predatory lenders often took full advantage of low-income neighborhoods' need for the investments that the Federal Housing Authority would not make. And, from Lenox Terrace in New York to the Fillmore District in San Francisco, communities of color were usually the first to see their homes and neighborhoods destroyed in the name of "urban renewal." "In retrospect," concluded a 2002 overview by the Poverty and Race Research Action Council, "it now seems apparent that public officials and policy makers, especially at the state and local level, used expressway construction to destroy low-income and especially black neighborhoods in an effort to reshape the physical and racial landscapes of the postwar American city."[21]

The phenomenon of white flight even further disrupted opportunities in America's inner cities. "The flight of the affluent from the city to the suburbs," said secretary of housing and development George Romney (father of Mitt) in 1971, "together with the influx of the poor into the central city, has created a white suburban noose around an impoverished black central core." When Romney tried to use the provisions of the 1968 Fair Housing Act, passed in the wake of Martin Luther King Jr.'s assassination, to reintegrate communities, allow for more affordable housing in the suburbs, and get rid of discriminatory zoning practices for good, he was blocked by no less than the president of the United States. "Stop this one," Richard Nixon informed his top aide, John Erlichman. "I realize this position will lead us to a situation in which blacks will continue to live for the most part in black neighborhoods."[22]

For decades thereafter, those neighborhoods were often in our inner cities, so much so that "inner city" became a euphemism for race. Now that those same inner cities are experiencing a welcome revitalization and seeing an influx of white people of means, it is unfair and unacceptable for the communities of color who lived there for generations to simply be forced out. The rising tides in historic neighborhoods must lift all boats.

Even if displacement levels do remain as low as many scholarly studies suggest, the influx of young, white Americans into historically ethnic neighborhoods often spurs anxiety, animosity, and distrust. The 2005 Rutgers study that found displacement accelerating also noted that many existing residents don't see gentrification as a "benevolent market force that gives them a reason to stay." Rather, they view it as a harbinger of their impending doom. "Residents who remain in gentrifying neighborhoods," the study noted, "fear that it is just a matter of time before they are displaced."[23]

This is especially true when little consideration is given to existing residents. One recent ad for a new luxury building urged New Yorkers to try out "Homesteading, Bushwick-Style." "Here in bohemian Bushwick, Brooklyn," it read, "you'll find a group of like-minded settlers, mixing the customs of their original homeland with those of one of NYC's most historic neighborhoods to create art, community, and a new lifestyle." Local residents rightfully found this talk of "settlers" colonizing an already existing neighborhood repellent. After another dustup in the same neighborhood over a "yarn mural" featuring characters from Wes Anderson's *Moonrise Kingdom* and Stanley Kubrick's *The Shining*, a local businessman wrote on Facebook, "Gentrification has gotten to the point where every time I see a group of young white millennials in the hood, my heart starts racing and a sense of anxiety starts falling over me."[24]

In a much-discussed 2014 tirade against these changes, writer-director Spike Lee referred to this sort of thinking as "Christopher Columbus syndrome." "You can't discover this! We've been here!" said Lee. "You can't just come and bogart. There were brothers playing . . . African drums in Mount Morris Park for 40 years and now they can't do it anymore because the new inhabitants said the drums are loud. . . . I'm for democracy and letting everybody live but you've got to have some respect." Lee was referring to a confrontation in which new white arrivals to a rapidly gentrifying part of Harlem demanded—sometimes extremely belligerently—that the drum circle that had been a daily event in the park for years be stopped. "I hope you all agree that the best thing that has happened to Harlem is gentrification," one new resident e-mailed his neighbors. "Let's get rid of these 'people' and improve the neighborhood once and for all."[25]

New York City is far from alone in these sorts of cultural clashes. The revitalization of H Street in Washington, D.C., was discussed in chapter 2, and although many longtime residents say the neighborhood's transformation from 94 percent African American to 63 percent African American and falling between 1990 and 2010 has been relatively benign, there have nonetheless been some sticking points that are cause for concern. One of the most alarming to longtime black residents is an increase in racial profiling by Washington, D.C., police. "You have a lot of people here who haven't lived in an urban neighborhood who are calling police for a lot of new things," said chief of police Cathy Lanier. Local residents agree. "A couple of guys walk through an alley like they've done their whole lives, and the newly arrived neighbors think something untoward is happening," said Philip Johnson, a seventy-one-year-old financial consultant and longtime resident. "These new people just got here two months ago, and we're getting all this drama. . . . The colonists have arrived and we have an occupying army enforcing the rules."[26]

This sudden police presence on H Street also testifies to another common and valid complaint about an influx of white residents into a community of color: often, only then does an area begin to see the level of social services that should have been its due from the very beginning. "I grew up here in Fort Greene," Spike Lee told his Brooklyn audience in 2014. "Why does it take an influx of white New Yorkers in the south Bronx, in Harlem, in Bed Stuy, in Crown Heights for the facilities to get better? The garbage wasn't picked up every . . . day when I was living in 165 Washington Park. P.S. 20 was not good. P.S. 11. Rothschild 294. The police weren't around."[27]

Just as city services have not kept pace in majority-minority communities, these same communities often are not afforded the same protections from development as those with more resources. As reported in *Politico*, a 2010 New York University study of the 188,000 lots rezoned in New York City between 2003 and 2007 found that "upzoned lots tended to be in areas that were less white and less wealthy. . . . Downzoned lots tended to be areas that were more white and had both higher incomes and higher rates of homeownership. In other words, more privileged people were more likely to have the city change the zoning of their neighborhoods to preserve them exactly as they were."[28]

Meanwhile, the residents of those "upzoned" areas often faced renewed pressure of displacement. As Ned Kaufman noted in *Race, Place, and Story*, a policy "which subsidizes the construction of luxury apartments, bends planning and zoning rules to shoehorn them into low- and moderate-income neighborhoods, and then fails to control their impact on nearby rents . . . will inevitably produce less, not more, affordable housing. It will also destroy historically valuable buildings, networks of social connections, local traditions, and patterns of place affection—all vital dimensions of the city's heritage."[29]

This is also far from just a black-and-white issue: ethnic communities of all kinds are seeing an influx of younger, richer, whiter residents. In Washington, D.C., the transformation of the Chinatown district—which began in earnest with the opening of the Verizon Center in 1997—has become evidence of the district's resurgent success. At the same time, as one journalist wrote, Chinatown has gone from "an ethnic enclave of mom-and-pop storefronts . . . into a kitschy block where Chipotle is written in Chinese characters." By 2015, the local Chinese population had dwindled by 90 percent, to just three hundred citizens, and roughly half of them were in serious danger of being displaced by the sale of the Museum Square Apartments, one of the few remaining affordable housing developments in the neighborhood.[30]

The same thing is happening in Washington, D.C.'s Mount Pleasant neighborhood, as well as in Miami's Little Havana, Chicago's Humboldt Park, Little Tokyo in Los Angeles, East Austin, and plenty of other places across the United States: all are seeing the ethnic character and culture that have long defined them draining away. It's true that neighborhoods have always changed over time—and ethnic neighborhoods are no exception—but the pace of change across the country appears to be systemic and accelerating.

"A neighborhood in transition is like a bus," argued Wellington Chen, executive director of the Chinatown Business Improvement District in New York, one of the few ethnic neighborhoods that has remained relatively stable. "The Germans got on, and then they got off. The Jewish population, same thing. The Italians succeeded and moved out to Howard Beach. . . . The battle that we are fighting right now is: Can we stay on a little bit longer? Now, that is a trickier riddle. No group so far has managed to hang on."[31]

Preservation and Affordability

The disproportionate downzoning revealed by the 2010 Rutgers study suggests that, sometimes, preservation tools have been culpable in the disparities that shape our cities. Some urban economists have taken that argument much further, insisting that historic preservation itself is one of the primary drivers of the current affordability crisis.

One of the foremost advocates of this line of thinking is Harvard urban economist Edward Glaeser, who wrote a well-received hymn to urban living called *Triumph of the City: How Our Greatest Invention Makes Us Richer, Smarter, Greener, Healthier, and Happier.* In that book and elsewhere, Glaeser often makes *Freakonomics*-style counterintuitive arguments about cities, such as "there's a lot to like about urban poverty"—to Glaeser, it means a city is doing what it should and attracting poor people who believe there are better opportunities to be had there— and "there are cities in America that may not be worth rebuilding in the wake of a disaster," such as New Orleans after Hurricane Katrina.[32]

In *Triumph of the City*, Glaeser offered some compelling arguments about the inherent social, environmental, and economic benefits of city living. When it comes to preservation, though, he is mostly wrong-headed. "New York's vast historic districts," he suggested, "impede new construction, keeping real estate in New York City enormously expensive . . . especially in its most desirable, historically protected areas." Noting that nearly 16 percent of Manhattan's 7,700 acres below 96th Street are historically protected, he argued that "preservation is freezing large tracts of land, rendering them unable to accommodate the thousands of people who would like to live in Manhattan but can't afford to." This preservation "drives up the price of housing" and "increasingly makes those districts exclusive enclaves of the well-to-do, educated, and white."[33]

Glaeser also cited "an aesthetic reason to be skeptical" about historic districts: he believes they "protect an abundance of uninteresting buildings that are less attractive and exciting than new structures that could replace them." "The real question," he concluded, echoing Le Corbusier, "is whether these vast districts should ever have been created and whether they should remain protected ground in the years ahead. No living city's future should become prisoner to its past."[34]

Glaeser pinned these perceived flaws of preservation on mistakes made by Jane Jacobs. "Because she saw that older, shorter buildings were cheaper," he wrote, "she incorrectly believed that restricting heights and preserving old neighborhoods would ensure affordability. That's not how supply and demand work. . . . Perhaps a forty-story building won't itself house any quirky, less profitable firms, but by providing new space, the building will ease pressure on the rest of the city's real estate. Growth, not height restrictions and a fixed building stock, keeps space affordable and ensures that poorer people and less profitable firms can stay." In sum, "limiting high-rise development doesn't guarantee interesting, heterogeneous neighborhoods. It just guarantees high prices," and thus "preserving vast numbers of postwar glazed-brick buildings is absurd."[35]

It is interesting to note that this charge was leveled at Jacobs's ideas even at the time. "I think it should be obvious," said one official on the other end of her attempts to protect her "blighted" neighborhood, "that, if the Village area is left alone and no middle-income housing is projected by the board, which is the only way it can be, eventually the Village will consist solely of luxury housing, which we, of course, will be powerless to prevent. That trend is already quite obvious and would itself destroy any semblance of the present village [Jacobs et al.] seem so anxious to preserve."[36]

Glaeser is not alone in raising these kinds of questions against both Jacobs and historic preservation in general. In a piece for *The Daily Beast* entitled "What Jane Jacobs Got Wrong about Cities," urban theorist Joel Kotkin argued that, for similar reasons, places like New York and San Francisco are now and will continue to be preserves of the rich, young, and childless and that "we are not seeing a renaissance of the kind of middle-class urbanity that she loved and championed. That city has passed into myth." In the *CityLab*, journalist Kriston Capps made the case that historic preservation districts are anathema to affordable housing and should probably go the way of the dinosaur. "When local- and state-government bodies grant preservation status to *historic districts*—sometimes entire neighborhoods," he wrote, "they do not always simply protect culture, architecture, and history. Sometimes they also shore up wealth, status, and power."[37]

On the surface, these arguments seem to make a good bit of sense. As Glaeser said, simple supply and demand: if historic preservation constrains the supply, then demand, and thus prices, will go up. But when you dig a little deeper, this attempt to scapegoat the affordability crisis on historic preservation is deeply flawed for a number of reasons.

First, as Georgetown Law professor J. Peter Byrne noted in his own response, "Glaeser's assault . . . greatly mischaracterizes preservation law both in its effects and in its role in urban life. He surely exaggerates the effect of preservation laws on urban house prices." If almost 16 percent of Manhattan below 96th Street is protected, Byrne pointed out, more than 84 percent of the island is not. In fact, less than 0.3 percent of the properties on New York City's tax survey—29,000 buildings—have received their own historic designation. "Even if these districts were frozen in amber," Byrne wrote, "developers would have nearly the entire city in which to build without preservation restraint." Of course, as noted in chapter 4, more often than not these districts are *not* frozen in amber. Instead, alterations and even appropriate new construction are allowed in historic districts all the time, including even the tall additions that Glaeser believes will solve the affordability issue.[38]

In chapter 2, I mentioned another problem with this line of argument with regard to the Height of Buildings Act in Washington, D.C. As the *Older, Smaller, Better* research and any number of historic neighborhoods across the country attest, achieving density in urban areas does not necessarily require towering skyscrapers. The streetcar suburbs of many cities, for example—many of which are still with us today only because they were protected—allow for considerably more population density than areas built with cars in mind a few decades later. The streetcar suburbs of Boston, for example—Roxbury, West Roxbury, and Dorchester—included twice as many two-family homes (4,000) and three times as many three-family homes (6,000) as single-family housing (2,000).[39]

Because they were designed to hold multiple families and uses, older buildings in these streetcar suburbs and across the country are often very well equipped to provide affordable housing. That is why, as we saw in chapter 4, creative adaptive reuse projects all over the United States are converting historic schools, warehouses, hotels, and other buildings to lofts, apartments, and homes.

"We used to build lots of in-between housing in this country: row houses, duplexes, apartment courts," journalist Amanda Kolson Hurley observed in *Next City*, but even though the nations of Europe have continued these traditions, "the United States stopped building this way decades ago." Instead of building skyscrapers, Hurley argued, creative "missing middle" infill projects, that take their cues from the existing historic fabric, can help neighborhoods reach what writer Lloyd Alter has coined "goldilocks density"—not too dense, not too sprawling.[40]

This notion of "goldilocks density" points to another problem with Glaeser's contention that skyscrapers will save the city. Sometimes too much density is counterproductive and detrimental to quality of life. Just imagine living in a New York City tenement in 1900, where often a dozen people shared a room 13 feet across![41]

"What we need," theorist Richard Florida offered, "are new measures of density that do not simply count how many people we can physically cram into a space but that accounts of how well the space is utilized."

Once again, historic places are instructive here. In the words of Urban Land Institute's Ed McMahon, "One block of an older neighborhood might include a community theatre, a coffee shop, an art gallery, two restaurants, a bicycle shop, ten music rehearsal studios, a church, twenty apartments, and a couple of bars, and all with much more 24/7 activity and intensity of use than one block of (much taller) office buildings on K Street."[42]

"Skyscrapers are a dime a dozen in today's world," said McMahon. "Once a low rise city or town succumbs to high-rise mania, many more towers will follow, until the city becomes a carbon-copy of every other city in a 'geography of nowhere.'" McMahon is right: demolishing historic buildings for giant towers throws out the baby with the bathwater. Going back to the Sasaki poll I mentioned in the introduction, 57 percent of city residents said they especially adore the historic buildings in their city, and 54 percent said they want to see more adaptive reuse projects that restore these buildings to life. By contrast, fewer than one in six—Glaeser presumably among them—preferred the skyscrapers in their midst, and fewer than one in five wanted to see more of them in their city.[43]

In other words, people—both residents and tourists—come to cities *because* of their historic character. Is it possible that everyone could live more affordably if we converted every block of our cities into giant residential skyscrapers, as Le Corbusier envisioned a century ago? Perhaps it's possible, but at what cost? Even notwithstanding the irreparable damage to the city's character, the quality of life would be vastly diminished such that, eventually, nobody would want to live there anymore anyway. The city would no longer need all its sparkling new towers.

In any event, the simple supply-and-demand thesis used against historic preservation does not reflect what's actually happening in cities today. In fact, despite the outsized demand for affordable housing, new construction has been almost exclusively focused on luxury homes and apartments. Of 370,000 multifamily rental units built between 2012 and 2014 in fifty-four different cities, one survey determined, 82 percent—more than four of every five—were luxury units. Cities such as Denver, Tampa, Baltimore, and Phoenix saw almost all their new units built for their richest residents. In New York City, residential construction spending jumped to $11.9 billion in 2014, the first time ever that more than $7 billion was spent in a year. At the same time, only 20,329 housing units were created, far below the more than 30,000 built a year between 2005 and 2008. In sum, more money was spent to build fewer units, because those units were mainly built for the rich. "You can just simply make much more money building for a luxury market," said Karen Chapple, a professor of planning at the University of California, Berkeley.[44]

Some cities have tried to partially offset these trends through a tool called inclusionary zoning, which allows developers to build bigger buildings if a certain percentage of its units are designated for affordable housing. However good the intentions, though, today's affordability crisis clearly indicates that inclusionary zoning has not been keeping pace with need. Under the voluntary inclusionary zoning system in New York City, affordable housing units represented just 1.7 percent of housing growth—fewer than three thousand homes—between 2005 and 2013. And many of those units, although "affordable" compared to the price of their neighbors, remained out of reach for many families.[45]

In any event, despite the criticisms of historic districts' impact on affordability, it is highly probable that were more older buildings in gentrifying areas protected, more affordable housing would still exist in and around them. In *Race, Place, and Story*, preservationist Ned Kaufman talked about the rapid transformation of communities in New York like the Lower East Side, Harlem, Greenpoint, and the Atlantic Avenue area, whose hub is now the Barclays Center, home of the Brooklyn Nets and New York Islanders. "At first glance," he argued, "the sweeping changes . . . appear to be market-driven, the natural results of free-market capitalism allowed to take its course. But this is not really the case: government and public money are behind them." In other words, simple supply-and-demand questions are a little bit less simple when there's a thumb on the scale.[46]

On Atlantic Avenue and in other neighborhoods like Battery Park City and Times Square, Kaufman noted, the "changes are largely government-driven. There are developers, and they stand to make a substantial return, but the public is underwriting the risks, absorbing the negative consequences, and subsidizing the profits," mainly through favorable zoning and tax policies as well as infrastructure improvements to support luxury residences. Meanwhile, "historic preservation has been almost entirely absent from these conflicted zones. Had these neighborhoods been declared historic districts, their social fabric might still have been transformed, but some portion of their physical fabric would have been protected. There would have been a public debate about the history and its importance to the city. But this did not happen." A chance to preserve "an equitable history" while "assuring an equitable future" slipped away.[47]

Even as luxury condos have become the norm for new construction, many existing properties have been left vacant, often as a result of real estate speculation and "warehousing," the practice of keeping a property off the market in case future opportunities emerge. Working with Hunter College, the advocacy group Picture the Homeless conducted a partial survey of vacant and underused properties in New York in 2011. After looking over a third of the city, the group found more than 3,500 vacant buildings and close to 2,500 vacant lots, enough to house 200,000 people comfortably. The group's report has encouraged the rethinking of the city's warehousing policies and has spurred Mayor Bill de Blasio to ask for a comprehensive study of all vacant sites in the city.[48]

Historic buildings should not be left abandoned and empty as investment vehicles. They should be places for families to live, innovators to create, and communities to gather. They should serve the needs of neighborhoods, including affordable housing. Cities can either help facilitate this process through historic tax credits and all the other tools discussed in chapter 3, or they can follow the path we are seeing in too many neighborhoods today: give tax and zoning boons to luxury development instead, encourage the use of buildings as speculative vehicles, and demolish the existing fabric to make way for hyperdevelopment.

If cities choose the latter course, more than just the buildings are lost. So are all the many benefits of old places I have discussed over the course of this book—all the ways older buildings help facilitate vibrant and dynamic communities.

As Jane Jacobs told us in *Death and Life*, thriving, mixed-use, residential-commercial corridors cannot simply be fashioned out of whole cloth. They can only come together over the process of time. If they are removed to make way for a few cookie-cutter high-rises, with room for a few chain stores at the base, cities lose more than just character. The engine itself that keeps neighborhoods growing, innovating, and thriving is disrupted.

Preventing Displacement

The job of historic preservation is not to try to prevent change—communities are always in the process of change. Rather, it is to leverage the tools, techniques, and habits of our field to help neighborhoods move forward in a positive direction, in a way that minimizes community disruption and helps facilitate equity, affordability, and harmony among old residents and new arrivals. Most important, in all the work we do, we can try to mitigate the displacement of existing residents.

There are many ways we can achieve these goals. We can make sure that beloved old buildings are still fulfilling needed uses in their communities, including the need for affordable housing. As in the Historic

Macon example I discussed in chapter 3, we can use tools like property tax freezes, down-payment assistance, and energy-efficiency loans to help low-income homeowners stay in a reviving neighborhood. We can also use the traditional tools of rent control, homeownership assistance, rehabilitation grant programs, zoning, historic districting, and others to help stabilize communities without contributing to unwanted displacement.

We can also work harder to listen to communities' concerns about a particular preservation project, and see that those concerns have a voice at the table where decisions are being made. As the National Trust has advocated with the Main Street program for decades, building and supporting organizations that are composed of community leaders will help ensure the brightest future for threatened neighborhoods. These Main Street organizations, like neighborhood associations, watch out for the needs of their residents and provide an important forum for discussion and community decision making. In many neighborhoods, community development corporations—such as the Seattle Chinatown International District Preservation and Development Authority—fulfill a similar role.

At the National Trust, we have been meeting with these and other local leaders and community advocates across the country to get a better sense of how preservation can help encourage equity and affordability, as well as mitigate displacement in transitioning neighborhoods. In these discussions, other tools have come up that could well prove fruitful.

Community Benefits Agreements
Many major construction projects in recent years have been accompanied with a community benefits agreement, or CBA. This agreement stipulates, before ground is broken, how and in what ways the finished project will improve the existing neighborhood. The first major CBA came into being in Los Angeles in 2001 when the Figueroa Corridor

Coalition, a network of local and labor organizations, struck a deal with developers on the building of a multipurpose sports, entertainment, and retail complex adjacent to the Staples Center. That CBA included a hiring program and additional affordable housing for low-income residents, a promise that at least 70 percent of the jobs at the complex would pay a living wage, and money would be set aside for parks, parking, and other community needs.[49]

Since then, CBAs have been used in a number of cities across the United States. When Wal-Mart negotiated a deal to bring its stores to Washington, D.C., in 2011, for example, it first signed a CBA promising to hire local firms for construction work and local residents in "a majority of available positions" when the stores were up and running. Wal-Mart also promised to fund a citywide workforce development program, install bike-share stations and bus shelters at its stores, and make $21 million worth of "charitable partnerships" over the next seven years.[50] (Subsequently, Wal-Mart decided not to build two of the originally planned five stores.)

Over in Washington's Southwest, where the DC United soccer team is constructing a new stadium at Buzzard Point, the team agreed through a CBA to make its facility available to the community, hire locals, look for small-business and nonprofit partnerships in the neighborhood, and create a summer jobs program. In the Motor City, meanwhile, lawmakers and activists have been pushing to make Detroit the first city to make CBAs mandatory for any new project with an investment of at least $15 million, any renovations or additions that will cost at least $3 million, or any projects that will receive at least $300,000 in public subsidies.[51]

Although a relatively new tool, there's no reason CBAs couldn't be part and parcel of every major historic redevelopment project going forward. For a good example of how it could work, look at the new-economy companies that have moved into San Francisco's Mid-Market. Or consider the Kingsbridge Armory, a community landmark in the

Northwest Bronx for more than a century. ("It's a miracle that [Robert] Moses didn't put a road through it," quipped one local journalist.) In 2014, developers began working to reconvert this massive structure into the 750,000-square-foot, nine-rink Kingsbridge National Ice Center.[52]

An earlier attempt to redevelop the armory as a shopping mall in 2009 foundered when local residents balked at the lack of proposed benefits for the surrounding neighborhood. This time, developers and community leaders met for months to craft a twenty-seven-page CBA first. It includes 50,000 square feet of community space, a minimum wage for permanent workers of $10 an hour, and $1 million spent each year for the next ninety-nine years on free ice time for local children. Although the project hit some funding snags in the spring of 2016, the agreed-upon CBA is nonetheless a model for future historic projects. "The Armory CBA is really pivotal for New York City, for the Bronx, and for CBAs," argued Julian Gross, a lawyer who's been working on CBAs since their inception. "It's New York City's first real CBA . . . driven by a legitimate community coalition." Let's hope there are many more to come.[53]

Commercial Protections and Heritage Business Laws

Often, when it comes to significant displacement in a neighborhood, the canaries in the coal mine are local small businesses. Bodegas, hair salons, or quirky record shops that have been around for decades suddenly disappear, replaced by banks, fast-food restaurants, or chain stores. When these new commercial tenants don't hire the old workers, those local residents no longer have jobs, and soon they cannot make the rent themselves.

This same sad story plays out every single day in our largest cities, and mainly for one key reason: although residential renters usually have at least a few protections against unreasonable rent hikes, commercial renters often do not. So landlords—eager to make more money from higher-paying tenants—start increasing the rent to absurd proportions. As Tim Wu explained it in the *New Yorker*: "If you're a landlord, why would you keep renting to a local café or restaurant at five thousand or ten thousand dollars a month when you might get twenty thousand or even forty thousand dollars a month from Chase [Bank]?"[54]

So local businesses suffer. Take Avignone on Bleecker, a 184-year-old pharmacy that had maintained the same West Village location since 1929. It closed in 2015 after a new landlord suddenly tripled the rent from $20,000 to $60,000 a month. Two of its West Village neighbors, Gray's Papaya and Café Angelique, also closed after rent hikes of $20,000 and $26,000 a month, respectively. In Brooklyn's Boerum Hill, the owner of Jesse's Deli, a neighborhood staple for twenty-five years, suddenly found out his rent was going from $4,000 to $10,000 a month. In Washington Heights, after saving up for ten years, José Alvarrado finally secured a five-year lease to open a bodega. Then, just six months after the 3 Brothers Mini Market opened its doors, he was told his lease would not be renewed—and the rent started going up $100 at a clip. "The problem isn't business. It's a good business," he told the *New York Times*. He could not afford the rent increases or fight what was happening in City Hall, though, so he too planned to give up his store.[55]

In our biggest cities, this dismal cycle of rent hikes and closings has reached epidemic proportions. New York City sees nearly five hundred store closings a month. (Not coincidentally, it has also seen seven consecutive years of chain store growth.) With the exception of the Times Square area, where rents stayed flat at the already high level of more than $2,400 a square foot, every single major retail corridor in Manhattan saw retail rents increase in 2015, often by outlandish amounts. On the Upper West Side, rents on Broadway increased by 37 percent over the year before; on Third Avenue and the Upper East Side, they jumped 39 percent. On East 57th Street, they soared 60 percent—in one year![56]

San Francisco is experiencing the same trends. Between 1992 and

2011, business closures and relocations increased 884 percent there. Since 1999, commercial rents have gone up by 250 percent, and 2014 saw an estimated thirteen thousand businesses close, including four thousand that had been open for more than five years. According to San Francisco's Office of Small Business, businesses involved in lease renewals regularly see rent hikes of 30 to 50 percent. When these stores close, they are often replaced by chains or businesses serving an upscale or luxury market. "Rents are no longer affordable for the average neighborhood-serving businesses," said San Francisco Small Business Commissioner Kathleen Dooley. "The basic needs have to be replaced by more and more restaurants, bars, and expensive boutiques. You kind of have to be expensive because the rents are so high."[57]

To help mitigate these losses, Mike Buhler, executive director of San Francisco Heritage, worked with the city's board of supervisors to create a Legacy Business Preservation Fund, an idea that's also been used in other white-hot markets like London and Barcelona. They first created a Legacy Business Registry of businesses and nonprofit organizations in San Francisco that are more than thirty years old and can prove, before the Small Business Commission, that they have had a significant cultural or historical impact on their local neighborhood. Enterprises on the registry must promise they will maintain their name and current focus. Approved legacy businesses on the registry will then receive grants from the city of $500 per full-time employee per year, up to $50,000 a year. Landlords who extend the leases of these businesses for at least ten years will receive $4.50 per square foot of leased space per year, up to $22,500 a year.[58]

In this way, the city is supporting its older small businesses while giving landlords a further incentive to do right by them. "We're not talking about propping up failing enterprises," noted Anthony Veerkamp, the National Trust's field director in San Francisco, who was active in the push for the fund. "These are businesses that were doing just fine . . . but they are dealing with catastrophic rent increases that they can't bridge the gap on." Unanimously endorsed by the board of supervisors, the Preservation Fund passed a citywide vote in November 2015. Now, other cities such as Los Angeles, Houston, and New York City are contemplating similar legislation.[59]

Community advocates in New York are also pushing for a local bill called the Small Business Jobs Survival Act (SBJSA), which would help close the disparity in protections for residential and commercial renters. This act would give commercial tenants the right to a minimum ten-year lease with right to renewal and ensure that they have access to a fair negotiation, with third-party arbitration if necessary, when renewal time comes. The bill has faced considerable headwinds since it was first introduced in 1986, but it has gained added urgency as the pace of change accelerates in the city. "When you have a big-box tenant whose corporate office is in another part of the country, you lose that neighborhood flavor," said Paul Bodley, a member of the advisory board of New York's Real Estate Investors Association. "You don't establish that back-and-forth relation you have with a small business in the neighborhood. That's what SBJSA is trying to preserve."[60]

Of course, businesses will come and go based on how well they serve the needs of their community. In our biggest cities, however, these mass closures clearly have more to do with speculative rent hikes than the desires of local customers. When all the quirky, independent mom-and-pop stores on a block are eventually replaced with high-end chains, its inherent character and cultural fabric are lost. The neighborhood becomes just like every other place and, thus, no place at all.

Community Land Trusts

Given the hypergentrification so evident in so many neighborhoods, a September 2015 *New York Magazine* piece by Nick Tabor asked a question that many in New York were probably wondering, too: How has

Chinatown stayed Chinatown? Even as other areas in Lower Manhattan are being completely overhauled and nearby Little Italy has all but disappeared, the streets of New York's Chinatown have mostly resisted the dissolution happening in so many other ethnic neighborhoods across the United States. Here, small, locally owned Chinese American businesses and restaurants are still the norm rather than the rapidly disappearing exception. What's the community's secret? "How," Tabor asked, "can this possibly be the state of one of the most desirable tracts of real estate in all of Manhattan?"[61]

The article offers several answers, but the main one is both prosaic and illuminating: "During the 1960s and '70s," Tabor explained, Chinese American family associations "bought up about 60 buildings in Chinatown's historic core. . . . They rent out the bottom floors to stores and restaurants, and the rest they use as apartments, many for the elderly." In addition, local advocacy organizations like Asian Americans for Equality (AAFE) and the Chinese Staff and Workers Association are constantly working to build out the real estate holdings of the community. "Since 1995, [AAFE] has pulled down more than $100 million in grants, donations, and loans to buy tenement buildings and restore them—ensuring that developers won't raze them instead—and to build affordable housing," said Tabor.[62]

In other words, Chinatown has stayed relatively affordable and stable because New York's Chinese American community collectively owns many of the buildings in the neighborhood. This ownership ensures that they are serving communal needs and cannot be sold easily for an individual payday. ("Because dozens of people have shares in the family associations' buildings," wrote Tabor, "they're almost impossible to sell.")[63]

Chinatown's relative success in retaining its existing historic and cultural fabric might be a hard thing for other neighborhoods to replicate, especially because the idea of community ownership wouldn't seem to jibe particularly well with traditional American views on property rights. There is, however, an increasingly popular approach to affordable housing that approximates this sort of ownership system: the community land trust.

A community land trust (CLT) is a nonprofit organization—sometimes created with the help of city officials, sometimes just by neighborhood advocates—that, after buying or otherwise acquiring land, promises to then use that land to serve the community. Often working with a mutual housing association, the CLT will develop properties on this land and then sell or rent these properties, all the while continuing to hold title to the land itself. (Usually the CLT will offer a ninety-nine-year lease on the land to the homeowner in question.) In this manner, CLTs keep housing affordable while letting buyers earn equity on their homes and ensuring that land stays in the hands of local residents.[64]

Put another way, CLTs break the usual connection between land and the houses on it: residents can buy or rent the homes, but the land remains owned by the community. (When I said this concept doesn't jibe with the "traditional" sense of American property rights, that isn't quite true. In fact, the idea that the land is for everyone, and cannot be owned by any one individual, was an American idea before the first European settlers ever arrived here. As one journalist has noted, when the Lenape Indians sold Manhattan to the Dutch in 1626 for $24, they probably had the CLT model in mind.)[65]

Community land trusts began being used as an affordable housing tool in the 1980s and have been growing in popularity over the years. As of 2012, there were 258 community land trusts in the United States, in cities like Boston, New York, Irvine, Austin, Chicago, and Las Vegas. They collectively oversee roughly 13,000 housing units and 25,000 rental units. (As it happens, the largest and to-date most successful urban CLT, in Burlington, Vermont, was in part established by Mayor Bernie Sanders.)[66]

THE PROBLEMS OF AFFORDABILITY AND DISPLACEMENT   231

Although it is still only a drop in the bucket in terms of the total housing market, the results so far have been very promising. A 2010 study by the Lincoln Institute of Land Policy found that homeowners in a CLT were one-tenth as likely to default on their homes as owners in the private market. "One of the things that we think is great about community land trusts," said Armando Carbonell of the Lincoln Institute, "is that they are pretty stable even in the face of tough economic conditions." That holds true, he noted, "even though CLT property tends to be owned by lower-income people, who might be under more stress than the average mortgage holder."[67]

From Roxbury in Boston to New York's Cooper Square to East Austin, Texas, community land trusts are helping neighborhoods retain their existing socioeconomic demographic, preserve their character, and resist mass displacement. This model seems to have great potential going forward, especially if municipalities work with local neighborhood advocates to build them out. For example, rather than simply auctioning off land that comes to the city through foreclosures and tax liens to the highest bidder, cities could donate or sell it at a discount to their local CLTs.

To some, things like increased protections for commercial renters and community land trusts may seem well outside the boundaries of traditional historic preservation. That, indeed, is the point.

As preservation is helping revitalize cities, we also need to be concerned about how that revitalization is affecting families. As historic buildings are creatively repurposed in ways that will attract new residents to a neighborhood, we should also make sure we are doing right by existing residents, and keeping them involved in the community's future. And while we think about how best to bring history into the present, we also need to confront related issues of equity and affordability, and make common cause with those who are already working hard to address these problems.

An artist's rendering of the proposed 11th Street Bridge Park in Washington, D.C. (© OMA & Luxigon)

In Washington, D.C., plans are now under way for a creative repurposing of the old 11th Street Bridge, which spans the Anacostia River. Very soon, it will become the 11th Street Bridge Park, a strip of green space—with playgrounds, outdoor classrooms, performance spaces, and other public amenities—that will reconnect communities east of the river to the rest of the city. Although the project is inspired by the tremendous success of the High Line in New York—one local writer has even dubbed it "the High Line on the Anacostia"—the developers, the city of Washington, D.C., and everyone involved are also very consciously working to learn from, and mitigate, the hyper-gentrification that ensued in that instance.[68]

To that end, an Equitable Development Task Force has been meeting with residents on both ends of the bridge, along with local community-minded nonprofits like LISC DC, to make sure the new park is a boon to everyone. "A key goal of the Bridge Park," reads the resulting Equitable Development Plan, "is to serve as an anchor for equitable and inclusive economic growth." Although everyone agrees that repurposing the bridge is a great idea, "more must be done to ensure that residents and small businesses nearby will continually benefit from the success of this signature new civic space."[69]

This agreed-upon plan—developed with the input of affected communities—prioritizes hiring local residents, at a living wage, for both construction and permanent jobs in the park. It sets up a workforce development program for training local residents in needed skills. It calls for using local small businesses to serve food in the park and for redeveloping nearby vacant properties as available and affordable commercial space for them. It also proposes creating a new community land trust, and using other tools like down-payment assistance, to ensure that affordable housing continues to be available on both sides of the river.[70]

"It's really critical," said Scott Kratz, director of the 11th Street project, "that we're thinking presciently about how to ensure that thousands of people who have helped shape this project can be the ones that benefit from it, while at the same time mitigating any potential displacement." So far, Amanda Stephenson, director of Anacostia's Small Business Development Center, has been impressed by what she's seen. "We definitely would have hoped that a lot of these things would have been considered in previous projects," she said. "But . . . a lot of the people have learned from the past and are expressing, 'More involvement, more inclusion.' I'm glad that at this time, we're at a time where we can say, 'Hey, we've made mistakes. Now let's move forward.'"[71]

CHAPTER 7

The Greenest Buildings: Preservation, Climate Change, and the Environment

It is far less costly to recycle a city than to build a suburb.

—Carla Hills, secretary of Housing and Urban Development, 1975[1]

H OW WELL DO YOU REMEMBER February 1985? I know that for more than a third of Americans—who are under the age of thirty-two—the answer is not at all. Journey back with me if you can. Ronald Reagan had just started his second term in office. Nelson Mandela was still in jail. Foreigner's "I Want to Know What Love Is" and George Michael's "Careless Whisper" were the big hits on the radio. At the movies, Harrison Ford was hiding out in Amish country in *Witness*, and the Brat Pack were figuring one another out and falling in love in *The Breakfast Club*. I myself was in college that month, at the University of Colorado Boulder.[2]

That month didn't seem like a particularly historic one at the time, but it holds a grim distinction. As of this writing, more than thirty years later, February 1985 was the last month that the surface temperature on Earth was colder than the twentieth-century average. Every single month since then has been warmer than that average. Writing on this phenomenon in July 2012, 327 months into the streak, author Bill McKibben pointed out in *Rolling Stone* that "the odds of [this] occurring by simple chance were 3.7×10^{99}, a number considerably larger than the number of stars in the universe." That was already years ago.[3]

A few years before writing that piece for *Rolling Stone*, McKibben started an advocacy website called 350.org, so named after the findings in a 2007 study by National Aeronautics and Space Administration (NASA) scientist James Hansen. The amount of carbon dioxide in the atmosphere before the Industrial Revolution was 275 parts per million (ppm). By 2008, it had reached 385 ppm. This number is important because more carbon in the atmosphere means more heat is trapped on Earth, thus warming the planet.[4]

Trying to figure how much atmospheric carbon would be too much, Hansen determined that "if humanity wishes to preserve a planet similar to that on which civilization developed and to which life on Earth is adapted, paleoclimate evidence and ongoing climate change suggest that CO^2 will need to be reduced from its current 385 ppm to at most 350 ppm, but likely less than that." Higher carbon dioxide levels, McKibben and Hansen pointed out, would mean melting ice caps and rising oceans, "something that would shake the foundations of the human enterprise should it happen again." The line had to be drawn, here and now. "Three hundred and fifty," McKibben said, "is the number every person needs to know."[5]

In March 2015, for the first time in recorded history, a reading of 400 ppm was measured for the entire month. By November 2015, scientists warned that 400 ppm and above would soon become a "permanent reality." Today, 350—the number that could very well mean catastrophe—is in the rearview mirror.[6]

Also in early 2015, two separate and independent analyses of climate data by NASA and the National Oceanic and Atmospheric Administration determined that 2014, the year that had just passed, was the warmest year ever recorded, going back to 1880. What's more, all ten of the hottest years on record had taken place since 1998. That dubious record lasted all of 365 days. A year later, scientists announced that 2015 had blown past 2014 as the hottest year ever, by the biggest margins ever seen. Said one scientist at the National Center for Atmospheric Research, "The whole system is warming up, relentlessly." And 2016 began even hotter still.[7]

I know there are those on Capitol Hill, in some state legislatures, and on talk radio who still question whether climate change is actually happening, but that is not a luxury we really have time for anymore. In the field of preservation, we are already starting to experience and grapple with climate change in very concrete ways. Beloved destinations are confronting the new reality of rising sea levels. Powerful superstorms like Katrina and Sandy are damaging historic places with increasing regularity. Roughly one hundred of the National Park Service's more than four hundred park units are already experiencing climate-related transformations.[8]

Climate change is real. It is happening. Its impact on all our communities is only going to grow stronger in the years to come. To address it head-on—and save the most important historic place there is, our planet—we are going to have to reshape our cities and neighborhoods to reduce carbon emissions and make them more green, sustainable, and energy efficient. Historic preservation has a huge part to play in this transformation.

Even beyond all the many social, economic, and community benefits of historic fabric I have already discussed, here is where reusing our older buildings becomes an absolute necessity for our future.

The Greenest Buildings . . .

Although climate change has added additional urgency to our efforts, the idea that older buildings have a key role to play in forging greener, more sustainable communities has been around for a while. In 1980—when President Jimmy Carter first made energy efficiency a national focus—the National Trust had a poster that showed a building in the shape of a gasoline can. It read: "It takes energy to construct a new building—it saves energy to preserve an old one." That, in a sentence, is why preservation is so fundamentally important to our future health and well-being.[9]

According to the US Department of Energy, building operations account for 41 percent of the nation's energy consumption, 72 percent of its electricity consumption, and 38 percent of its carbon dioxide emissions. In urban areas, these numbers are even higher. Commercial buildings are estimated to be responsible for 70 percent of Chicago's total carbon emissions and 80 percent of New York's. Given these statistics, there is no way to feasibly address the climate crisis without changing how we manage our urban landscape.[10]

At the same time, roughly one billion square feet of buildings are demolished and replaced every year in the United States. According to an analysis by the Brookings Institution, the country is in the midst of demolishing and replacing 82 billion square feet of existing space—nearly one-fourth of the existing building stock—by 2030.[11]

That is an astonishing amount of waste. In fact, the energy used to demolish and rebuild that much space could power the entire state of California for a decade! According to a formula produced for the Advisory Council on Historic Preservation, about 80 billion British thermal units (Btus) of energy are embodied in a typical 50,000-square-foot commercial building. As my predecessor Richard Moe pointed out in 2008, that's "the equivalent of 640,000 gallons of gasoline. And if you tear the building down, all the energy that went into creating the build-

The gas can featured on a 1980 National Trust for Historic Preservation poster: It takes energy to construct a new building—it saves energy to preserve an old one. (© National Trust for Historic Preservation)

ing is wasted. Demolishing that same 50,000-square-foot building also creates nearly 4,000 tons of waste. That's enough debris to fill 26 railroad boxcars—a train nearly a quarter of a mile long, headed for a landfill that is already almost full."[12]

It simply does not make sense to recycle cans and newspapers to save energy and not recycle buildings. As architect and green advocate Carl Elefante wrote in a 2009 essay, "Taking into account the massive investment of materials and energy in existing buildings, it is both obvious and profound that extending the useful service of life of the building stock is common sense, good business, and sound resource management." Put simply, he said, "the Greenest Building is the one that's already built."[13]

This holds particularly true when you consider that it takes decades for even most of the new efficient buildings to recover the carbon that is expended in their construction. In short, we cannot build our way to sustainability. In a perfect world, every new building going forward would be net zero—meaning it produces as much as energy as it consumes. But even if that were the case, it would have the same effect over a full year as cutting energy use of all existing buildings by just 1 percent. "Seeking salvation through green building," wrote Elefante, "fails to account for the overwhelming vastness of the existing building stock. [That] is the elephant in the room: Ignoring it, we risk being trampled by it. We cannot build our way to sustainability; we must conserve our way to it."[14]

That is why what we do with our existing fabric is so important. In our rush to embrace green construction, we cannot lose sight of the tremendous value of saving and reusing buildings that have already been built.

In January 2012, a few years before conducting the *Older, Smaller, Better* research cited throughout this book, the National Trust's Preservation Green Lab published its first major report, entitled *"The Greenest Building: Quantifying the Environmental Value of Building Reuse"*, on this nexus of preservation and sustainability. The Green Lab first looked at the full life-cycle—from the extraction and transportation of the raw materials used in construction through decades of use—of different types of buildings, such as single-family and multifamily homes, schools, warehouses, and offices.[15]

To ensure that their data accounted for different climates and a variable mix of energy sources, Green Lab researchers surveyed buildings in four US cities: Chicago, Atlanta, Phoenix, and Portland, Oregon. Using this life-cycle analysis methodology, they then compared the relative environmental impacts of building reuse and renovation versus demolition and new construction over the course of a seventy-five-year life span.[16]

In almost all cases, when they compared buildings of similar size and functionality, they found that building reuse yields fewer environmental impacts than new construction. In fact, depending on the type of structure, it takes between ten and eighty years for a new "green" building that is 30 percent more energy efficient than the existing one to make up for the amount of carbon unleashed through its construction. These findings accord with other studies on the subject. For example, a report by Britain's Empty Homes Agency found that it takes thirty-five to fifty years for a new, green home to recover the initially expended carbon as well.[17]

The range of environmental savings varies based on building type, location, and presumed level of energy efficiency, but when comparing buildings with the same energy performance level, the environmental savings from reuse are between 4 and 46 percent over new construction. The one exception is when industrial warehouses are converted into multifamily residential units, which resulted in a 1 to 6 percent greater environmental impact. Foremost among the reasons for this difference are the amount and type of materials used for rehab, which can significantly mitigate or even cancel out the energy savings from recycling buildings.[18]

So it is important to use the right materials—and minimize the amount of new materials—in renovation projects. If done correctly, however, the impact reductions of reusing old buildings can be substantial, particularly when taken to scale.

To take just one example, if the city of Portland, Oregon, were to retrofit and reuse the single-family homes and commercial office buildings that it is otherwise likely to demolish over the next ten years, based on its demolition rates from 2003 to 2011, the potential impact reduction would total approximately 231,000 metric tons of carbon dioxide. This figure is about 15 percent of Portland's stated carbon reduction target over the next decade. The city could save 15 percent immediately just by conserving and reusing its already existing buildings.[19]

What is true in Portland can be true all over the United States. In 2014, as part of the United Nations Climate Summit, 451 cities around the world—including 122 in the United States—pledged to reduce their carbon emissions and begin preparing for climate change. Similarly, in 2015, a number of US and Chinese cities agreed to deep cuts in carbon emissions as part of a bipartisan climate summit in Los Angeles—a city that, like New York, has pledged to cut its emissions by 80 percent by 2050. As noted earlier, Seattle has gone a step even further and declared that it will be completely carbon neutral by 2050. All these cities can get a leg up on reaching these necessary emissions cuts by stopping demolition and working with their existing building fabric.[20]

Ultimately, we can't build our way out of the global warming crisis. We have to save our way out. That means we have to make better, wiser use of what we've already built.

"Original Green"

There's another factor to consider here as well, what author and architect Stephen Mouzon has called "original green" in a book and blog by that name. "Originally, before the Thermostat Age," Mouzon wrote, "the places . . . and buildings we built had no choice but to be green, otherwise people would freeze to death in the winter, die of heat strokes by summer, starve to death, or other really bad things would happen." Put another way, many older buildings are inherently green by design through features like thick walls, high ceilings, use of daylight, operable windows, awnings, generous eaves, and porches. They reflect the wisdom—wisdom that has sometimes been lost—of earlier generations

The Greenest Building: Implications
Portland, Oregon

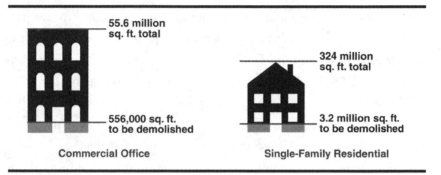

1% of the building stock in Portland (within Multnomah County) is expected to be demolished over the next 10 years.

55.6 million
sq. ft. total

556,000 sq. ft.
to be demolished

Commercial Office

324 million
sq. ft. total

3.2 million sq. ft.
to be demolished

Single-Family Residential

15% of the county's total CO_2 reduction targets, over the coming decade, could be met by retrofitting and reusing existing buildings rather than demolishing and building new, efficient ones.

The implications of the Green Lab's *"The Greenest Building"* study for the city of Portland. In short, reusing existing buildings can help Portland and other cities meet their carbon reduction goals much more easily. (© National Trust for Historic Preservation)

to keep places naturally warm in winter and cool in summer. "Early American homes were designed with the empirical knowledge gained from thousands of trials and errors," argued a 1982 US Department of Housing and Urban Development report on this subject. "The only problem with these features is that they may not be recognized as energy conserving because they are not understood."[21]

In fact, a 2003 study by the US Energy Information Administration bears this "wisdom of the past" thesis out. It found that commercial buildings constructed before 1920 were more energy efficient than those built over the next seventy years; only relatively new innovations in green-building have resulted in a more efficient building overall. Results from New York City—which passed a first-in-the-nation law mandating the disclosure of buildings' energy performance data in 2009—also demonstrate that the "older," pre-1920 buildings are far from the biggest energy hogs, and when these older buildings receive investment in energy-efficiency upgrades, they can become models of energy efficiency. After some insulation and mechanical upgrades, the Empire State Building and Chrysler Building even outperformed new, Gold-LEED (Leadership in Energy and Environmental Design)-certified skyscrapers in the city. This result is more common than you might think, argued Mouzon. "Buildings must perform twice as well as the average LEED building," he asserted, "to be equal to unmodified (but well-maintained, of course) historic buildings" in terms of energy efficiency.[22]

The inherent sustainability of older fabric even goes beyond the bricks and mortar of individual buildings. It is about how the buildings are sited and oriented to take advantage of sun and shade. It is also about how older neighborhoods tend to be more walkable and transit-oriented, and more likely to facilitate mixed-use functions. When people talk about smart growth today, what they often mean is a return to the dense, multiuse, mass transit-oriented urban layout of the city before automobiles. "Why are we even discussing the carbon footprint of a building," asked Mouzon in *Original Green*, "if it is built somewhere that requires you to drive everywhere?"[23]

In his book, Mouzon talked about how "gizmo green"—the opposite of his "original green"—is often seen as the ultimate solution to the sustainability crisis. "Buy compact fluorescent light bulbs. Buy a Prius. Buy some bamboo . . . and everything will be okay," he characterizes this tendency. "The solution to everything is to go shopping." Yet although new technologies can be very helpful in mitigating carbon emissions—and by all means let's keep them coming!—ultimately the key to real sustainability is in fashioning neighborhoods where you can get around without using gas or electricity at all.[24]

Mouzon uses himself as an example. Before he and his wife, Wanda, moved to Miami Beach, they drove 48,000 miles a year in two cars. Now that they live in a dense, walkable downtown area, they drive fewer than 6,000 miles per year. "If we wanted to achieve the same reduction in gasoline use with a more efficient car instead, while still driving 48,000 miles a year," he argued, "we'd have to have a car that was *8 times as efficient* as my Accord and Wanda's CRV." Their Accord "would need to get about 240 miles per gallon to have the same effect. . . . It's actually more effective to change our minds (and then to change our behavior) than it is to change our gadgets."[25]

That is not to say we should give up on green innovations like the electric car. We are going to need many more energy-saving technologies before the day is done to get our carbon emissions where they need to be. And, as we saw in chapter 6, many poor and even middle-class families are currently being priced out of walkable, transit-oriented downtowns and being forced to relocate to car-dependent suburbs. To get to real sustainability, the affordability issue must be tackled as well. Mouzon is right, however, when he says that really improving the sustainability of our neighborhoods means, along with taking more advantage of existing historic fabric, going back to the example of our streetcar suburbs and other precar parts of our cities. Our urban past is in many ways the template of our smart growth future.

Saving Energy

Since the *"Greenest Building"* report came out in 2012, the National Trust has been working to bring about the best of both worlds. It is encouraging sustainable building reuse at scale while making the twenty-first-century upgrades and retrofits that make older buildings even more energy efficient.

In October 2012, the Green Lab's follow-up report, *"Saving Windows, Saving Money"*, provided owners of older buildings with tested and confirmed ways to increase the energy performance of original windows in existing buildings. They included cost-effective techniques such as adding storm windows, applying ultraviolet-light films, and installing insulating shades. In both hot and cold climates, retrofitting windows proves to be a far more cost-effective strategy than paying for expensive new replacement windows.[26]

Then, in June 2013, the Green Lab published *"Saving Energy, Money, and Jobs"*, a report highlighting the energy-efficiency potential of retrofitting small commercial buildings (less than 50,000 square feet). It found that potential energy savings for small businesses range from 27 to 59 percent, depending on the building. These savings total 1.07 quadrillion Btus annually, or 17 percent of commercial energy use. Small neighborhood businesses, like restaurants, grocers, and retailers, could improve their profitability by more than 10 percent through smart investments in energy savings.[27]

More than just having these data, we want to create a road map for delivering needed energy retrofits to these buildings. So, based on this report and working with a national team of experts, the National Trust developed and established a new national program, America Saves. Supported in part by the US Department of Energy, America Saves worked to improve the energy and economic performance of small businesses in Main Streets, eco-districts (neighborhoods committed to sustainability), and business improvement districts by uncovering the opportunity for long-term energy cost savings in existing buildings.[28]

Of course, every business would like to reduce its overhead, but many do not have the time or the expertise to figure out how to bring down energy costs on their own. So, after getting information about business energy usage and the building from community volunteers, the Green Lab used a remote auditing technology to analyze the data and reveal opportunities for cost-effective building retrofits. They included simple fixes like changing light bulbs, installing programmable thermostats, and adding occupancy sensors to more extensive changes like replacing out-dated equipment, upgrading heating, ventilation, and air-conditioning (HVAC) systems, and adding insulation.[29]

These businesses—with help from volunteers—could then apply for incentives from their utility providers to implement the identified upgrades. Here again, these retrofits could make a tremendous differ-ence for our communities if brought to scale: more than $240 billion in capital investment and 580,000 permanent jobs across the United States by 2050, as well as, again, 1.07 quadrillion Btus a year, or 17 percent of commercial energy use. That's quite a difference.[30]

Another good way to achieve impact at scale is through reforms to the rules guiding building construction and rehabilitation—for example, energy codes. At present, the nation's energy codes don't always fit very well with older buildings. They take a very prescriptive approach, often forcing owners and design teams to pursue specific retrofit measures with no regard for the way a change might compromise architectural integrity or the inherent "original green" qualities of these older build-ings. Often, there is no recognition that many older and historic build-ings have passive features that make them inherently energy efficient.

With that in mind, the National Trust has been working with green building advocates and preservationists to push for reforms that posi-tion older buildings as potential models of sustainable design, rather than as energy hogs that need exceptions from the rules. For example, in partnership with city officials and the New Buildings Institute, the Pres-ervation Green Lab drafted and piloted a new outcome-based energy code framework for the city of Seattle, one that we hope will be a model for other cities.[31]

In an outcome-based system, rather than judging energy code com-pliance based on whether an owner makes a particular retrofit, the codes monitor the actual performance of the building. In other words, owners agree to a predetermined set of performance outcomes, and they are then free to retrofit the building more creatively as long as it meets these specific performance targets.[32]

Evaluating energy efficiency by actual performance may seem like a no-brainer, but it is actually relatively new territory for building codes. As such, outcome-based codes have been a particularly hot topic in sustainability circles lately. There is a general agreement that the current prescriptive code system doesn't allow the level of flexibility required to get to net-zero carbon emissions.

Although the results of this pilot program are not in, the Seattle project should provide a good opportunity to demonstrate that older buildings can compete with, and even exceed, the kind of high performance often associated only with new construction. In addition, if outcome-based energy codes take hold in more places, they could make it possible to retrofit many historic buildings that might otherwise be left alone, left vacant, or even demolished to make way for "greener" structures.

In the meantime, we have also been working with groups like the US Green Building Council (USGBC) to see that its LEED standards do more to recognize the inherently green nature of preservation activities such as building reuse. Beginning in 2012, USGBC began making some significant alterations to its LEED rating system that reflect preservation's benefits and improve incentives to reuse existing buildings. For example, it began including credits for "whole building reuse" as a way of encouraging people to rehab and reuse older and historic structures. Partly as a result, we're now seeing more and more LEED-certified historic buildings across the United States.[33]

Another promising frontier in sustainability that hearkens back to the wisdom of an earlier time is the idea of district energy. As the scale of transformation necessary to tackle the impacts of climate change has come into scope, we've seen a shift in the way people are thinking about green buildings, from a building-by-building approach—which has proven to be difficult and expensive to implement—to district-level solutions. Now, businesses and neighborhoods are coming together to figure out how they can pool their resources to meet aggressive energy goals.[34]

Once again, this idea is not new. The idea of shared "city steam" systems goes back to the nineteenth century; Denver's 1880s system was the first example. Many of these citywide systems were abandoned in the 1950s, when suburban development began in earnest, but recent renewed interest in efficiency and alternative energy sources has brought the idea back. The difference now is that the energy sources being used are more efficient and even renewable than years ago. For example, at Taliesin West, the Frank Lloyd Wright–designed complex of buildings that served as the architect's winter home in scorching Scottsdale, Arizona, a new and totally hidden solar garden is now handling about 50 percent of the electrical needs for that entire National Historic Landmark campus.[35]

Another intriguing strategy for reducing energy consumption is the use of geothermal, or geo-exchange, systems. Again, this is an established, simple technology that is coming back into practice. One of my favorite examples comes from Texas, where county commissioners in several counties have decided to install geothermal systems as part of comprehensive courthouse rehabilitations. The design hides what is otherwise highly visible HVAC equipment on the courthouse lawn and saves tens of thousands of dollars annually in operating costs.[36]

Another example is one of the National Trust's own buildings, the Emerson School in Denver, Colorado. Originally built in 1885, the school now serves as a nonprofit campus, including both historic preservation and land conservation groups. As part of the LEED-certified rehabilitation of the school, we installed a geothermal heating and cooling system under the parking lot. Now instead of up to $3,000 in gas bills during the winter, we typically pay just a few hundred. Overall, energy consumption at the Emerson School is down 54 percent over prerehab levels, and that's with more people using the building than ever before.[37]

In sum, a number of energy-saving tricks that fell out of favor for a few decades can help us reach a more sustainable future. If we work to leverage these forgotten principles, take advantage of older buildings as the tremendous assets for energy efficiency they are, and combine them with new innovations as they come about, we can create a sustainable future that will see vastly reduced carbon emissions and a healthier quality of life for all.

Threats to Historic Areas

Alas, we also have to recognize that, in some ways, even these efforts will no longer be enough. As author and scientist John Englander pointed out in a sobering discussion at the 2014 National Preservation Conference, a certain amount of sea level rise is already "baked in" due to the warming that has already happened, regardless of anything we try to do to prevent future warming.

So far, the seas have only risen around 8 inches since 1880, but even that has taken its toll, especially in places where the land is sinking as well. Consider the current challenges faced by Annapolis, Maryland, a city with historic roots that go back centuries. In the early 1960s, it experienced nuisance flooding at high tide three days a year. Because it is experiencing subsidence—the land is sinking—while water levels are rising, today its historic downtown area floods between thirty and forty days a year. By 2030, according to a study by the Union of Concerned Scientists (UCS), it will flood every other day in downtown Annapolis, and by 2045, it will flood every single day.[38]

Annapolis prides itself on being America's sailing capital, but that is emphatically not what the city had in mind. And it is not alone. In its "Encroaching Tides" report, the UCS discovered that many communities along the Atlantic and Gulf Coasts have seen rates of tidal flooding

Because of rising sea levels and land subsidence, nuisance flooding in downtown Annapolis is an increasingly regular occurrence. By 2030, it will flood every other day. By 2045, it will flood every day. (©Union of Concerned Scientists, "Encroaching Tides")

quadruple since 1970. By 2045, places like Atlantic City and Cape May, New Jersey, will see near-constant flooding, and many other cities, from Savannah to Ocean City to Myrtle Beach to even Washington, D.C., will see tidal floods become a regular occurrence.[39]

In another 2014 report, the UCS identified thirty landmarks across the United States in serious danger as a result of accelerating climate change. It included Faneuil Hall in Boston, the Johnson Space Center in Houston, Historic Charleston and Historic Jamestown, the Cesar Chavez National Monument in California, and the Statue of Liberty. The danger is not always water. Sometimes it is drought. If the temperature of Earth rises by another 1.8 degrees Fahrenheit—which is less than is predicted—New Mexico can expect the number of wildfires it suffers in a year to quadruple. "Fire resets the clock. It removes artifacts from time," noted US Forest Service ecologist Rachel Loehman. "If we start losing the archaeological record, we're never going to get it back."[40]

It may be hard—and quite frankly depressing—to imagine what these floodings and droughts mean for both communities and beloved historic resources in the near future. But the fact is we don't have to imagine it. Even if seas have not yet risen, we are already witnessing the impacts of climate change on historic resources right here, right now, all over the United States. Native communities in particular have already faced significant losses, because so much of their history and culture is tied to the landscape.

At Cape Krusenstern on the coast of Alaska, where Inupiat Eskimos have lived for thousands of years, the shoreline is eroding so quickly that the National Park Service is now using climate models to direct its survey efforts, to find cultural resources before they are lost to the sea. At Tumacacori, a Spanish mission in Arizona, and throughout the Southwest, adobe structures are deteriorating rapidly because of rainfall changes. Sea-level rise is already threatening to swamp Fort Jefferson in the Florida Keys and many National Parks and sacred spaces in the Hawaiian Islands. In 2012, Hurricane Sandy pummeled Ellis Island near New York City and devastated its buildings and collections. The National Park Service moved many of these collections off-site for repair and had to consider, for a long time, whether moving them back was prudent given that more dangerous and climate-change-fueled super-storms will soon become the norm. (Three years later, in September 2015, these artifacts did in fact return to Ellis Island.)[41]

We cannot prevent all these losses, and nobody wants to think about the kind of triage we will likely face in the years ahead, but it is incumbent for both preservationists and communities to reckon bravely with what is coming. Going forward, we will have to consider new approaches to saving important and beloved places, like moving buildings, raising them up, moving utilities out of the basement, and implementing creative waterproofing and reinforcements to help them withstand flooding.

For example, in Plano, Illinois, the iconic Farnsworth House—completed in 1951 by architect Mies van der Rohe in the international style and owned and operated by the National Trust—has been threatened by severe and growing flooding in recent years. In this case, although increasing rainfalls in the Midwest are by no means helping, the flooding has more to do with urbanization and development in the watershed upstream than with climate change. The principle still stands, however: unchanged in its current location, Farnsworth House will be perennially flooded, causing hundreds of thousands of dollars of damage each time and placing this internationally recognized architectural treasure at risk. So, after creating a panel of architects and experts that looked at a number of options, including moving the house entirely, the National Trust is now exploring the possibility of raising the height of Farnsworth House as needed through hydraulic lifts.[42]

If the savior of Mount Vernon, Ann Pamela Cunningham, were around today, she might argue that creative waterproofing and other such tools are against the true spirit of historic preservation—let "no vandal hands desecrate [sites] with the fingers of progress!" she warned us. Nonetheless, we face hard choices in the years to come. We can make important alterations to critical historic places in danger, or we can keep them perfectly preserved, underwater.

Saving History, Saving Earth

Climate change poses a frightening challenge for communities all over the world, and we are in for some tough times ahead. This crisis is by no means insurmountable, however. Already it is spurring new ideas, new thinking, and new partnerships, and each and every year, more people are awakening to the situation we face.

This coming battle against climate change also gives us a chance to

Because of increasing urbanization and development in the watershed upstream, the historic Farnsworth House in Plano, Illinois, is increasingly threatened by damaging floods. (© National Trust for Historic Preservation)

repair a breach that, strangely enough, only seems to exist in the United States. In England, our organizational counterpart is called the National Trust for Places of Historic Interest or Natural Beauty. But although the United States was the first country in the world to set aside lands for conservation, the American environmental and historic preservation movements have evolved along separate paths.

As a result, American conservationists have often focused on landscapes, natural systems, and biological units, and preservationists on human impacts, culture, and history. Yet even when all of us have been working to save the exact same places, we haven't always been very good at working together. Too often in the past, historic preservationists have been extraordinarily concerned about saving a grand and beautiful building, with less thought put in to the importance of the surrounding landscape. At the same time, conservation organizations have saved the land surrounding an iconic farmstead, but have left the historic buildings unprotected.

We will be stronger and better able to accomplish what we need to do on climate change if we make common cause with our many friends in the conservation and environmental movements. As someone who worked at The Nature Conservancy for nearly two decades, I can tell you that we all have a keen appreciation for the fragility of our heritage, be it natural or man-made, and a strong desire to preserve the unique and irreplaceable. We are all committed to sustainable solutions and focused on helping communities take action to preserve what matters to them. And we all want to save the most important historic place there is, the planet we call home.

We know what we have to do to tackle climate change. Now we need the will to do it. In February 2015, a group of preservationists, architects, green builders, archaeologists, and environmental advocates—including representatives from the US Forest Service, World Monuments Fund, Union of Concerned Scientists, and the National Trust—gathered at the Pocantico Center, on the grounds of the historic Rockefeller estate, to affirm our commitment to confronting climate change's impact on the places that matter to us. "Cultural heritage is a human right," argued the ensuing Pocantico Call to Action, a human right now deeply threatened by the changing climate. As such, we will do everything in our power to "mobilize action addressing the risks to our shared heritage."[43]

Yes, we will. Going forward, we will work together to reduce our carbon emissions, recycle our existing fabric, and make the places we live and love more resilient against climate-related impacts. We will encourage sustainability in our cities, our culture, and our way of life. And we will help people save the places they can—and memorialize the places they cannot.

This work is incredibly important, and it will only grow more important in the years and decades to come.

The Future of the Past: Livable Cities and the Future of Preservation

In the end, our society will be defined not only by what we create, but by what we refuse to destroy.
  —John Sawhill[1]

AS THE DISCUSSION WE HAVE BEEN HAVING over the course of this book attests, historic preservation in the twenty-first century is a remarkably dynamic and vibrant field. All across the United States, preservationists are working in a host of ways to revitalize cities and communities, capture the contours of our shared past, address the most pressing challenges of today, and bring people together.

The key tool in accomplishing these goals is our historic fabric—the older and historic buildings that are all around us. When, through smart urban policy, the amazing potential of this fabric is realized, these buildings and communities can accelerate economic growth and attract residents and tourists, create opportunity and mitigate inequality, reduce energy costs and help save the planet, and create the foundations for a stronger American future.

The combination of preservation and adaptive reuse is not just the best way forward for our cities. It is in many ways the *only* way forward. This is in part—as mentioned at the end of chapter 7—because of the looming threat of climate change. It is also because it is the old, distinctive, and beloved places around us that even make us communities at all.

"The development of a real community takes *time*," wrote Tom Mayes in his "Why Do Old Places Matter?" essays. "Community develops through the interaction between people and place over *time*. We cannot build a community—we can only foster the conditions in which communities can grow and thrive." If communities can only form over time, preservation helps protect them as they grow, giving consistency to the landscape and a shared sense of history to its members. As Pope Francis put it in his 2015 encyclical, *Laudato Si*, we must "protect those common areas, visual landmarks, and urban landscapes which increase our sense of belonging, of rootedness, of 'feeling at home' within a city which includes us and brings us together." When we do, "others will then no longer be seen as strangers, but as part of a 'we' which all of us are working to create."[2]

Old places do that. They give us a collective memory and a sense of perspective. They offer us a source of wisdom and strength that we can draw on when we need it, including times like now, when the challenges we face can seem so complicated and intractable. We know we can navigate what's ahead of us because we know that the men and women of our community generations ago faced their own problems—oftentimes much worse ones, in fact—and stuck through. Today, with so many forces threatening to divide us, preservation is one of the few things that brings us together—as a nation, as communities, and as people.

The work of saving places speaks to so many of our fundamental needs: opportunity, identity, community, recognition, self-knowledge, mutual understanding. Over the years, though, its importance to our lives and our communities has often been hidden to us.

Five decades after the National Historic Preservation Act became law, preservation has in many ways been a victim of its success. Although the practice of saving and adaptively reusing historic places is much more common today than ever before, preservation has also become systematized and bureaucratized. We have adopted increasingly specialized jargon and have occasionally fallen into the trap of speaking to each other rather than speaking to the concerns of the community.

As a result, too many people today see preservation as something removed from their daily lives or not reflective of their cultural heritage. They feel shut out by the often complicated and expensive process of securing formal, legal designations for a place. To some Americans, the important work of saving historic places has even seemed like something that a preservation class inflicted on a town, rather than an organic outgrowth of the community's wants and needs.

One of the founding figures of the twentieth-century preservation movement, W. Brown Morton, captured this unfortunate shift in a little-heard 2014 speech. Forty years earlier, Morton had helped codify the work of saving places by drafting the secretary of the interior's standards for historic preservation, standards that still guide our work today. But, he argued, we had taken a wrong turn somewhere along the way. "I believe that historic preservation in the United States has become ossified," he said, "and needs a kick in the pants to regain its earlier excitement and reconnect people with their deepest hope." Too many preservation activities, Morton observed, "have lost their original sense of urgency. They have become unnecessarily frozen in a bureaucratic system of regulations, criteria, and standards which have become sclerotic, pro forma, and inflexible."[3]

It doesn't have to be this way, and indeed, there are signs all over the United States that preservation is shaking off this rust and returning to its roots. "What makes this possibility of change especially exciting at the present time," Morton continued, "is the growing awareness that historic preservation has moved in a very real sense beyond history. Our work is no longer perceived as preserving the past. It is more and more understood as wisely managing change."[4]

Morton is exactly right. Far too often in the past, preservation has been what I call a movement of no. It has focused mainly on stopping bad things from happening to old buildings and on telling people what they are not allowed to do to their historic homes. So, despite the current flourishing of ideas, innovation, and creativity in the preservation space, Americans tend to think that we are static, stuck-in-the-mud obstacles to change and progress. Often, even when I tell communities or developers that adaptive reuse is one of the cornerstones of historic preservation, people seem surprised to hear it.

To bury that incorrect stereotype for good, we need to break away even further from the old, bad habits and become a movement of yes. Of course, there is still an important place for local preservation controls. All too often, though, laudable preservation goals—once the bureaucracy gets involved—are experienced by the people involved as impractical, irritating, and even insignificant. There is so much more to preservation than that.

So, instead of being the ones who hold back change and say "no, you can't do that," let's jump in and find more ways to reuse historic buildings. We can seek out more partnerships with developers, property owners, real estate agents, city officials, and local advocacy organizations to modernize regulations, lift regulatory barriers, and make it easier to breathe new life into older buildings. We can work harder to help these places stay more relevant to the needs of the community they are in. We can keep moving beyond buildings and think about saving landscapes, character, and culture.

Most of all, we can break our bureaucratic constraints and recapture the grassroots energy that originally drove our work—that compelled Jane Jacobs to fight for Greenwich Village and Dana Crawford to

Residents of Ithaca, New York, stand up for a historic place that matters.
(Courtesy Historic Ithaca)

reshape her Denver neighborhood. And it is happening. We see it at the National Trust every day: in the throngs of young Americans who come out to save Cincinnati's Union Terminal, Houston's Astrodome, and a host of other places; in the dedication and commitment of HOPE Crew volunteers; and in all the ways communities all over the United States are restoring the places that matter to them.

We also see it in the extraordinary response to a recently relaunched National Trust campaign. In the fall of 2015, we printed up orange map pins, posters, and scarves with three simple words on them—This Place Matters—and encouraged Americans to tell us about the particular places that matter to them. We were soon inundated with Twitter testimonials and Facebook and Instagram posts as people showed love for the places in their communities.

When you cut away the cruft that has built up around historic preservation over the decades, that response is the heart of what we do and why we do it. We all have places that matter to us—places that define us, places that challenge us, places that bring us together and tell our story. These places help form our identity and our community. They create opportunities for growth and help us feel at home. They bind us to those who came long before us, and to those who will live in these very same places long after we are gone. They explain our past, and serve as the foundation of our future.

These places matter, and we are richer and stronger when they remain.

Notes

Introduction

1. LA Conservancy, "Japanese-American Heritage," https://www.laconser vancy.org/japanese-american-heritage. LA Conservancy, "The Maravilla Handball Court and El Centro Grocery Store," https://www.laconser vancy.org/locations/maravilla-handball-court-and-el-centro-grocery. "Old Homies Pay Tribute to History, Handball, and a Woman Named Michi," *Eastsider LA*, June 29, 2009, http://theeastsiderlahomehistory .blogspot.com/2009/06/old-hommies-play-tribute-to-history.html. Hec- tor Becerra, "Extending a Hand to a Faded East L.A. Handball Court," *Los Angeles Times*, February 14, 2010, http://articles.latimes.com/2010 /feb/14/local/la-me-handball14-2010feb14.

2. LA Conservancy, "The Maravilla Handball Court." Becerra, "Extending a Hand." "Old Homies Pay Tribute."

3. Becerra, "Extending a Hand." "Old Homies Pay Tribute." Newly Paul, "Group Works to Preserve East LA's Maravilla Handball Court," *KPCC*, February 23, 2010, http://www.scpr.org/news/2010/02/23/12216/group -works-preserve-east-las-maravilla-handball-c/.

4. Paul, "Group Works to Preserve East LA's Maravilla Handball Court."

5. Ibid.

6. Ibid. "East L.A. Handball Court Declared a State Historic Landmark," *Eastsider LA*, August 7, 2012, http://www.theeastsiderla.com/2012/08 /east-l-a-handball-court-declared-a-state-historic-landmark/.

7. Maria Lewicka, "Place Attachment: How Far Have We Come in the Last 40 Years?," *Journal of Environmental Psychology* 31 (2011): 211, 225; and Maria Lewicka, "Place Attachment, Place Identity, and Place Memory: Restoring the Forgotten City Past," *Journal of Environmental Psychology* 28 (2008): 211. Quoted in Tom Mayes, "Why Old Places Matter: Con-

tinuity," November 21, 2013, http://forum.savingplaces.org/blogs/forum
-online/2013/11/21/why-do-old-places-matter-continuity

8. Dylan Trigg, *The Memory of Place: A Phenomenology of the Uncanny* (Athens: Ohio University Press, 2013), 1; Introduction available at http://www.academia.edu/355785/The_Memory_of_Place_a_Phenomenology_of_the_Uncanny.

9. Katherine Mansfield, "Letter to Ida Baker," 1922, quoted at "Six Stories, Six Places," https://www.behance.net/gallery/5125053/-SIX-STORIES-SIX-PLACES-Katherine-Mansfield. The Beatles, "In My Life," *Rubber Soul*, EMI, 1965, compact disc.

10. Robert F. Kniesche, "Happy Birthday H. L. Mencken," *Baltimore Sun*, February 15, 2012, http://www.baltimoresun.com/entertainment/bal-hl-mencken-20120215-photo.html.

11. Jaime Lerner, *Urban Acupuncture: Celebrating Pinpricks of Change That Enrich City Life* (Washington, DC: Island Press, 2014), 98–99.

12. Trigg, *Memory of Place*, 1. Lily M. Cho, "The Turn to Diaspora," *Topia* 17, special issue on "Diaspora" (2007): 11–30, https://lucian.uchicago.edu/blogs/politicalfeeling/files/2007/10/cho-topia11-30.pdf. John Steinbeck, *The Grapes of Wrath* (1939; repr., New York: Penguin, 2006), 88.

13. "The Wheel," *Mad Men*, season 1, episode 13. Originally aired October 18, 2007. Pamela Petro, "Dreaming in Welsh," *Paris Review*, September 8, 2012, http://www.theparisreview.org/blog/2012/09/18/dreaming-in-welsh/.

14. Charles Montgomery, *Happy City: Transforming Our Lives through Urban Design* (New York: Farrar, Straus and Giroux, 2013), 130–33, 161. Alain de Botton, "The Architecture of Happiness," http://alaindebotton.com/architecture/; also cited in Kaid Benfield, "The Pursuit of Happiness: How Do Communities Make Us Happy?," *Atlantic*, June 29, 2011, http://www.theatlantic.com/health/archive/2011/06/the-pursuit-of-happiness-how-do-communities-make-us-happy/241201/.

15. Hippocrates, *On Airs, Water, and Places*, trans. Francis Adams, MIT Internet Classics Archive, http://classics.mit.edu/Hippocrates/airwatpl.html. Robert Ivy, "Healthy Living Choices—By Design," *Huffington Post*, February 13, 2014, http://www.huffingtonpost.com/robert-ivy-faia/healthy-living-choices-by_1_b_4777121.html.

16. US Census, "Growth in Urban Population Outpaces Rest of Nation, Census Bureau Reports," March 26, 2012, https://www.census.gov/newsroom

/releases/archives/2010_census/cb12-50.html. Leigh Gallagher, "The End of the Suburbs," *Time*, July 31, 2014, http://ideas.time.com/2013 /07/31/the-end-of-the-suburbs/. Joe Cortright, "The Dow of Cities," *City Observatory*, August 20, 2015, http://cityobservatory.org/dow-of -cities/. Sam Frizell, "The New American Dream Is Living in a City, Not Owning a House in the Suburbs," *Time*, April 25, 2014, http://time .com/72281/american-housing/.

17. Quoted in James A. Clapp, *The City: A Dictionary of Quotable Thoughts on Cities and Urban Life* (New Brunswick, NJ: Center for Urban Policy Research, 1984). Anthony Flint, *Wrestling with Moses: How Jane Jacobs Took on New York's Master Builder and Transformed the American City* (New York: Random House, 2009), 139–40.

18. Kenneth T. Jackson, "The Rise and Fall of Main Street," in *American Places: Encounters with History*, ed. William Leuchtenberg (New York: Oxford University Press, 2000), 182. Kenneth T. Jackson, *Crabgrass Frontier: The Suburbanization of the United States* (New York: Oxford University Press, 1985), 4.

19. Jackson, *Crabgrass Frontier*, 4.

20. Richard Moe and Carter Wilkie, *Changing Places: Rebuilding Community in the Age of Sprawl* (New York: Henry Holt, 1997), ix–x.

21. James Howard Kunstler, *The Geography of Nowhere: The Rise and Decline of America's Man-Made Landscape* (New York: Touchstone, 1993), 10.

22. Charles Montgomery, *Happy City*, 47.

23. Ibid., 47, 83, 95, 97.

24. Jackson, *Crabgrass Frontier*, 296.

25. Alan Ehrenhalt, *The Great Inversion and the Future of the American City* (New York: Knopf, 2012), 7, 12.

26. Frizell, "New American Dream." Carol Coletta, "How We Build Our Cities, What's at Stake," *City Observatory*, December 24, 2014, http:// cityobservatory.org/coletta-guest-post/.

27. Claire Cain Miller, "Where Young Graduates Are Choosing to Live," *New York Times*, October 20, 2014, http://www.nytimes.com/2014/10/20 /upshot/where-young-college-graduates-are-choosing-to-live.html. Stephanie Hanes, "The New 'Cool' Cities for Millennials," *Christian Science Monitor*, February 1, 2015, http://www.csmonitor.com/USA/Soci ety/2015/0201/The-new-cool-cities-for-Millennials.

28. Frizell, "New American Dream."

29. Hanes, "New 'Cool' Cities."

30. Ibid. Christopher Corbett, "The Charm City of H. L. Mencken," *New York Times*, September 4, 1988, http://www.nytimes.com/1988/09/04/travel/the-charm-city-of-h-l-mencken.html.

31. Jordan Teicher, "Millennials Are Moving to Buffalo and Living Like Kings," *Gothamist*, January 28, 2015, http://gothamist.com/2015/01/28/millennials_buffalo.php. Hanes, "New 'Cool' Cities."

32. Frizell, "New American Dream."

33. Sasaki Associates, "The State of the City Experience," http://www.sasaki.com/media/files/cities_survey_final-1.pdf. Sydney Brownstone, "4 Reasons Why People Love Cities and How We're Working on Ruining Them," *Co Exist*, August 6, 2014, http://www.fastcoexist.com/3033848/4-reasons-why-people-love-living-in-cities-and-how-were-working-on-ruining-them.

34. Sasaki Associates, "The State of the City Experience."

35. Sandra Shannon, "Why Old Places Matter: A Survey of the Public," *Preservation Leadership Forum*, May 7, 2015, http://forum.savingplaces.org/blogs/forum-online/2015/05/07/why-old-places-matter-a-survey-of-the-public. Kaid Benfield, "Why the Places We Live Make Us Happy," *City Lab*, February 2, 2012, http://www.citylab.com/design/2012/02/why-places-we-live-make-us-happy/1122/.

36. Stewart Brand, *How Buildings Learn: What Happens after They're Built* (New York: Penguin, 1994), 10–11.

37. Historic England, "The Value and Impact of Heritage," http://hc.historicengland.org.uk/content/pub/2190644/value-impact-chapter.pdf. Katey Amie, "Visiting Heritage Sites Makes People Happier," *Daily Mail*, November 13, 2014, http://www.dailymail.co.uk/travel/travel_news/article-2832875/Visiting-historical-towns-cities-makes-happy.html.

38. Alan Davies, "Why Do We Love Old Buildings So Much?," *Crikey*, May 11, 2011, http://blogs.crikey.com.au/theurbanist/2011/05/11/why-do-we-love-old-buildings-so-much/. Brand, *How Buildings Learn*, 90.

39. Ed McMahon, "Where Am I? The Power of Uniqueness," TedX Jacksonville, January 6, 2015, https://www.youtube.com/watch?v=qB5tH4rt-x8.

40. Ibid. Coletta, "How We Build Our Cities." Sam Brodey, "Forget Brooklyn: Could Columbus Be the Next 'Hot' Millennial Enclave?," *Mother Jones*, June 1, 2015, http://www.motherjones.com/media/2015/05/columbus-ohio-millennials-brooklyn.

41. McMahon, "Where Am I?"
42. John Kenneth Galbraith, "The Economic and Social Returns of Preservation," in *Preservation: Towards an Ethic in the 1980s* (Washington, DC: Preservation Press, 1980), 57–58. Arthur Frommer, "Viewpoint: Historic Preservation and Tourism," *Preservation Forum*, Fall 1988, http://forum.savingplaces.org/connect/community-home/librarydocuments/viewdocument?DocumentKey=97ff95cd-857c-4cef-ad21-61b8cb3682a9.
43. Roadside America, "Maps," http://www.roadsideamerica.com/location/. McMahon, "Where Am I?"
44. Edge Research, "National Trust for Historic Preservation Brand Elements Research," July 18, 2011.
45. Emily Potter, "Preservation-Themed Movies," *Preservation Nation*, February 19, 2014, https://savingplaces.org/stories/10-tuesday-preservation-themed-movies/.
46. Priya Chhaya and Will O'Keefe, "Preservation in Pop Culture: How I Met Your Mother," *Preservation Nation*, June 2, 2011, http://archive.mnpreservation.org/2011/06/02/preservation-in-pop-culture-how-i-met-your-mother/.
47. Cavan Wilk, "Has Preservation Become an Echo Chamber?," *Greater Greater Washington*, December 16, 2008, http://greatergreaterwashington.org/post/1501/has-preservation-become-an-echo-chamber/. David Lowenthal, "The Heritage Crusade and Its Contradictions," in *Giving Preservation a History: Histories of Historic Preservation*, ed. Max Page and Randall Mason (New York: Routledge, 2004), 9.
48. Nic Musolino, "Whenever Anyone Says 'Historic Preservation' I Reach for My Hoary Clichés," *Miss Representation*, May 23, 2007, http://www.missrepresentation.com/?p=440.
49. Lydia DePillis, "The Future of the Past," *Washington CityPaper*, September 29, 2011, http://www.washingtoncitypaper.com/blogs/housingcomplex/2011/09/29/the-future-of-the-past/.
50. Montgomery, *Happy City*, 42.
51. Ibid.
52. Jeff Speck, *Walkable City: How Downtown Can Save America, One Step at a Time* (New York: Northpoint Press, 2012), 4–5.

Chapter 1

1. Jane Jacobs, *The Death and Life of Great American Cities* (New York: Vintage Books, 1961), 238.

2. Jacobs, *Death and Life*, 187.

3. Anthony Flint, *Wrestling with Moses: How Jane Jacobs Took on New York's Master Builder and Transformed the American City* (New York: Random House, 2009), 122.

4. Le Corbusier, *The City of Tomorrow and Its Planning*, trans. Frederick Etchells (New York: Payson and Clarke Ltd., 1929), 244.

5. Le Corbusier, *The City of Tomorrow*, 62, 60, xxi, 15, 22, 12, 24. Jacobs, *Death and Life*, 21. Gili Merin, "AD Classics: Ville Radieuse/Le Corbusier," *Arch Daily*, August 11, 2013, http://www.archdaily.com/411878 /ad-classics-ville-radieuse-le-corbusier/. James Howard Kunstler, *The Geography of Nowhere: The Rise and Decline of America's Man-Made Landscape* (New York: Touchstone, 1993), 72–73, 78–80.

6. Kunstler, *Geography of Nowhere*, 78–79.

7. Paul Goldberger, "Robert Moses, Master Builder, Is Dead at 92," *New York Times*, July 30, 1981, http://www.nytimes.com/learning/general /onthisday/bday/1218.html. Anthony Flint, *Modern Man: The Life of Le Corbusier, Architect of Tomorrow* (New York: New Harvest, 2014), 52–53, 203. Flint, *Wrestling with Moses*, xv, 48–49. Robert Caro, *The Power Broker: Robert Moses and the Fall of New York* (New York: Vintage, 1974), 829, 834, 839, 909. Flint, *Wrestling with Moses*, 51. Goldberger, "Robert Moses, Master Builder."

8. Flint, *Wrestling with Moses*, 106, 142. Kunstler, *Geography of Nowhere*, 100.

9. Flint, *Wrestling with Moses*, xv, 106, 188, 142. Kunstler, *Geography of Nowhere*, 100. Robert Moses, "Are Cities Dead?," *Atlantic*, January 1962, http://www.theatlantic.com/magazine/archive/1962/01/are-cities-dead /306546/.

10. Caro, *The Power Broker*, 848, 866–67.

11. Flint, *Wrestling with Moses*, 9. Robert Brandes Gratz, "Planners and the Jane Jacobs Conundrum," *Planetizen*, April 25, 2011, http://www.plan etizen.com/node/49100.

12. Flint, *Wrestling with Moses*, 19–20. Christopher Pierznik, "The Father of Modern Philadelphia: The (Un-)making of a City," *Medium*, February 13, 2015, https://medium.com/@pierzy/the-father-of-modern-phil

adelphia-cc2373717a45. National Building Museum, "The Father of Modern Philadelphia," January 22, 2014, http://www.nbm.org/about-us/national-building-museum-online/the-legacy-of-urban-renewal.html. Robin Pogrebin, "Edmund Bacon, 95, Urban Planner of Philadelphia, Dies," *New York Times*, October 18, 2005, http://www.nytimes.com/2005/10/18/arts/design/edmund-bacon-95-urban-planner-of-philadelphia-dies.html.

13. Pierznik, "Father of Modern Philadelphia." National Building Museum, "Father of Modern Philadelphia." Pogrebin, "Edmund Bacon."

14. Gratz, "Planners." Flint, *Wrestling with Moses*, 19–20.

15. Flint, *Wrestling with Moses*, 19–20.

16. Flint, *Wrestling with Moses*, 27. Jane Jacobs, "Downtown Is for People," *Fortune*, 1958; reprinted by Nin-Hai Tseng, *Fortune Magazine*, September 18, 2011, http://fortune.com/2011/09/18/downtown-is-for-people-fortune-classic-1958/.

17. Jacobs, "Downtown Is for People."

18. Ibid.

19. Ibid. Flint, *Wrestling with Moses*, 28.

20. Flint, *Wrestling with Moses*, 63–65.

21. Ibid. Chris Pomorski, "Power Couple: The Feud between Jane Jacobs and Robert Moses Becomes Operatic," *New York Observer*, May 29, 2015, http://observer.com/2015/05/power-couple-the-feud-between-jane-jacobs-and-robert-moses-becomes-operatic/.

22. Flint, *Wrestling with Moses*, 80–87. Robert Fishman, "Revolt of the Urbs: Robert Moses and His Critics," in *Robert Moses and the Modern City: The Transformation of New York*, ed. Hilary Ballon and Kenneth T. Jackson (New York: W. W. Norton, 2007), http://macaulay.cuny.edu/eportfolios/rodberg15/files/2015/01/Robert-Fishman-Revolt-of-the-Urbs.pdf. Pomorski, "Power Couple."

23. Flint, *Wrestling with Moses*, 99–115.

24. Flint, *Wrestling with Moses*, 153–57, 177.

25. Jacobs, *Death and Life*, 12–13. Flint, *Wrestling with Moses*, 91.

26. Jacobs, *Death and Life*, 34, 37, 448.

27. Flint, *Wrestling with Moses*, 95–96.

28. Jacobs, *Death and Life*, 90–91, 99, 140, 144, 150–51.

29. Ibid., 187–88.

30. Ibid., 188.

31. Ibid., 189, 191, 193.

32. Ibid., 338, 343, 357, 384.

33. Ibid., 198–99.

34. Flint, *Wrestling with Moses*, 121–25.

35. Lloyd Rodwin, "Neighbors Are Needed," *New York Times*, November 5, 1961, https://www.nytimes.com/books/97/08/17/reviews/jacobs.html. Flint, *Wrestling with Moses*, 129.

36. Hilary Ballon, *New York's Pennsylvania Stations* (New York: W. W. Norton, 2002), 97–100.

37. Ibid., 101. Flint, *Wrestling with Moses*, 130–31. David W. Dunlap, "50 Years Ago, Sharply Dressed Protesters Stood Up for a Train Station They Revered," *New York Times*, July 31, 2012, http://cityroom.blogs.nytimes .com/2012/07/31/50-years-ago-sharply-dressed-protesters-stood-up-for -a-train-station-they-revered/.

38. Ada Louise Huxtable, "Farewell to Penn Station," *New York Times*, October 30, 1963, https://nycarchitectureandurbanism.files.wordpress .com/2015/03/huxtable-farewell-to-penn-station-1963.pdf. Ballon, *New York's Pennsylvania Stations*, 102.

39. Isaac Kremer, "The NHPA at 50: The Williamsburg Conference and *With Heritage So Rich*," *Place Promotion*, June 21, 2013, http://placepro motion.blogspot.com/2013/06/nhpa50-williamsburg-conference-and -with.html.

40. New York City Landmarks Commission, "What Happened in 1965?," http://www.nyclandmarks50.org/history_and_education.html.

41. Kremer, "The NHPA at 50."

42. Special Committee on Historic Preservation, *With Heritage So Rich* (New York: Random House, 1966), 17–20.

43. Advisory Council on Historic Preservation, "National Historic Preservation Act," 1966, http://www.achp.gov/NHPA.pdf. Advisory Council on Historic Preservation, "Section 106 Regulations Summary," http://www .achp.gov/106summary.html/. Advisory Council on Historic Preservation, "Section 106 Success Stories," http://www.achp.gov/sec106_suc cesses.html. Adam Jones, "Transportation Legislation Threatens Section 4(f)," *Preservation Leadership Forum*, October 27, 2015, http://forum .savingplaces.org/blogs/forum-online/2015/10/27/transportation-legis lation-threatens-section-4f. Stephanie Meeks, "The DRIVE Act Throws His

tory Out the Window," *Hill*, July 29, 2015, http://thehill.com/blogs
/congress-blog/249489-the-drive-act-throws-history-out-the-window.

44. Stewart Brand, *How Buildings Learn: What Happens after They're Built*
(New York: Penguin, 1994), 88–89.

Chapter 2

1. James A. Clapp, *The City: A Dictionary of Quotable Thought on Cities
and Urban Life* (New Brunswick, NJ: Center for Urban Policy Research,
1984), 259.

2. Aaron Lubeck, *Green Restorations: Sustainable Building and Historic
Homes* (Gabriola Island, BC: New Society, 2010), 29.

3. Kenneth Neal Cukier and Viktor Mayer-Schoenberger, "The Rise of Big
Data," *Foreign Affairs*, May/June 2013, https://www.foreignaffairs.com
/articles/2013-04-03/rise-big-data. Mike Powe, "Big Data: A New Frontier in Historic Preservation?," *Preservation Leadership Forum*, March 4,
2014, http://forum.savingplaces.org/blogs/forum-online/2014/03/04
/big-data-a-new-frontier-in-historic-preservation

4. For those who are interested, the full *Older, Smaller, Better* report—available at the Preservation Green Lab and the National Trust for Historic
Preservation's websites—goes into much more detail about the Green
Lab's specific methodology. Preservation Green Lab, *Older, Smaller, Better: Measuring How the Character of Buildings and Blocks Influences Urban
Vitality*, May 2014, http://forum.savingplaces.org/act/pgl/older-smaller
-better.

5. H Street Neighborhood News, "USA Today—H Street Ten Best Neighborhoods to Explore," February 1, 2012, http://hstreet.org/usa-today-h
-street-10-best-neighborhoods-to-explore/. Maya Rhodan, "Forbes Names
H Street Sixth 'Hippest Hipster' Neighborhood in America," *Washingtonian*, September 21, 2012, http://www.washingtonian.com/2012/09/21
/forbes-names-h-street-6th-hippest-hipster-neighborhood-in-america/.

6. Katie Dennis and Sheryl Poe, "Riots to Revitalization: The Difference
on H Street Is Night and Day," *Free Enterprise*, November 14, 2013,
http://archive.freeenterprise.com/entrepreneur/riots-revitalization-differ
ence-h-street-night-and-day. H Street Main Street, http://hstreet.org/h
-street/hsms/. Stephanie Meeks, "Urban CPR: Community, Preservation, Resurgence," Detroit Economic Club, May 19, 2014, https://saving

placcs.org/press-center/media-resources/urban-cpr-community-preserva
tion-resurgence

7. Preservation Green Lab, *Older, Smaller, Better*, 66–67. Missy Frederick, "Rose's Luxury Tops Bon Appetit Best Restaurant List," *Washington DC Eater*, August 19, 2014, http://dc.eater.com/2014/8/19/6168979/roses -luxury-tops-bon-appetit-best-restaurant-list.

8. Michael Nelbauer, "National Community Church to Acquire Blue Castle, Expand Barracks Row Portfolio," *Washington Business Journal*, November 4, 2014, http://www.bizjournals.com/washington/breaking _ground/2014/11/national-community-church-to-acquire-blue-castle .html.

9. Matthew Yglesias, "Washington D.C.'s Aversion to Skyscrapers Has Turned It into an American Versailles," *de Zeen*, June 19, 2015, http:// www.dezeen.com/2015/06/19/washington-dc-height-buildings-act-sky scrapers-inequality-housing-american-versailles/. Preservation Green Lab, *Older, Smaller, Better*, 57.

10. Lydia DePillis, "What Does Ed Glaeser Have against Planning?," *Washington City Paper*, February 14, 2011, http://www.washingtoncitypaper.com /blogs/housingcomplex/2011/02/14/what-does-ed-glaeser-have-against -planning/.

11. Ibid. Jeff Speck, *Walkable City: How Downtown Can Save America, One Step at a Time* (New York: Northpoint Press, 2012), 220–21.

12. Speck, *Walkable City*, 220–21.

13. Preservation Green Lab, *Older, Smaller, Better*, 82–84. J. P. Mangalinden, "Suitcase of Body Parts Found a Block from Twitter HQ," *Mashable*, January 29, 2015, http://forum.savingplaces.org/blogs/forum-online/2015 /10/09/witnessing-how-older-and-smaller-is-better

14. Preservation Green Lab, *Older, Smaller, Better*, 82–84. Kristina Shevory, "Twitter Helps to Revive a Seedy San Francisco Neighborhood," *New York Times*, November 2, 2013, http://www.nytimes.com/2013/11/02 /business/twitter-helps-revive-a-seedy-san-francisco-neighborhood.html.

15. Preservation Green Lab, *Older, Smaller, Better*, 82–84. Kim Mai-Cutler, "How Burrowing Owls Led to Vomiting Anarchists (or the S.F. Housing Crisis Explained)," *TechCrunch*, April 14, 2014, http://techcrunch .com/2014/04/14/sf-housing/.

16. Preservation Green Lab, *Older, Smaller, Better*, 82–84. Mai-Cutler, "How Burrowing Owls."

17. Joe Garofoli, "Twitter Opens $3 Million Tech Skills Center for SF Poor, Homeless," *San Francisco Chronicle*, May 20, 2015, http://www.sfgate .com/business/article/Twitter-opens-3-million-tech-skills-center-for -6276841.php.

18. Ibid. Heather Somerville, "Four Years after Mid-Market Tax Break, Zendesk Wins Over Community," *Mendocino Beacon Journal*, February 21, 2015, http://www.mendocinobeacon.com/business/20150221/four -years-after-mid-market-tax-break-zendesk-wins-over-community.

19. Sam Gustin, "Google Buys Giant New York Building for $1.9 Billion," *Wired*, December 22, 2010, http://www.wired.com/2010/12/google-nyc/. Roger Vincent and Andrea Chang, "Google Buys 12 Acres in Playa Vista, Vastly Expands Presence in L.A," *Los Angeles Times*, December 3, 2014, http://www.latimes.com/business/realestate/la-fi-playa-property-sale -20141203-story.html.

20. Stewart Brand, *How Buildings Learn: What Happens after They're Built* (New York: Penguin, 1994), 23–24.

21. Talia Avakian, "America's Most Expensive Cities for Renters," *Business Insider*, August 25, 2015, http://www.businessinsider.com/americas-20 -most-expensive-cities-for-renters-2015-8. Mai-Cutler, "How Burrowing Owls." Derek Thompson, "Why Middle-Class Americans Can't Afford to Live in Liberal Cities," *Atlantic*, October 29, 2014, http://www.the atlantic.com/business/archive/2014/10/why-are-liberal-cities-so-unaf fordable/382045/.

22. Mai-Cutler, "How Burrowing Owls." SPUR and San Francisco Archi-tectural Heritage, "Historic Preservation in San Francisco: Making the Preservation Process Work for Everyone," July 2013, http://www.spur .org/sites/default/files/publications_pdfs/SPUR_Historic_Preservation _in_SF.pdf.

23. Preservation Green Lab, *Older, Smaller, Better*, 77. SPUR and San Fran-cisco Architectural Heritage, "Historic Preservation in San Francisco."

24. Preservation Green Lab, *Older, Smaller, Better*, 38–40. "Amazon Leases Supply Laundry," *Daily Journal of Commerce*, June 11, 2014, http://www .djc.com/news/re/12066610.html.

25. Preservation Green Lab, *Older, Smaller, Better*, 38–40.

26. Ibid., 44.

27. Ibid. Charles Montgomery, *Happy City: Transforming Our Lives through Urban Design* (New York: Farrar, Strauss and Giroux, 2013), 136–37.

28. First Hill Streetcar, http://www.seattlestreetcar.org/firsthill.htm.
29. Preservation Green Lab, *Older, Smaller, Better*, 49–51.
30. Ibid.
31. Ibid.
32. Kathryn Schultz, "The Really Big One," *New Yorker*, July 20, 2015, http://www.newyorker.com/magazine/2015/07/20/the-really-big-one. Kara Bloomgarden-Smoke, "Digital Publications Won Big at the Magazine Awards," *Observer*, February 2, 2016, http://observer.com/2016/02/digital-publications-won-big-at-the-magazine-awards/. Preservation Green Lab, *Older, Smaller, Better*, 49–51.
33. Preservation Green Lab, *Older, Smaller, Better*, 49–51.
34. Partnership for Building Reuse, "Building on Baltimore's History," November 2014, http://forum.savingplaces.org/connect/community-home/librarydocuments/viewdocument?DocumentKey=81d17447-80d8-429d-acbd-a82649e94120
35. Partnership for Building Reuse, "Retrofitting Philadelphia," September 2014, http://forum.savingplaces.org/connect/community-home/librarydocuments/viewdocument?DocumentKey=981d6c61-aefb-4a18-a34b-c6098a82b178
36. Sam Zacher, "Witnessing How Older and Smaller Is Better," *Preservation Nation*, October 19, 2015, http://blog.preservationleadershipforum.org/2015/10/09/witnessing-how-older-and-smaller-is-better/.

Chapter 3

1. Petula Clark and Tony Hatch, *Downtown*, Warner Bros.-Seven Arts, 1965.
2. Jeff Speck, *Walkable City: How Downtown Can Save America, One Step at a Time* (New York: Northpoint Press, 2012), 3.
3. Partnership for Building Reuse, "Learning from Los Angeles," October 2013, http://forum.savingplaces.org/connect/community-home/librarydocuments/viewdocument?DocumentKey=41dc24dd-bef7-404a-97d3-480cbfa4a871
4. Jane Jacobs, "Downtown Is for People," *Fortune*, 1958; reprinted by Nin-Hai Tseng, *Fortune Magazine*, September 18, 2011, http://fortune.com/2011/09/18/downtown-is-for-people-fortune-classic-1958/.
5. Ellie Violet Bramley, "Is Jan Gehl Winning His Battle to Make Our Cities Livable?," *Guardian*, December 8, 2014, http://www.theguardian.com

/cities/2014/dec/08/jan-gehl-make-cities-liveable-urban-rethinker. Gehl Architects, "Our Story," http://gehlarchitects.com/story/.

6. Bramley, "Is Jan Gehl Winning." Gehl Architects, "Our Story."
7. Jan Gehl, *Life between Buildings* (Washington, DC: Island Press, 2011), 14, 22.
8. Speck, *Walkable City*, 8.
9. Preservation Green Lab, *Older, Smaller, Better: Measuring How the Character of Buildings and Blocks Influences Urban Vitality*, May 2014, http://forum.savingplaces.org/act/pgl/older-smaller-better.
10. Stephanie K. Meeks, "Step Boldly and Bring the Past Forward," National Preservation Conference, Savannah, Georgia, November 12, 2014, http://forum.savingplaces.org/blogs/forum-online/2014/11/12/step-forward-boldly-and-bring-the-past-forward
11. Ibid.
12. Ibid.
13. Ibid. David J. Barboza, "SurveyLA Training Preps Group 4 Survey Teams," *SurveyLA Blog*, May 8, 2012, https://surveyla.wordpress.com/2012/05/08/surveyla-training-preps-group-4-survey-teams/. SurveyLA, "Why a City-Wide Survey?," http://preservation.lacity.org/survey/why. SurveyLA, "Project Description," http://preservation.lacity.org/survey/description.
14. SurveyLA, "SurveyLA Facts," http://preservation.lacity.org/files/04%20MyHistoricLA%20SurveyLA%20Facts_0.pdf.
15. James Fink, "Hundreds of Buffalo Buildings May Qualify for Incentives," *Buffalo Business First*, April 4, 2014, http://www.bizjournals.com/buffalo/news/2014/04/14/hundreds-of-buffalo-buildings-may-qualify-for.html. "Buffalo Property Eligibility for Historic Tax Credit Incentives," *Buffalo News*, http://data.buffalonews.com/databuff/government/buffalo-property-eligibility-historic-tax-credits-incentives/.
16. Civil War Trust, "Wal-Mart Controversy Finally Resolved," *Hallowed Ground*, Spring 2014, http://www.civilwar.org/hallowed-ground-magazine/spring-2014/walmart-controversy-fully.html.
17. Preservation Green Lab, *Older, Smaller, Better*, 93–94.
18. Stewart Brand, *How Buildings Learn: What Happens after They're Built* (New York: Penguin, 1994), 73. Francisco J. Matta-Bermudez, "From Hammurabi to the International Building Code: A Brief History of Construction Law and Regulation," *Construction Law Depot*, September 22, 2013, https://constructionlawdepot.wordpress.com/2013/09/22/833/.

19. Charles Montgomery, *Happy City: Transforming Our Lives through Urban Design* (New York: Farrar, Straus and Giroux, 2013), 283. Sonia Hirt, *Zoned in the U.S.A.: The Origins and Implications of American Land-Use Regulation* (Ithaca, NY: Cornell University Press, 2015), 3–5.

20. Kevin C. Murphy, "Uphill All the Way: The Fortunes of Progressivism, 1920–1929," February 2013, http://www.kevincmurphy.com/uatw-1924-schism.html. "No Way Out: Two New York City Firemen Testify about the 1911 Shirtwaist Fire," *History Matters*, http://historymatters.gmu.edu/d/57/.

21. Robert R. Weyeneth, "Ancestral Architecture: The Early Preservation Movement in Charleston," in *Giving Preservation a History: Histories of Historic Preservation*, ed. Max Page and Randall Mason (New York: Routledge, 2004), 257–78.

22. Ibid.

23. Partnership for Building Reuse, "Learning from Los Angeles," 24.

24. Hirt, *Zoned in the U.S.A.*, 5–8.

25. Speck, *Walkable City*, 106.

26. Ibid., 24, 32–34. "Building on Baltimore's History," 79–80. Preservation Green Lab, *Older, Smaller, Better*, 93–94.

27. Partnership for Building Reuse, "Learning from Los Angeles," 24, 32–34. "Building on Baltimore's History," 49.

28. Partnership for Building Reuse, "Building on Baltimore's History," 49–50, 79–80. Natalie Sherman, "Groups Pressure City Council on New Zoning Code," *Baltimore Sun*, August 21, 2015, http://www.baltimoresun.com/business/bs-bz-baltimore-zoning-20150820-story.html.

29. California Office of Historic Preservation, "State Historic Building Code," http://ohp.parks.ca.gov/?page_id=21410.

30. Preservation Green Lab, *Older, Smaller, Better*, 92–94. Montgomery, *Happy City*, 283. Chicago Metropolitan Agency for Planning, "Form-Based Codes: A Step-by-Step Guide for Communities," November 2013, http://formbasedcodes.org/content/uploads/2013/11/CMAP-GuideforCommunities.pdf.

31. US Government Accountability Office, "Key Issues—Food Safety," http://www.gao.gov/key_issues/food_safety/issue_summary.

32. Partnership for Building Reuse, "Learning from Los Angeles," 24, 32–34. Partnership for Building Reuse, "Retrofitting Philadelphia," September 2014, http://forum.savingplaces.org/connect/community-home/library

documents/viewdocument?DocumentKey=981d6c61-aefb-4a18-a34b
-c6098a82b178.

33. Jane Jacobs, *The Death and Life of Great American Cities* (New York: Vintage Books, 1961), 190. Preservation Green Lab, *Older, Smaller, Better*, 93–94.

34. Rebecca Lubens and Julia Miller, "Protecting Older Neighborhoods through Conservation District Programs," *Preservation Law Reporter*, January–March 2002/2003, http://forum.savingplaces.org/connect/community-home/librarydocuments/viewdocument?DocumentKey=fb1 88e94-8dba-4717-9476-c62cf17c4314. Preservation Green Lab, *Older, Smaller, Better*, 92–94. Jay Walljasper, "9 Lessons We Can Learn from Seattle," *Minneapolis Post*, June 5, 2014, https://www.minnpost.com/politics -policy/2014/06/9-lessons-we-can-learn-seattle. City of Dallas, "Current Planning: Conservation Districts," http://dallascityhall.com/depart ments/sustainabledevelopment/planning/Pages/Conservation-Districts .aspx.

35. Preservation Green Lab, *Older, Smaller, Better*, 92–94.

36. Brand, *How Buildings Learn*, 17–20.

37. Ibid., 57–61.

38. Speck, *Walkable City*, 141. Murphy, "Uphill All the Way," http://www .kevincmurphy.com/uatw-culture-distracted.html. Max Fisher, "It's Official: Western Europeans Have More Cars Per Person Than Americans," *Atlantic*, August 14, 2012, http://www.theatlantic.com/international /archive/2012/08/its-official-western-europeans-have-more-cars-per-per son-than-americans/261108/.

39. Emily Badger, "The Myth of the American Love Affair with Cars," *Washington Post*, January 27, 2015, https://www.washingtonpost.com/news /wonk/wp/2015/01/27/debunking-the-myth-of-the-american-love -affair-with-cars/. Montgomery, *Happy City*, 186.

40. Speck, *Walkable City*, 78, 141. Badger, "The Myth of the American Love Affair with Cars." James Howard Kunstler, *The Geography of Nowhere: The Rise and Decline of America's Man-Made Landscape* (New York: Touchstone, 1993), 87–92.

41. Kunstler, *Geography of Nowhere*, 86. Badger, "The Myth of the American Love Affair with Cars." Murphy, "Uphill All the Way". Speck, *Walkable City*, 142.

42. Speck, *Walkable City*, 90–91. Jane Jacobs, *Dark Age Ahead* (New York: First Vintage Books, 2004), 74–76.

43. Kunstler, *Geography of Nowhere*, 99–100. Robert Caro, *The Power Broker: Robert Moses and the Fall of New York* (New York: Vintage, 1974), 903–4.

44. Anthony Flint, *Wrestling with Moses: How Jane Jacobs Took on New York's Master Builder and Transformed the American City* (New York: Random House, 2009), 191–92. Caro, *The Power Broker*, 834, 903–4, 916–17. Kunstler, *Geography of Nowhere*, 100.

45. Speck, *Walkable City*, 80–82.

46. Ibid., 80, 89, 97.

47. Ibid., 91–92. Angie Schmitt, "Wider Lanes Make City Streets More Dangerous," *Greater Greater Washington*, May 29, 2015, http://greater greaterwashington.org/post/26921/wider-lanes-make-city-streets-more -dangerous/. Jeff Speck, "Why 12-Foot Lanes Are Disastrous for Safety and Must Be Replaced Now," *CityLab*, October 6, 2014, http://www .citylab.com/design/2014/10/why-12-foot-traffic-lanes-are-disastrous -for-safety-and-must-be-replaced-now/381117/.

48. Gehl, *Life between Buildings*, 34–37. Montgomery, *Happy City*, 168–70.

49. Peter Simek, "What Other Cities Learned," *D Magazine*, May 2014, http://www.dmagazine.com/publications/d-magazine/2014/may/what -other-cities-learned-tearing-down-highways. Speck, *Walkable City*, 94–95.

50. Simek, "What Other Cities Learned."

51. C. J. Hughes, "A Plan in New Haven to Right a Highway's Wrong," *New York Times*, July 18, 2012, http://www.nytimes.com/2012/07/18 /realestate/commercial/a-plan-in-new-haven-to-right-a-highways-wrong .html. Rachel Sadon, "Five Things to Know about the Capitol Crossing Project," *DCist*, May 12, 2015, http://dcist.com/2015/05/x_things_to _know_about_capitol_cros.php. Bridget Bowman, "D.C. Officials Break Ground on Capitol Crossing," *Roll Call*, May 12, 2015, http://www.roll call.com/hill-blotter/d-c-officials-break-ground-on-capitol-crossing/.

52. Justine Hofherr, "Can We Talk Rationally about the Big Dig Yet?," *Boston Globe*, January 5, 2015, http://www.boston.com/cars/news-and -reviews/2015/01/05/can-talk-rationally-about-the-big-dig-yet /0BPodDnlbNtsTEPFFc4i1O/story.html.

53. David Roberts, "Seattle's Unbelievable Transportation Megaproject Fus- tercluck," *Grist*, June 5, 2015, http://grist.org/cities/seattles-unbelievable- transportation-megaproject-fustercluck/. Speck, *Walkable City*, 95–96. David Z. Morris, "Seattle's Massive(ly Troubled) Tunnel Drill Is About

to Restart," *Fortune*, December 3, 2015, http://fortune.com/2015/12/03/seattle-tunnel-drill-restarting/.

54. David Dunlap, "No Vehicles—But Plenty of People on Broadway," *New York Times*, May 24, 2009, http://www.nytimes.com/2009/05/25/nyregion/25bway.html. Laura Stampler, "This Map Shows the Most Popular Attractions in Every State," *Time*, March 28, 2014, http://time.com/42038/map-popular-attractions-united-states/. Montgomery, *Happy City*, 223–24. Jan Gehl, Jeff Risom, and Julia Day, "Times Square: The Naked Truth," *New York Times*, August 31, 2015, http://www.nytimes.com/2015/08/31/opinion/times-square-the-naked-truth.html.

55. Smart Growth America National Complete Streets Coalition, "Fundamentals," http://www.smartgrowthamerica.org/complete-streets/complete-streets-fundamentals. Barbara McCann, *Completing Our Streets: The Transition to Safe and Inclusive Transportation* (Washington, DC: Island Press, 2013), 9.

56. Speck, *Walkable City*, 98–99. Jenn Stanley, "Closing Streets to Cars for Walkers and Bicyclists Is Getting More Popular by the Minute," *Next City*, June 19, 2015, https://nextcity.org/daily/entry/san-jose-street-event-new-york-central-park-closed-to-cars.

57. Partnership for Building Reuse, "Retrofitting Philadelphia," 18.

58. Richard Willson, *Parking Reform Made Easy* (Washington, DC: Island Press, 2013), 2. Speck, *Walkable City*, 116–17. Michael Kimmelman, "Paved but Still Alive," *New York Times*, January 8, 2012, http://www.nytimes.com/2012/01/08/arts/design/taking-parking-lots-seriously-as-public-spaces.html.

59. Speck, *Walkable City*, 118–20, 129. Willson, *Parking Reform Made Easy*, 2.

60. Speck, *Walkable City*, 118–20, 129.

61. Willson, *Parking Reform Made Easy*, xvii.

62. Speck, *Walkable City*, 122–23. Brian Meyer, "Plenty of Space to Park: Lobbying Group Blames Planning for Excessive Lots," *Buffalo News*, July 21, 2013, https://www.highbeam.com/doc/1P2-22574066.html. Kimmelman, "Paved but Still Alive."

63. Speck, *Walkable City*, 124, 121. Kimmelman, "Paved but Still Alive."

64. Willson, *Parking Reform Made Easy*, xviii.

65. Partnership for Building Reuse, "Building on Baltimore's History," 49–50. Montgomery, *Happy City*, 170.

66. Gehl, *Life between Buildings*, 31–33. Montgomery, *Happy City*, 161.
67. Montgomery, *Happy City*, 161.
68. Ibid., 162–63.
69. Speck, *Walkable City*, 37–39.
70. Montgomery, *Happy City*, 7. Speck, *Walkable City*, 142–43.
71. Montgomery, *Happy City*, 262–63. Joseph Minicozzi, "The Smart Math of Mixed-Use Development," *Planetizen*, January 23, 2012, http://www .planetizen.com/node/53922.
72. Montgomery, *Happy City*, 262–63. Minicozzi, "The Smart Math."
73. Montgomery, *Happy City*, 262–63. Minicozzi, "The Smart Math."
74. Minicozzi, "The Smart Math."
75. Main Street America, "National Main Street Center," http://www.preser vationnation.org/main-street/.
76. Main Street America, "History of the National Main Street Center," http://www.preservationnation.org/main-street/about-main-street/the -center/history.html.
77. Ibid.
78. Ibid.
79. Ibid.
80. Ibid.
81. Main Street America, "National Main Street Center."
82. Main Street America, "The Main Street Approach," http://www.pres ervationnation.org/main-street/about-main-street/main-street-america /the-main-street-approach.html.
83. Ibid.
84. Main Street America, "Manassas, Virginia," http://www.preservationna tion.org/main-street/awards/gamsa/2003/manassas-virginia.html.
85. Main Street America, "Frederick, Maryland," http://www.preservation nation.org/main-street/awards/gamsa/2005/frederick-maryland.html.
86. Ibid.
87. Ibid.
88. Main Street America, "Rawlins DDA/Main Street, Wyoming," http:// www.preservationnation.org/main-street/awards/gamsa/2015/rawlins .html. "Rawlins Chosen as Semi-Finalist for National Main Street Award," *County10*, October 18, 2014, http://archive.county10.com/2014/10/18 /rawlins-chosen-semifinalist-national-main-street-award/.
89. Main Street America, "Rawlins DDA." "Rawlins Chosen as Semi-Finalist."

90. Main Street America, "Rawlins DDA." "Rawlins Chosen as Semi-Finalist."
91. Place Economics and the National Trust for Historic Preservation, "The Federal Historic Tax Credit: Transforming Communities," June 2014, 3–6.
92. Ibid.
93. Ibid.
94. Ibid.
95. Ibid.
96. Ibid. Stephanie Meeks, "Urban CPR: Community, Preservation, Resurgence," Detroit Economic Club, May 19, 2014, https://savingplaces.org/press-center/media-resources/urban-cpr-community-preservation-resurgence
97. Stephanie Meeks, "Older Buildings, Livable Cities," Grain Exchange, Milwaukee, Wisconsin, March 19, 2015, http://forum.savingplaces.org/blogs/forum-online/2015/03/20/meeks-older-buildings-livable-cities
98. Ibid. Meeks, "Urban CPR." Partnership for Building Reuse, "Building on Baltimore's History," 14.
99. "National Trust Community Investment Corporation," http://ntcic.webfactional.com/.
100. Meeks, "Urban CPR." National Trust for Historic Preservation, "Protect Historic Tax Credits," http://www.preservationnation.org/take-action/advocacy-center/policy-resources/historic-tax-credits.html.
101. Meeks, "Urban CPR."
102. Partnership for Building Reuse, "Building on Baltimore's History," 14, 61.
103. Ibid. Partnership for Building Reuse, "Retrofitting Philadelphia," 10–11, 23. City of Philadelphia Office of Property Assessment, "Homestead Exemption," http://www.phila.gov/OPA/AbatementsExemptions/Pages/Homestead.aspx.
104. Partnership for Building Reuse, "Building on Baltimore's History," 61. City of Phoenix, "Historic Preservation Incentive Programs," https://www.phoenix.gov/pdd/historic/historicincentives. City of Boulder, "Incentives for Historic Preservation," https://bouldercolorado.gov/historic-preservation/incentives-for-historic-preservation.
105. Jonathan D. Epstein, "Renovation Projects Bring Back Character of Buffalo's Historic Buildings," *Buffalo News*, April 19, 2014, http://www.buffalonews.com/city-region/development/renovation-projects-bring-back-character-of-buffalos-historic-buildings-20140419.
106. Partnership for Building Reuse, "Building on Baltimore's History," 61.

Evan Thompson, "What Is So Magical about the Abandoned Buildings Revitalization Act?," *Charleston City Paper*, January 29, 2014, http://www.charlestoncitypaper.com/charleston/what-is-so-magical-about-the-abandoned-building-revitalization-act/Content?oid=4853196.

107. South Carolina Association for Community and Economic Development, "South Carolina Community Development Tax Credit," http://www.communitydevelopmentsc.org/CD-Tax-Credits.html. Massachusetts Office of Housing and Economic Development, "Community Investment Tax Credit Program (CITC)," http://www.mass.gov/hed/community/funding/community-investment-tax-credit-program.html. Indiana Economic Development Corporation, "Community Revitalization Enhancement District Tax Credit," http://iedc.in.gov/assets/files/Docs/2015%20downloads/CReEd_01-15.pdf. New Jersey Department of Community Affairs, "Neighborhood Revitalization Tax Credit Program," http://www.state.nj.us/dca/divisions/dhcr/offices/nrtc.html. Melissa Jest, "Community Development Corporations Embrace Historic Rehabs," *Preservation Forum Journal* 29, no. 1 (Fall 2014): 31–39.

108. ReNewSA, http://www.renewsa.com/About.aspx. City of San Antonio, "Funding Sources," http://www.sanantonio.gov/GMA/About/Funding-Source.aspx. Preservation Green Lab, *Older, Smaller, Better*, 92–94.

109. J. Myrick Howard, *Buying Time for Heritage: How to Save an Endangered Historic Property* (Chapel Hill: University of North Carolina Press, 2007). National Trust for Historic Preservation, "The Importance of Preservation Revolving Funds," http://forum.savingplaces.org/connect/community-home/librarydocuments/viewdocument?DocumentKey=77c915a8-a6b5-4966-94d0-2254721e29af

110. Winslow Hastie and April Wood, "The Evolving Revolving Fund: Historic Charleston Foundation Revamps Its Pioneering Program," *Preservation Forum Journal* 29, no. 1 (Fall 2014): 10–12.

111. Ibid. Howard, *Buying Time for Heritage*. "SCAD Measures Revolving Fund Impacts," *Preservation Forum Journal* 29, no. 1 (Fall 2014): 40–41, http://forum.savingplaces.org/HigherLogic/System/DownloadDocumentFile.ashx?DocumentFileKey=a80aa93f-9424-4d79-65f3-dd7ed6efe032

112. Stephanie Meeks, "Step Forward Boldly and Bring the Past Forward," Savannah, Georgia, November 12, 2014, http://blog.preservationleadershipforum.org/2014/11/12/2014-pastforward-stephanie-meeks-keynote-address/. Nicole Motter, "Why Program-Related Investments Are

Not Risky Business," *Forbes*, February 21, 2013, http://forum.saving
places.org/blogs/forum-online/2014/11/12/step-forward-boldly-and
-bring-the-past-forward

113. Meeks, "Step Forward Boldly." Ethiel Garlington, "Program-Related
Investments: 'Groan' for Preservation," November 24, 2014, http://
forum.savingplaces.org/blogs/forum-online/2014/11/24/program
-related-investments-groan-for-preservation.

114. Meeks, "Step Forward Boldly." Garlington, "Program-Related Investments."

115. Meeks, "Step Forward Boldly." Garlington, "Program-Related Investments."

116. Meeks, "Step Forward Boldly." Garlington, "Program-Related Investments."

117. Meeks, "Step Forward Boldly." Garlington, "Program-Related Investments."

118. Meeks, "Step Forward Boldly." Garlington, "Program-Related Investments."

119. City of San Antonio, "About the Vacant Building Registration Pilot Program," http://www.sanantonio.gov/VacantBuilding/About.aspx. Preservation Green Lab, "The Greenest Building: Quantifying the Environmental Value of Building Reuse," January 2012, http://www.preserva
tionnation.org/information-center/sustainable-communities/green-lab
/lca/The_Greenest_Building_lowres.pdf.

120. Tom Mayes, "Changing the Paradigm from Demolition to Reuse—Building Reuse Ordinances," in *Bending the Future: Fifty Ideas for the Next Fifty Years of Preservation*, ed. Max Page and Marla Miller (Amherst: University of Massachusetts Press, 2016).

121. Isaac Kremer, "How Tactical Urbanism Can Help Build a #BetterMain Street," *Main Street Story of the Week*, August 7, 2014, http://www.pre
servationnation.org/main-street/main-street-news/story-of-the-week
/2014-/how-tactical-urbanism-can.html.

122. Ibid. Nate Berg, "The Official Guide to Tactical Urbanism," *CityLab*, March 3, 2012, http://www.citylab.com/design/2012/03/guide-tactical
-urbanism/1387/.

123. Berg, "The Official Guide."

124. Laura Mills Simpson, "Pop-Up Art," *Main Street Story of the Week*, October 2, 2015, http://www.preservationnation.org/main-street/main-street
-news/story-of-the-week/2015/pop-up-art-tour.html.

125. David Weible, "7 Tips for Creating a Preservation Pop-Up Shop," *Preservation Nation*, https://savingplaces.org/stories/preservation-tips-tools
-7-tips-creating-preservation-pop-shop. Marisa Holden, "Friday Find: 'Pop-Up' Preservation!" Nantucket Preservation Trust, October 24, 2014,

https://www.nantucketpreservation.org/friday-find-pop-up-preservation
-3598. Kremer, "How Tactical Urbanism Can Help Build a #BetterMain
Street."

126. Stephanie Meeks, "Older Buildings, Livable Cities—Denver," Economic
Club of Colorado, October 27, 2015. Blair Shiff, "Denver Is One of the
Fastest Growing Economies in the U.S.," KUSA, September 29, 2015,
http://www.9news.com/story/money/2015/09/29/fast-growing-large
-cities/73019934/. Ana Campoy and Dan Frosch, "Denver Job Market
Lures Millennials," *Wall Street Journal*, July 23, 2015, http://www.wsj
.com/articles/denver-job-market-lures-millennials-1437698907. Adazeh
Ansari, "The Fittest Cities in the U.S., and Why," *CNN*, May 19, 2015,
http://www.cnn.com/2015/05/19/health/fit-city/.

127. Judy Mattivi Morley, "Making History: Historic Preservation and Civic
Identity in Denver," in *Giving Preservation a History: Histories of Historic
Preservation*, ed. Max Page and Randall Mason (New York: Routledge,
2004), 284.

128. Ibid., 283–85. Marik Jaffe, "Denver's Union Station a 30-Year Barn-
Raising," *Denver Post*, July 15, 2014, http://www.telegram.com/article
/20140715/NEWS/307159745.

129. Morley, "Making History," 283–87. Jaffe, "Denver's Union Station."

130. Morley, "Making History," 283–87. Jaffe, "Denver's Union Station."

131. Morley, "Making History," 288–93.

132. Ibid., 294–98. Jaffe, "Denver's Union Station."

133. Morley, "Making History," 294–98. Meeks, "Older Buildings, Livable
Cities—Denver." Denver Public Library, "LoDo: Denver's Lower Downtown Success Story," https://history.denverlibrary.org/lodo-denvers-lower
-downtown-success-story.

134. Meeks, "Older Buildings, Livable Cities—Denver." Jaffe, "Denver's Union
Station."

135. Jaffe, "Denver's Union Station." Meeks, "Older Buildings, Livable Cities—Denver." Morley, "Making History," 297–98.

136. Meeks, "Older Buildings, Livable Cities—Denver."

137. Ibid.

138. Kaid Benfield, "A Closer Look at a Smart Growth Icon: Denver's Highlands' Garden Village," *NRDC Switchboard*, July 20, 2010, https://web
.archive.org/web/20150723022413/http://switchboard.nrdc.org/blogs
/kbenfield/a_close_look_at_a_smart_growth.html. Jonathan Rose Com-

panies, "Highlands' Garden Village Mixed-Use and Mixed-Income Community," http://www.rosecompanies.com/all-projects/highlands-garden-village-mixed-use-and-mixed-income-community.

139. Jaffe, "Denver's Union Station." Jay Walljasper, "6½ Lessons the Twin Cities Can Learn from Denver," *Minneapolis Post*, June 4, 2014, https://www.minnpost.com/politics-policy/2014/06/6-lessons-twin-cities-can-learn-denver.

140. Walljasper, "6½ Lessons."

141. History Colorado, "State Historical Fund," http://www.historycolorado.org/oahp/state-historical-fund. John Murray, "Denver's $500 'Mini-Bonds' Sell Out in First Hour, Raising $12 Million," *Denver Post*, August 4, 2014, http://www.denverpost.com/news/ci_26272746/denvers-500-mini-bonds-sell-out-first-hour.

142. History Colorado, "Preservation Tax Credits," http://www.historycolorado.org/oahp/preservation-tax-credits.

143. Morley, "Making History," 305.

Chapter 4

1. Jane Jacobs, "Downtown Is for People," *Fortune*, 1958; reprinted by Nin-Hai Tseng, *Fortune Magazine*, September 18, 2011, http://fortune.com/2011/09/18/downtown-is-for-people-fortune-classic-1958/.

2. Jane Jacobs, *The Death and Life of Great American Cities* (New York: Vintage Books, 1961), 194–95.

3. Stewart Brand, *How Buildings Learn: What Happens after They're Built* (New York: Penguin, 1994), 104–5.

4. Special Committee on Historic Preservation, *With Heritage So Rich* (New York: Random House, 1966), 17. Renee Brincks, "How San Francisco's Ferry Building Became a Can't Miss Attraction," *Where Traveler*, August 19, 2015, http://www.wheretraveler.com/san-francisco/how-san-franciscos-ferry-building-became-cant-miss-attraction.

5. Mount Vernon, "Ann Pamela Cunningham," http://www.mountvernon.org/research-collections/digital-encyclopedia/article/ann-pamela-cunningham/. Richard Moe, "Are There Too Many House Museums?," *Preservation Forum Journal* 27, no. 1 (Fall 2012): 55–61.

6. Mount Vernon, "Ann Pamela Cunningham."

7. Ibid.

8. Stephanie Meeks, "House Museums: A 20th Century Paradigm," National

Preservation Conference, Indianapolis, Indiana, October 30, 2013, https://savingplaces.org/press-center/media-resources/house-museums -a-20th-century-paradigm. Ruth Graham, "The Great Historic House Museum Debate," August 9, 2014, https://www.bostonglobe.com/ ideas/2014/08/09/the-great-historic-house-museum-debate/jzFwE9tvJd HDCXehIWqK4O/story.html.

9. Meeks, "House Museums."

10. Ibid.

11. Ibid.

12. Ibid.

13. Donna Ann Harris, *New Solutions for House Museums* (Lanham, MD: Altamira Press, 2007), 4.

14. Ibid.

15. Meeks, "House Museums." "Robert E. Lee's Childhood Home Is Sold," *New York Times*, March 12, 2000, http://www.nytimes.com/2000/03/12 /us/robert-e-lee-s-childhood-home-is-sold.html. Sarah Lauren Wade, "The Privatization of American House Museums: Three Case Studies," University of Pennsylvania, January 1, 2008, http://repository.upenn .edu/cgi/viewcontent.cgi?article=1117&context=hp_theses.

16. Susan Svrluga, "Colonial Williamsburg Sells Carter's Grove Planta- tion after Bankruptcy," *Washington Post*, September 19, 2014, https:// www.washingtonpost.com/local/colonial-williamsburg-sells-carters -grove-plantation-after-bankruptcy/2014/09/19/ebe79418-403b-11e4 -b0ea-8141703bbf6f_story.html. Historic New England, "History of the Preservation Easement Program," http://www.historicnewengland .org/preservation/preservation-easements/history-of-the-stewardship -program. Rob Bear, "Louis Kahn's Fisher House on the Market for the First Time," *Curbed*, July 10, 2012, http://www.curbed.com/2012/7/10 /10353670/louis-kahns-fisher-house-now-on-the-market-for-first-time.

17. Graham, "Great Historic House Museum Debate."

18. Jose Mateo Ballet Theatre, "Sanctuary Theatre," http://www.ballettheatre .org/sanctuary-theatre/. "KC Ballet's New Home, a Former Electric Plant, Has a Power All Its Own," *Kansas City Star*, August 20, 2011, http://www .kansascity.com/entertainment/article299225/KC-Ballet%E2%80%99s -new-home-a-former-electric-plant-has-a-power-all-its-own.html. "Power Ballad: A Kansas City Energy Plant Is Converted into a Stunning

Performance Hall," April 18, 2014, http://architizer.com/blog/kansas -city-ballet/.

19. Park Avenue Armory, "Park Avenue Armory Drill Hall and Interiors Guide," http://www.armoryonpark.org/downloads/ArmoryInteriorsGuide.pdf.

20. Ibid.

21. David Dunlap, "A Landmark Restored, from Mosaic Marble Floor to Grand Dome," *New York Times*, March 13, 2014, http://www.nytimes .com/2014/03/13/nyregion/a-landmark-restored-from-mosaic-marble -floor-to-grand-dome.html. National Trust for Historic Preservation, "Williamsburgh Savings Bank," http://www.preservationnation.org /resources/training/awards/2014-national-presrvation-awards/William sburgh-Savings-Bank.html. NY Landmarks Conservancy, "The 24th Lucy G. Moses Preservation Awards," May 6, 2014, http://www.nyland marks.org/events/moses_awards/the_24th_lucy_g._moses_preservation _awards/. Jeremiah Budin, "Inside the Painstaking Williamsburgh Savings Bank Restoration," September 19, 2013, *Curbed*, http://ny.curbed .com/archives/2013/09/19/inside_the_painstaking_williamsburgh_sav ings_bank_restoration.php.

22. Weylin B. Seymours, http://www.weylinbseymours.com/accolades/.

23. Christopher Gray, "When Banks Looked Like a Million Bucks," *New York Times*, June 13, 2010, http://www.nytimes.com/2010/06/13/realestate /13scapes.html. Skylight One Hanson, http://skylightnyc.com/onehan son/about-onehanson.html.

24. Kings Theatre, "History behind Kings Theatre," http://www.kingsthe atre.com/info/history. Nathaniel Adams, "Across the New York Area, Restoring 'Wonder Theater' Movie Palaces to Glory," *New York Times*, January 15, 2015, http://www.nytimes.com/2015/01/18/nyregion/across-the-new -york-area-restoring-wonder-theater-movie-palaces-to-glory.html.

25. Fox Oakland Theater, "History of the Fox Oakland Theater," http:// www.thefoxoakland.com/history.html. National Park Service, "Fox Theater—Atlanta," http://www.nps.gov/nr/travel/atlanta/fox.htm. Historic Detroit, "Fox Theatre," http://www.historicdetroit.org/building/fox-the atre/.

26. Howard Theater, "History," http://thehowardtheatre.com/history/. Howard Theatre, "Historic Howard Theatre Opens April 9th," http://www .howardtheatre.org/Press_Releases/HowardTheatreOpensApril9.pdf.

Danielle Douglas, "Ground Broken on Restoration of Historic Howard Theatre," *Washington Post*, September 6, 2010, http://www.washingtonpost.com/wp-dyn/content/article/2010/09/03/AR2010090305370.html.

27. Adams, "Across the New York Area."

28. Jose Mateo Ballet Theatre, "Sanctuary Theatre."

29. David Weible, "Learning by Design: Baltimore Design School," April 1, 2014, *Preservation*, https://savingplaces.org/stories/learning-by-design-baltimore-design-school. Marianne Amoss, "How Architects Transformed This Former Set from 'The Wire' into a Training Ground for Tomorrow," *FastCo Design*, November 21, 2013, http://www.fastcodesign.com/3021481/how-architects-transformed-this-former-set-from-the-wire-into-a-training-ground-for-tomorrow.

30. Weible, "Learning by Design." Amoss, "How Architects Transformed." Baltimore Design School, "Our History," http://baltimoredesignschool.com/?page_id=225.

31. Mapos LLC, "The Lessons of Savannah," May 25, 2010, http://studiomapos.com/spamos/the-lessons-of-savanah/. Julia Ritchey, "Savannah Tourism Industry Shows Gains, 13 Million Visitors in 2013," *Savannah Morning News*, June 13, 2014, http://savannahnow.com/exchange/2014-06-13/savannah-tourism-industry-shows-gains-13-million-visitors-2013.

32. Adam Bluestein, "Paula Wallace Is the Reason These Art-Kids Mean Business," *Fast Company*, May 24, 2012, http://www.fastcompany.com/1838339/paula-wallace-reason-these-art-kids-today-mean-business.

33. Savannah College of Art and Design, "The History of SCAD's Buildings," *Foursquare*, May 6, 2012, https://foursquare.com/p/scad/4428248/list/the-history-of-scads-buildings. SCAD Museum of Art, "About the Museum," http://www.scadmoa.org/about/about-museum. "SCAD Receives Award for Sustainability and Reuse of Historic Properties," *Editor at Large*, October 24, 2009, http://www.editoratlarge.com/articles/scad-receives-award-for-sustainability-and-reuse-of-historic-properties.

34. "SCAD Receives Award for Sustainability." Susan S. Szenazy, "Q&A: SCAD President Paula Wallace," *Metropolis*, February 26, 2015, http://www.metropolismag.com/Point-of-View/February-2015/Q-A-SCAD-President-Paula-Wallace/. "The Empire SCAD Built," *Savannah Morning News*, May 5, 2005, http://savannahnow.com/stories/050505/3009744.shtml.

35. McMenamins, "Kennedy School," http://www.mcmenamins.com/Ken
nedySchool. Artspace, "El Barrio's Artspace PS109: An Artspace Project for East Harlem," http://www.artspace.org/our-places/el-barrio-s-art
space-ps109.

36. Cassie Keener, "Churches Turned Restaurants: The Answer to Your Historic Dining Prayers," *Preservation Nation*, September 9, 2014, https://
savingplaces.org/stories/churches-turned-restaurants-answer-historic
-dining-prayers. Freemason Abbey, http://www.freemasonabbey.com/.
National Trust for Historic Preservation, "Reusing Historic Religious Properties," http://www.preservationnation.org/information-center/saving
-a-place/historic-houses-of-worship/additional-resources/worship_reus
ing_summary.pdf. Christopher Mote, "How to Reuse a Church: Our Top
Ten," *Hidden City*, June 21, 2013, http://hiddencityphila.org/2013/05
/how-to-reuse-a-church-our-top-ten/. Daniel Nairn, "Planning for Adaptive Post Office Re-Use," *Discovering Urbanism*, May 19, 2010, http://
discoveringurbanism.blogspot.com/2010/05/planning-for-adaptive
-post-office-reuse.html. "The Old Post Office Restaurant," http://www
.theoldpostofficerestaurant.com/.

37. Ron Dewey, "Iconic Michigan Bell Building Re-Dedicated as Center
for Homeless," *CBS Detroit*, October 23, 2013, http://detroit.cbslocal
.com/2013/10/23/iconic-michigan-bell-building-rededicated-as-center
-for-homeless/. Neighborhood Service Organization, "NSO Bell Building," http://www.nso-mi.org/bell-building.php.

38. Jacques Kelly, "Changes a Long Time Brewing," *Baltimore Sun*, November
16, 2008, http://www.baltimoresun.com/news/maryland/baltimore-city
/bal-md.ci.brewery16nov16-story.html. Humanim, "American Brewery,"
http://www.humanim.com/social-enterprise/american-brewery. Andrew
Price, "A Rebuilt Baltimore Brewery Renews a Neighborhood," *Fast Company*, February 1, 2012, http://www.fastcoexist.com/1679234/a-rebuilt
-baltimore-brewery-renews-a-neighborhood.

39. Kelly, "Changes a Long Time Brewing." Price, "A Rebuilt Baltimore
Brewery."

40. Leigh Franke, "Harvest Commons Apartments Offers More Than Just
a Room of One's Own," *AIArchitect*, September 13, 2013, http://www
.aia.org/practicing/AIAB099982. Heartland Housing, "Case Study: The
Viceroy Hotel," http://www.heartlandhousing.org/case-studies/harvest
-commons%E2%80%94-fresh-start-viceroy-hotel.

41. Hayley Fox, "Historic Dunbar Hotel Set to Reopen as Part of $30 Million Apartment Complex," KPCC 89.3, June 24, 2013, http://www.scpr.org/blogs/southla/2013/06/24/14043/historic-dunbar-hotel-set-to-reopen-as-part-of-30/. James Brasuell, "Renovation of 1889 Boyle Hotel Set to Finish Up This Month," *Curbed*, May 3, 2012, http://la.curbed.com/archives/2012/05/renovation_of_1889_boyle_hotel_set_to_finish_up_this_month.php. East Bay Asian Local Development Corporation, "California Hotel," http://ebaldc.org/home/california-hotel-0. East Bay Asian Local Development Corporation, "San Pablo Hotel," http://ebaldc.org/home/san-pablo-hotel.

42. Meeks, "House Museums." Tammy Walquist, "Renovating Ottinger Hall: Historic S.L. Building Will House YouthCity After-School Programs," *Deseret News*, June 9, 2006, http://www.deseretnews.com/article/635212177/Renovating-Ottinger-Hall.html?pg=all.

43. Ferry Building Marketplace, "Visitor Information," http://www.ferrybuildingmarketplace.com/faq.php. Brincks, "How San Francisco's Ferry Building Became a Can't Miss Attraction."

44. Ferry Building Marketplace, "Visitor Information." Brincks, "San Francisco's Ferry Building."

45. Wayne Curtis, "Music City Marvel: Acme Feed and Seed's New Gig," *Preservation*, Fall 2015, https://savingplaces.org/stories/music-city-marvel-acme-feed-seed. Acme Feed and Seed, http://theacmenashville.com/.

46. Ibid.

47. Stephanie Meeks, "Older Buildings, Livable Cities," Grain Exchange, Milwaukee, Wisconsin, March 19, 2015, http://forum.savingplaces.org/blogs/forum-online/2015/03/20/meeks-older-buildings-livable-cities.

48. Ibid. Kaid Benfield, "A Spectacular Green Neighborhood Brewing in Milwaukee," *NRDC Switchboard*, September 22, 2011, https://web.archive.org/web/20150906232652/http://switchboard.nrdc.org/blogs/kbenfield/a_spectacular_green_neighborho.html. Tom Held, "Pabst to Brew Beer in Milwaukee Once Again," *Milwaukee Business-Journal*, July 15, 2015, http://www.bizjournals.com/milwaukee/news/2015/07/15/pabst-to-brew-beer-in-milwaukee-once-again.html.

49. David Weible, "Ponce City Market: Atlanta's History in the Making," *Preservation Nation*, November 29, 2013, https://savingplaces.org/stories/ponce-city-market-atlantas-history-making.

50. Ibid. David Weible and Blake Burton, "Photo Essay: Atlanta's Ponce City

Market," *Saving Places*, January 7, 2016, https://savingplaces.org/stories
/photo-essay-atlantas-ponce-city-market.

51. Weible, "Ponce City Market."

52. Meeks, "House Museums."

53. Ibid.

54. Ibid.

55. Ibid. Brucemore, http://www.brucemore.org/.

56. Meeks, "House Museums."

57. Stephanie Meeks, "The Future of Preservation," National Cathedral, Washington, DC, November 13, 2015, https://savingplaces.org/press -center/media-resources/pastforward-2015-keynote-speech

58. Richard Moe, *Forum News* 7, no. 2 (November/December 2000): 1. Rhonda Sincavage, "Building Communities through Historic Preservation," *Preservation Nation*, August 9, 2011, http://www.preservation nation.org/main-street/main-street-news/story-of-the-week/2011/11 0809/building-community-though.html.

59. Julia Christensen, "Big Box Reuse," http://www.bigboxreuse.com/. "Used to Be a Pizza Hut," http://usedtobeapizzahut.blogspot.com/.

60. Woodward, "Hibernia Tower," http://www.woodwarddesignbuild.com /projects/313-carondelet/.

61. Katharine Flynn, "New Orleans' Saenger Theater Weathers the Storm," *Preservation*, October 4, 2014, https://savingplaces.org/stories/new-or leans-saenger-theater-weathers-storm.

62. April Siese, "A Look Inside the Transformed Myrtle Banks Building," *Curbed*, November 11, 2014, http://nola.curbed.com/2014/11 /11/10024756/a-look-inside-the-completely-transformed-myrtle -banks-building. Richard Webster, "O. C. Haley Renaissance Continues with Future Opening of Jack & Jake's," *New Orleans Times-Picayune*, June 23, 2014, http://www.nola.com/business/index.ssf/2014/06/oc _haley_renaissance_continues.html.

63. Jaime Lerner, *Urban Acupuncture: Celebrating Pinpricks of Change That Enrich City Life* (Washington, DC: Island Press, 2014), 43.

Chapter 5

1. David McCullough, "45th National Preservation Conference," 1991, quoted in South Carolina State Historic Preservation Office, "Quotes," http://shpo.sc.gov/about/Documents/Quotes.pdf.

2. Tom Mayes, "Why Old Places Matter: Economics," April 16, 2015, http://forum.savingplaces.org/blogs/forum-online/2015/04/16/why-do-old-places-matter-economics .

3. Jaime Lerner, *Urban Acupuncture: Celebrating Pinpricks of Change That Enrich City Life* (Washington, DC: Island Press, 2014), 86. William Cronon, "Quotations," http://www.williamcronon.net/quotations.htm. Keith H. Basso, *Wisdom Sits in Places: Landscape and Language among the Western Apache* (Albuquerque: University of New Mexico Press, 1996), 105.

4. William H. Frey, "A Demographic Tipping Point among America's Three-Year-Olds," Brookings Institution, February 7, 2011, http://www.brookings.edu/research/opinions/2011/02/07-population-frey. Eric Kayne, "Census: White Majority Gone by 2043," *NBC News*, June 13, 2013, http://usnews.nbcnews.com/_news/2013/06/13/18934111-census-white-majority-in-us-gone-by-2043.

5. Tinner Hill Heritage Foundation, "Our History," http://tinnerhill.org/about/history. Beverly Bunch-Lyons and Nakeina Douglas, "The Falls Church Colored Citizens Protective League," in *Long Is the Way and Hard: One Hundred Years of the NAACP*, ed. Kevern Verney and Lee Sartain (Fayetteville: University of Arkansas Press, 2009), 92–95. Stephanie Meeks, "Visiting Tinner Hill: Local History, National Significance," *Preservation Nation*, February 25, 2015, https://savingplaces.org/stories/visiting-tinner-hill-local-history-national-significance/.

6. Tinner Hill Heritage Foundation, "Our History." Bunch-Lyons and Douglas, "The Falls Church Colored Citizens Protective League." Meeks, "Visiting Tinner Hill."

7. Tinner Hill Heritage Foundation, "Our History." Bunch-Lyons and Douglas, "The Falls Church Colored Citizens Protective League." Meeks, "Visiting Tinner Hill."

8. Jack Broom, "Seattle's Panama Hotel Deemed a National Treasure," *Seattle Times*, July 26, 2015, http://www.seattletimes.com/seattle-news/seattles-panama-hotel-deemed-a-national-treasure/. Kyle Jensen, "Seattle's Panama Hotel Is a National Treasure That Needs a New Owner," *Seattle Post-Intelligencer*, April 13, 2015, http://www.seattlepi.com/local/article/Seattle-s-Panama-Hotel-is-a-national-treasure-6197611.php. Historic Panama Hotel Bed and Breakfast, http://www.panamahotel.net/history.htm. National Park Service, "Panama Hotel," http://www.nps.gov/nr/travel/Asian_American_and_Pacific_Islander_Heritage/Panama-Hotel.htm.

9. Broom, "Seattle's Panama Hotel." Jensen, "Seattle's Panama Hotel." National Park Service, "Panama Hotel." Charles Wilson, "Heartbreak Hotel—Japanese Artifacts Left in a Seattle Basement Freeze a Moment in Time," *Preservation*, March/April 1999, http://www.preservationnation.org/magazine/1999/heartbreak-hotel.html.

10. Broom, "Seattle's Panama Hotel." Jensen, "Seattle's Panama Hotel." National Park Service, "Panama Hotel." Wilson, "Heartbreak Hotel."

11. Broom, "Seattle's Panama Hotel."

12. Andrew O'Reilly, "Hispanic Heritage Profile: Ken Salazar Fights for the American Landscape," *FOX News Latino*, October 7, 2013, http://latino.foxnews.com/latino/lifestyle/2013/10/07/hispanic-heritage-month-profile-ken-salazar-fights-for-american-landscape/. Ken Salazar, "America's Diversity—A History Worth Preserving," *Preservation Forum Journal* 28, no. 3 (Spring 2014), http://www.preservationnation.org/assets/pdfs/FJ_SPRING_14.pdf.

13. Stephanie Meeks, "A More Perfect Union: Toward a More Inclusive History, and a Preservation Movement That Looks Like America," King Center, Atlanta, Georgia, March 31, 2015, https://savingplaces.org/press-center/media-resources/a-more-perfect-union-towards-a-more-inclusive-history-and-a-preservation-movement-that-looks-like-america. Martin Luther King Jr., "Remaining Awake through a Great Revolution," National Cathedral, Washington, DC, March 31, 1968, http://kingencyclopedia.stanford.edu/encyclopedia/documentsentry/doc_remaining_awake_through_a_great_revolution.1.html.

14. Meeks, "A More Perfect Union." Martin Luther King Jr., *Where Do We Go from Here—Chaos or Community?* (Boston: Beacon Press, 2010).

15. Martin Luther King Jr., "I Have a Dream," Lincoln Memorial, Washington, DC, August 28, 1963, https://www.archives.gov/press/exhibits/dream-speech.pdf. Henry Louis Gates Jr., "Did MLK Improvise the 'I Have a Dream' Speech?," *Root*, August 26, 2013, http://www.theroot.com/articles/history/2013/08/100_amazing_facts_about_the_negro_what_led_to_it_and_how_some_famous_lines_nearly_didnt_happen.html. Stephanie Meeks and Marita Rivero, "How We Can Achieve a More Inclusive History," *Huffington Post*, January 16, 2015, http://www.huffingtonpost.com/national-trust-for-historic-preservation/how-we-can-achieve-a-more_b_6482008.html.

16. King, "I Have a Dream."

17. Ibid.

18. Gates, "Did MLK Improvise?"

19. Ibid.

20. Cesar Chavez, *Education of the Heart*, quoted at Cesar Chavez Foundation, "Speeches and Writings," http://www.chavezfoundation.org/_cms.php?mode=view&b_code=001008000000000&b_no=2197&page=1&field=&key=&n=1.

21. Christopher Beagan, "Freedom's Fortress," at National Park Service, "Stories: Social Injustice in the Landscape," http://www.nps.gov/cultural_landscapes/stories-FtMonroe.html.

22. Meeks, "A More Perfect Union." National Park Service, *Five Views: An Ethnic Historic Site Survey for California*, December 1988, http://www.nps.gov/parkhistory/online_books/5views/5views0.htm.

23. Ned Kaufman, *Race, Place, and Story: Essays on the Past and Future of Historic Preservation* (New York: Routledge, 2009), 225–26, 232.

24. Meeks, "A More Perfect Union." Stephanie Meeks, "Expanding Our Outlook," *Preservation*, November 1, 2014, https://savingplaces.org/stories/expanding-our-outlook/.

25. National Trust for Historic Preservation, "National Treasures," https://savingplaces.org/national-treasures.

26. Ibid.

27. Ibid.

28. Ibid.

29. National Trust for Historic Preservation, "Villa Lewaro," https://savingplaces.org/places/villa-lewaro-madam-c-j-walker-estate. Stephanie Meeks, "Walker, Whitman, and Other American Women Whose Stories Need Celebrating," *Preservation Nation*, March 19, 2015, https://savingplaces.org/stories/walker-whitney-american-women-stories-celebrating. Historic Hudson River Towns, "Estates of the Hudson Valley," http://www.hudsonriver.com/hudson-river-estates.

30. National Trust for Historic Preservation, "Villa Lewaro." Meeks, "Walker, Whitman." Historic Hudson River Towns, "Estates of the Hudson Valley."

31. Carolyn Brackett, "Whitney Studio: Haven and Legacy for Early 20th Century Art," *Preservation Nation*, October 8, 2014, https://savingplaces.org/stories/whitney-studio-haven-legacy-early-20th-century-american-art/. Meeks, "Walker, Whitman."

32. Brackett, "Whitney Studio." Meeks, "Walker, Whitman."

33. National Trust for Historic Preservation, "Pauli Murray House," https:// savingplaces.org/places/pauli-murray-house. Pauli Murray Project, "Biography," http://paulimurrayproject.org/pauli-murray/biography/.

34. National Trust for Historic Preservation, "Pauli Murray House." Pauli Murray Project, "Biography."

35. National Park Service, "American Latino Theme Study," http://www.nps .gov/history/heritageinitiatives/latino/latinothemestudy/.

36. United States House of Representatives, "Emancipation Hall: A Tribute to the U.S. Slaves Who Built the U.S. Capitol," September 25, 2007, https://www.gpo.gov/fdsys/pkg/CHRG-110hhrg38171/html/CHRG -110hhrg38171.htm. Architect of the Capitol, "History of the U.S. Capitol Building," http://www.aoc.gov/history-us-capitol-building. Architect of the Capitol, "Brumidi Corridors," http://www.aoc.gov/capitol-build ings/brumidi-corridors. Architect of the Capitol, "U.S. Capitol Visitor Center," http://www.aoc.gov/capitol-buildings/us-capitol-visitor-center. Vivien Green Fryd, "Lifting the Veil of Race at the U.S. Capitol," *Commonplace* 10, no. 4 (July 2010), http://www.common-place-archives.org /vol-10/no-04/fryd/.

37. Architect of the Capitol, "Martin Luther King Jr. Bust," http://www.aoc .gov/capitol-hill/busts/martin-luther-king-jr-bust. Kristi Keck, "Truth Comes to the U.S. Capitol," *CNN*, April 28, 2009, http://www.cnn .com/2009/POLITICS/04/28/sojourner.truth/. Jilian Fama, "Rosa Parks: First Statue of African-American Female to Grace Capitol," *ABC News*, February 27, 2013, http://abcnews.go.com/Politics/OTUS/rosa-parks -full-bodied-statue-african-american-depicted/story?id=18608892. Lucia Raatma, *Shirley Chisholm* (New York: Marshall Cavendish, 2011), 85. Ben Pershing, "Frederick Douglass Statue Unveiled in the Capitol," *Washington Post*, June 19, 2013, https://www.washingtonpost.com/local/dc -politics/frederick-douglass-statue-unveiled-in-the-capitol/2013/06/19 /a64916cc-d906-11e2-a9f2-42ee3912ae0e_story.html.

38. Brett Zongker, "Slave Quarters to Be Rebuilt at Madison's Va. Home," *USA Today*, November 2, 2014, http://www.usatoday.com/story/news /nation/2014/11/02/slave-quarters-montpelier/18366999/.

39. Ibid. Montpelier, "Paul Jennings," https://www.montpelier.org/research -and-collections/people/african-americans/montpelier-slaves/paul-jen nings. History of American Women, "The Pearl Incident," http://www .womenhistoryblog.com/2015/01/pearl-incident.html.

40. Zongker, "Slave Quarters to Be Rebuilt."

41. Associated Press, "Thomas Jefferson's Home Unveils Rebuilt Slave Quarters to Tell Fuller Tale of Past," May 2, 2015, http://www.theguardian.com/us-news/2015/may/02/thomas-jefferson-monticello-slaves-quarters. Faiza Elmasry, "Harsh Life of Washington's Slaves Revealed," *Voice of America*, November 29, 2010, http://www.voanews.com/content/harsh-life-of-washingtons-slaves-revisited-111032034/163434.html.

42. National Park Service, "How to Evaluate the Integrity of a Property," http://www.nps.gov/nr/publications/bulletins/nrb15/nrb15_8.htm #seven aspects. Stephanie Meeks, "Towards a More Perfect Union: Engaging a More Diverse Community in Preservation," Hampton University, Hampton, Virginia, October 10, 2014, https://savingplaces.org/press-center/media-resources/towards-a-more-perfect-union-engaging-a-more-diverse-community-in-preservation

43. Meeks, "Towards a More Perfect Union."

44. Michael Holleran, "Roots in Boston, Branches in Planning and Parks," in *Giving Preservation a History: Histories of Historic Preservation*, ed. Max Page and Randall Mason (New York: Routledge, 2004), 85.

45. National Trust for Historic Preservation, "La Laguna de San Gabriel," http://www.preservationnation.org/information-center/saving-a-place/modernism-recent-past/Case-Studies/la-laguna-de-san-gabriel.html. Alex Smith, "Monster Mash—Conservation Wins the Day in San Gabriel, California," *Playgroundology*, July 1, 2010, https://playgroundology.wordpress.com/2010/07/01/monster-mash-conservation-wins-the-day-in-san-gabriel-california/.

46. National Trust for Historic Preservation, "La Laguna de San Gabriel." Smith, "Monster Mash." Friends of La Laguna, "Benjamin Dominguez," http://www.friendsoflalaguna.org/about/artist.htm.

47. Friends of Miami Marine Stadium, http://www.marinestadium.org/. Lauren Walser, "If Seats Could Talk: Richard Nixon and Sammy Davis Jr. Share the Stage at Miami Marine Stadium," *Preservation Nation*, April 18, 2013, https://savingplaces.org/stories/if-seats-could-talk-richard-nixon-and-sammy-davis-jr-share-the-stage-at-miami-marine-stadium. Stephanie Meeks, "Step Forward Boldly and Bring the Past Forward," Savannah, Georgia, November 12, 2014, http://forum.savingplaces.org/blogs/forum-online/2014/11/12/step-forward-boldly-and-bring-the-past-forward

48. Meeks, "Step Forward Boldly."

49. Meeks, "Towards a More Perfect Union." Barack Obama, "Remarks by the President at the Designation of Three National Monuments," Chicago, Illinois, February 19, 2015, https://www.whitehouse.gov/the-press-office/2015/02/19/remarks-president-designation-three-new-national-monuments.

50. Obama, "Designation of Three National Monuments."

51. US Census Bureau, "2010 Census Shows America's Diversity," March 24, 2011, https://www.census.gov/newsroom/releases/archives/2010_census/cb11-cn125.html.

52. Tal Trachtman Alroy, "Stonewall Inn Granted Landmark Status by New York Landmarks Commission," *CNN*, June 23, 2015, http://www.cnn.com/2015/06/23/us/stonewall-inn-landmark-status/. David-Elijah Nahmod, "Tenderloin Pride: Remembering the Compton's Cafeteria Riot," *Hoodline*, June 26, 2015, http://hoodline.com/2015/06/tenderloin-pride-remembering-the-compton-s-cafeteria-riot. Nicole Pasulka, "Ladies in the Streets: Before Stonewall, Transgender Uprising Changed Lives," *NPR*, May 5, 2015, http://www.npr.org/sections/codeswitch/2015/05/05/404459634/ladies-in-the-streets-before-stonewall-transgender-uprising-changed-lives.

53. National Park Service, "Lesbian, Gay, Bisexual, Transgender, and Queer (LGBTQ) Heritage Initiative," http://www.nps.gov/history/heritageinitiatives/LGBThistory/.

54. National Trust for Historic Preservation, "HOPE Crew," https://savingplaces.org/hope-crew. Stephanie Meeks, "A Year of Hope," *Preservation Magazine*, Spring 2015, https://savingplaces.org/stories/presidents-note-year-hope.

55. Meeks, "A Year of Hope."

56. Ibid.

57. Ibid. Meeks, "Towards a More Perfect Union."

58. Meeks, "Towards a More Perfect Union." Max Page, "Sites of Conscience: Shockoe Bottom, Manzanar, and Mountain Meadows," *Preservation Magazine*, Fall 2015, https://savingplaces.org/stories/sites-of-conscience. Meeks and Rivero, "How We Can Achieve a More Inclusive History." Erica Stewart, "A Letter from Lupita: Why Shockoe Bottom Deserves—and Demands—Protection," *National Trust for Historic Preservation*, January 5, 2015, http://www.huffingtonpost.com/national-trust-for-historic-preservation/a-letter-from-lupita-why_b_6481896.html.

59. Stewart, "A Letter from Lupita."

60. James C. Cobb, "Confronting the Future of New Orleans' Confederate Past," *Time*, January 14, 2016, http://time.com/4179175/new-orleans-confederate-statues-2/.

61. Brent Staples, "Confederate Memorials as Instruments of Racial Terror," *New York Times*, July 25, 2015, http://www.nytimes.com/2015/07/25/opinion/confederate-memorials-as-instruments-of-racial-terror.html.

62. Drew Gilpin Faust, *This Republic of Suffering: Death and the American Civil War* (New York: Alfred A. Knopf, 2008), xi–xviii, http://www.nytimes.com/2008/01/27/books/chapters/1st-chapter-this-republic-of-suffering.html.

63. David Blight, *Race and Reunion: The Civil War in American Memory* (Cambridge: Harvard University Press, 2001).

64. James W. Loewen, "Why Do People Believe Myths about the Confederacy? Because Our Textbooks and Monuments Are Wrong," *Washington Post*, July 1, 2015, https://www.washingtonpost.com/posteverything/wp/2015/07/01/why-do-people-believe-myths-about-the-confederacy-because-our-textbooks-and-monuments-are-wrong/. Perry Stein, "Confederate Soldier Statue in Montgomery Spray-Painted with 'Black Lives Matter,'" *Washington Post*, July 27, 2015, https://www.washingtonpost.com/news/local/wp/2015/07/27/confederate-soldier-statue-in-montgomery-spray-painted-with-black-lives-matter/.

65. Ethan J. Kytle and Blain Roberts, "Take Down the Confederate Flags, but Not the Monuments," *Atlantic*, June 25, 2015, http://www.theatlantic.com/politics/archive/2015/06/-confederate-monuments-flags-south-carolina/396836/.

66. "Faithful Slaves Monument—Thanks but No Thanks," *All Other Persons*, February 3, 2010, https://allotherpersons.wordpress.com/2010/02/03/faithful-slaves-monument-thanks-but-no-thanks/. Greg Tasker, "Tribute to Victim of Brown's Raid Still Controversial," *Baltimore Sun*, September 3, 1995, http://articles.baltimoresun.com/1995-09-03/news/1995246078_1_brown-raid-monument-john-brown.

67. Lerner, *Urban Acupuncture*, 91.

68. Cobb, "Confronting the Future."

69. Doyle Rader, "Let's Turn Our Confederate Monuments into Collaborative Art Spaces," *Dallas Magazine*, August 3, 2015, http://frontrow.dmagazine.com/2015/08/lets-turn-our-confederate-monuments-into-collaborative-art-spaces/. Jill Ogline Titus, "Why Confederate Monu-

ments Are Different from the Flag," *Real Clear Politics*, July 6, 2015, http://www.realclearpolitics.com/articles/2015/07/06/why_confeder ate_monuments_differ_from_the_flag_127257.html.

70. Meeks, "Visiting Tinner Hill."

71. Ibid.

Chapter 6

1. Alan Ehrenhalt, *The Great Inversion and the Future of the American City* (New York: Knopf, 2012), 233. Tom Slater, "A Literal Necessity to Be Re-Placed: A Rejoinder to the Gentrification Debate," *International Journal of Urban and Regional Research* 32, no. 1 (March 2008): 212–23, http://www.geos.ed.ac.uk/homes/tslater/evictionrejoinder.pdf.

2. Michael Kimmelman, "The Climax in a Tale of Green and Gritty," *New York Times*, September 19, 2014, http://www.nytimes.com/2014/09/20/arts/design/the-high-line-opens-its-third-and-final-phase.html. Paul Goldberger, "Miracle Above Manhattan," *National Geographic*, April 2011, http://ngm.nationalgeographic.com/2011/04/ny-high-line/goldberger-text.

3. Goldberger, "Miracle Above Manhattan."

4. Ibid. Michael Bourne, "The High Line: New York's Monument to Gentri-fication," *Millions*, June 29, 2012, http://www.themillions.com/2012/06/the-high-line-new-yorks-monument-to-gentrification.html. Carl T. Hyden and Theodore F. Sheckels, *Public Places: Sites of Political Commu-nication* (New York: Rowman and Littlefield, 2016), 159–60.

5. Goldberger, "Miracle Above Manhattan." Bourne, "The High Line." Hyden and Sheckels, *Public Places*. Kimmelman, "The Climax in a Tale."

6. Eric Jaffe, "How Parks Gentrify Neighborhoods, and How to Stop It," *Fast Company*, October 15, 2014, http://www.fastcodesign.com/3037135/evi dence/how-parks-gentrify-neighborhoods-and-how-to-stop-it. Bourne, "The High Line." Jeremiah Moss, "Disney World on the Hudson," *New York Times*, August 22, 2012, http://www.nytimes.com/2012/08/22/opinion /in-the-shadows-of-the-high-line.html. Charles Montgomery, *Happy City: Transforming Our Lives through Urban Design* (New York: Farrar, Straus and Giroux, 2013), 245.

7. Jeremiah Moss, *Jeremiah's Vanishing New York*, http://vanishingnewyork .blogspot.com/.

8. Ibid. Max Page and Timothy Mennel, *Reconsidering Jane Jacobs* (Chicago:

American Planning Association, 2011), 3–5. Anthony Flint, *Wrestling with Moses: How Jane Jacobs Took on New York's Master Builder and Transformed the American City* (New York: Random House, 2009), 191. Tim Wu, "Why Are There So Many Shuttered Storefronts in the West Village?," *New Yorker*, May 24, 2015, http://www.newyorker.com/business/currency/why-are-there-so-many-shuttered-storefronts-in-the-west-village. Jane Jacobs, *The Death and Life of Great American Cities* (New York: Vintage Books, 1961), 282. Jeremiah Moss, "More Jane, Less Marc," *Jeremiah's Vanishing New York*, October 16, 2009, http://vanishingnewyork.blogspot.com/2009/10/more-jane-less-marc.html.

9. Tracy Elsen, "San Francisco's Median Rent Hits Yet Another New High," *Curbed*, September 3, 2015, http://sf.curbed.com/archives/2015/09/03/san_franciscos_median_rent_hits_yet_another_new_high.php. Abigail Sindzinski, "Why Homes in Major U.S. Cities Are Almost Impossible to Afford," *Curbed*, January 27, 2016, http://curbed.com/archives/2016/01/27/buying-homes-major-cities-unaffordable-new-york-san-francisco-la.php. Richard Florida, "The Complicated Link between Gentrification and Displacement," *Citylab*, September 18, 2015, http://www.citylab.com/housing/2015/09/the-complicated-link-between-gentrification-and-displacement/404161/.

10. Sindzinski, "Why Homes in Major U.S. Cities."

11. Alex Proud, "'Cool' London Is Dead, and the Rich Kids Are to Blame," *Telegraph*, April 7, 2014, http://www.telegraph.co.uk/men/thinking-man/10744997/Cool-London-is-dead-and-the-rich-kids-are-to-blame.html.

12. John Buntin, "The Myth of Gentrification," *Slate*, January 14, 2015, http://www.slate.com/articles/news_and_politics/politics/2015/01/the_gentrification_myth_it_s_rare_and_not_as_bad_for_the_poor_as_people.html.

13. Ibid. Florida, "The Complicated Link."

14. Ehrenhalt, *The Great Inversion*, 234. Florida, "The Complicated Link."

15. Tracy Elsen, "San Francisco's Median Rent Hits Yet Another New High," December 13, 2015, http://www.nbcnews.com/business/economy/its-not-just-poor-who-cant-make-rent-n478501. Jordan Weissman, "An Occasion to Weep about the Cost of Rent," *Slate*, January 28, 2016, http://www.slate.com/blogs/moneybox/2016/01/28/u_s_rents_hit_20_year_high.html. Martha White, "It's Not Just the Poor Who Can't Make

Rent," *NBC News*, December 13, 2015, http://www.nbcnews.com/busi
ness/economy/its-not-just-poor-who-cant-make-rent-n478501. Sindzinski, "Why Homes in Major U.S. Cities."

16. Jeremiah Moss, "On Spike Lee & Hyper-Gentrification, the Monster
That Ate New York," *Jeremiah's Vanishing New York*, March 3, 2014,
http://vanishingnewyork.blogspot.com/2014/03/on-spike-lee-hyper
-gentrification.html.

17. Ned Kaufman, *Race, Place, and Story: Essays on the Past and Future of Historic Preservation* (New York: Routledge, 2009), 320.

18. Ehrenhalt, *The Great Inversion*, 3–4, 232–33.

19. Ibid. Centers for Disease Control, "Health Effects of Gentrification,"
http://www.cdc.gov/healthyplaces/healthtopics/gentrification.htm.

20. Ta-Nehisi Coates, "The Case for Reparations," *Atlantic*, June 2014,
http://www.theatlantic.com/magazine/archive/2014/06/the-case-for
-reparations/361631/. Alexis Madrigal, "The Racist Housing Policy That
Made Your Neighborhood," *Atlantic*, May 22, 2014, http://www.the
atlantic.com/business/archive/2014/05/the-racist-housing-policy-that
-made-your-neighborhood/371439/.

21. Madrigal, "The Racist Housing Policy." Raymond Mohl, "The Interstates and the Cities: Highways, Housing, and the Freeway Revolt," Poverty and Race Research Action Council, 2002, http://www.prrac.org/pdf
/mohl.pdf.

22. James A. Clapp, *The City: A Dictionary of Quotable Thoughts on Cities
and Urban Life* (New Brunswick, NJ: Center for Urban Policy Research,
1984), 204–5. Nikole Hannah-Jones, "Living Apart: How the Government Betrayed a Landmark Civil Rights Law," *ProPublica*, June 25, 2015,
https://www.propublica.org/article/living-apart-how-the-government
-betrayed-a-landmark-civil-rights-law.

23. Kaufman, *Race, Place, and Story*, 320.

24. Sarah Goodyear, "Gentrification Backlash Has Inspired Its Own Backlash,"
CityLab, October 1, 2015, http://www.citylab.com/politics/2015/10/gentri
fication-backlash-has-inspired-its-own-backlash/408388/.

25. Ibid. Joe Coscarelli, "Spike Lee's Amazing Rant about Gentrification,"
New York Magazine, February 25, 2014, http://nymag.com/daily/intel
ligencer/2014/02/spike-lee-amazing-rant-against-gentrification.html. Moss,
"On Spike Lee & Hyper-Gentrification." Timothy Williams, "An Old

Sound in Harlem Draws New Neighbors' Ire," *New York Times*, July 6, 2008, http://www.nytimes.com/2008/07/06/nyregion/06drummers.html?_r=0.

26. David Schultz, "On H Street, Gentrification Not as Simple as Black and White," March 2, 2012, https://www.washingtonpost.com/local/on-h-street-gentrification-not-as-simple-as-black-and-white/2012/03/02/gIQAwRsBvR_story.html. Andrea Swalec, "Racial Profiling Is Worse after H Street Development, Locals Tell Police Chief," *HillNow*, December 12, 2014, https://www.hillnow.com/2014/12/12/police-chief-fields-racial-profiling-questions-near-h-street-ne/.

27. Coscarelli, "Spike Lee's Amazing Rant about Gentrification."

28. Sarah Laskow, "The Quiet, Massive Rezoning of New York," *Politico*, February 24, 2014, http://www.capitalnewyork.com/article/city-hall/2014/02/8540743/quiet-massive-rezoning-new-york?page=all.

29. Kaufman, *Race, Place, and Story*, 327.

30. Yanan Wang, "D.C.'s Chinatown Has Only 300 Residents Left, and They're Fighting to Stay," *Washington Post*, July 16, 2015, https://www.washingtonpost.com/lifestyle/style/dcs-chinatown-has-only-300-chinese-americans-left—and-fighting-to-stay/2015/07/16/86d54e84-2191-11e5-bf41-c23f5d3face1_story.html.

31. Rachel Reichard, "Oh, Gentrification: Latino Neighborhoods That Are Now Too Pricey," *Latina*, October 21, 2015, http://www.latina.com/lifestyle/our-issues/gentrification-latino-neighborhoods#1. Nick Tabor, "How Has Chinatown Stayed Chinatown?" *New York Magazine*, September 24, 2015, http://nymag.com/daily/intelligencer/2015/09/how-has-chinatown-stayed-chinatown.html.

32. Edward Glaeser, *Triumph of the City: How Our Greatest Invention Makes Us Richer, Smarter, Greener, Healthier, and Happier* (New York: Penguin, 2011), 9. Ashley Pettus, "Rethinking New Orleans," Harvard Magazine, January–February 2006, http://harvardmagazine.com/2006/01/rethinking-new-orleans.html.

33. Edward Glaeser, "Preservation Follies," *City Journal*, Spring 2010, http://www.city-journal.org/html/preservation-follies-13279.html.

34. Ibid. Glaeser, *Triumph of the City*, 119.

35. Glaeser, *Triumph of the City*, 11, 147.

36. Flint, *Wrestling with Moses*, 113.

37. Joel Kotkin, "What Jane Jacobs Got Wrong about Cities," *Daily Beast*, August 1, 2015, http://www.thedailybeast.com/articles/2015/08/01 /what-jane-jacobs-got-wrong-about-cities.html. Kriston Capps, "Why Historic Preservation Districts Should Be a Thing of the Past," *CityLab*, January 29, 2016, http://www.citylab.com/housing/2016/01/why-his toric-preservation-districts-should-be-a-thing-of-the-past/431598/.

38. J. Peter Byrne, "Historic Preservation and Its Cultured Despisers: Reflec- tions on the Contemporary Role of Preservation Law in Urban Develop- ment," *Georgetown University Law Center*, 2012, http://scholarship.law .georgetown.edu/cgi/viewcontent.cgi?article=1786&context=facpub.

39. Amanda Kolson Hurley, "Will U.S. Cities Design Their Way Out of the Affordable Housing Crisis?" *Next City*, January 18, 2016, https://next city.org/features/view/cities-affordable-housing-design-solution-missing -middle.

40. Ibid.

41. Edward Glaeser, "How Skyscrapers Will Save the City," *Atlantic*, March, 2011, http://www.theatlantic.com/magazine/archive/2011/03/how-sky scrapers-can-save-the-city/308387/. Snejana Farberov, "Immigrant Lives Frozen in Time: Never-Before-Seen Photos from Inside Manhattan's Ten- ement Museum Shed Light on Lower East Side's Notorious Turn-of-the- Century Slum," *Daily Mail*, December 25, 2014, http://www.dailymail .co.uk/news/article-2886995/Immigrant-lives-frozen-time-Never-seen -photos-inside-Manhattan-s-Tenement-Museum-shed-light-Lower-East -s-notorious-turn-century-slum.html. "Tenements," *History Channel*, 2010, http://www.history.com/topics/tenements.

42. Richard Florida, "The Limits of Density," *CityLab*, May 16, 2012, http:// www.citylab.com/design/2012/05/limits-density/2005/.

43. Ibid. Sasaki Associates, "The State of the City Experience," http://www .sasaki.com/media/files/cities_survey_final-1.pdf.

44. Laura Kusisto, "New Luxury Rental Projects Add to Rent Squeeze," *Wall Street Journal*, May 20, 2015, http://www.wsj.com/articles/new-luxury -rental-projects-add-to-rent-squeeze-1432114203. Alan Pyke, "America's Housing Developers Are Almost Exclusively Building Luxury Units," *ThinkProgress*, May 22, 2015, http://thinkprogress.org/economy/2015 /05/22/3662239/luxury-housing-80-percent-developers/. David M. Levitt, "New York Construction Booms with Focus on Luxury Housing,"

Bloomberg, April 30, 2015, http://www.bloomberg.com/news/articles /2015-04-30/new-york-construction-booms-with-focus-on-luxury-hous ing. Florida, "The Complicated Link."

45. Josh Barro, "Affordable Housing That's Very Costly," *New York Times*, June 8, 2014, http://www.nytimes.com/2014/06/08/upshot/affordable-hous ing-thats-very-costly.html. Samuel Stein, "DeBlasio's Doomed Housing Plan," *Jacobin*, October 2014, https://www.jacobinmag.com/2014/10 /de-blasios-doomed-housing-plan/.

46. Kaufman, *Race, Place, and Story*, 324.

47. Ibid.

48. India Rogers, "Banking on Vacancy: Groundbreaking Report from Pic ture the Homeless," *WhyHunger.Org*, February 13, 2012, http://www .whyhunger.org/connect/item/2435-banking-on-vacancy-groundbreak ing-report-from-picture-the-homeless.

49. Partnership for Working Families, "Los Angeles Sports and Entertainment District CBA," http://www.forworkingfamilies.org/resources/staples-cba. Michael Neibauer, "Wal-Mart, D.C., Strike Community Benefits Deal," *Washington Post*, November 22, 2011, http://www.bizjournals.com /washington/blog/2011/11/wal-mart-dc-strike-community.html. Mike DeBonis, "Read Wal-Mart's DC Community Benefits Deal," *Washington Post*, November 22, 2011, https://www.washingtonpost.com/blogs/mike -debonis/post/read-wal-marts-dc-community-benefits-deal/2011/11/22 /gIQAfL6alN_blog.html.

50. Partnership for Working Families, "Los Angeles Sports and Entertain ment District CBA." Neibauer, "Wal-Mart, D.C., Strike Community Benefits Deal." DeBonis, "Read Wal-Mart's."

51. "DC United, Southwest Residents Forge Community Benefits Agree ment," *DC United*, December 18, 2014, http://www.dcunited.com /post/2014/12/18/dc-united-southwest-residents-forge-community -benefits-agreement. Alexis Stephens, "Detroit Is Taking the Lead in the Community Benefits Movement," *Next City*, March 10, 2015, https:// nextcity.org/daily/entry/detroit-community-benefits-agreement.

52. Laura Flanders, "After 20-Year Fight, Bronx Community Wins Big on Development Project Committed to Living Wages and Local Economy," *YES Magazine*, January 3, 2014, http://www.yesmagazine.org/commo nomics/kingsbridge-armory-community-benefits-agreement.

53. Ibid.

54. Wu, "Why Are There So Many Shuttered Storefronts?"

55. Kate Rogers, "Small Businesses Push to Keep NYC from Becoming 'Cement City,'" *CNBC*, March 12, 2015, http://www.nbcnews.com /business/consumer/small-businesses-push-keep-nyc-becoming-cement -city-n322156. Wu, "Why Are There So Many Shuttered Storefronts?" Elizabeth Miller, "Neighbors of Brooklyn Deli Fight Gentrification with Grass-Fed Tuna Salad," NPR, June 19, 2015, http://www.npr.org/sec tions/thetwo-way/2015/06/19/415006564/neighbors-of-brooklyn-deli -fight-gentrification-with-grass-fed-tuna-salad. Tatiana Schlossberg, "Bodegas Declining in Manhattan as Rents Rise and Chains Grow," *New York Times*, August 4, 2015, http://www.nytimes.com/2015/08/04/ny region/bodegas-declining-in-manhattan-as-rents-rise-and-chains-grow .html.

56. Christian González-Rivera, "State of the Chains 2015," Center for an Urban Future, December 2015, https://nycfuture.org/research/publica tions/state-of-the-chains-2015. Lois Weiss, "Rent Skyrockets in Man-hattan Retail Zones," *New York Post*, May 18, 2015, http://nypost .com/2015/05/18/rent-skyrockets-in-manhattan-retail-zones/.

57. Marisa Lagos and J. K. Dineen, "Taking Care of Business in S.F.'s High-Turnover Climate," *San Francisco Chronicle*, October 12, 2014, http:// www.sfgate.com/politics/article/Taking-care-of-business-in-S-F-s-high -turnover-5818417.php.

58. San Francisco Heritage, "Legacy Business Registry and Preservation Fund," http://www.sfheritage.org/legacy/legacy-business-registry-preser vation-fund/. J. K. Dineen, "Is Prop J for Preservation, or a Slush Fund?," *San Francisco Chronicle*, October 6, 2015, http://www.sfchronicle.com /bayarea/article/Is-Prop-J-for-preservation-or-a-slush-fund-6554711. php. Broke-Ass Stuart, "Voters Must Protect the City's Legacy," *San Francisco Examiner*, October 8, 2015, http://www.sfexaminer.com/vot ers-must-protect-the-citys-legacy/.

59. Dineen, "Is Prop J for Preservation?" Stuart, "Voters Must Protect."

60. Take Back NYC, "About the Small Business Jobs Survival Act," http:// takebacknyc.nyc/. Peter Rugh, "The Battle to Save the Businesses That Make New York Unique," *Vice*, August 17, 2015, http://www.vice.com /en_uk/read/it-was-nice-knowing-you-new-york-253.

61. Tabor, "How Has Chinatown?"

62. Ibid.

63. Ibid.

64. Alana Semuels, "Affordable Housing, Always," *Atlantic*, July 6, 2015, http://www.theatlantic.com/business/archive/2015/07/affordable-housing-always/397637/. National Community Land Trust Network, "FAQ," http://cltnetwork.org/faq/. Jake Blumgart, "How Bernie Sanders Made Burlington Affordable," *Slate*, January 19, 2016, http://www.slate.com/articles/business/metropolis/2016/01/bernie_sanders_made_burlington_s_land_trust_possible_it_s_still_an_innovative.html.

65. Jamiles Lartey, "Cooper Square Is Here to Stay," *Bedford and Bowery*, January 1, 2015, http://bedfordandbowery.com/2015/01/cooper-square-is-here-to-stay-but-first-they-had-to-go-on-the-warpath/.

66. Rich Jacobus and Michael Brown, "City Hall Steps In," National Housing Institute, Spring 2007, http://www.nhi.org/online/issues/149/cityhall.html. Blumgart, "How Bernie Sanders."

67. Alexis Stephens, "Should Community Land Trusts Rank Higher in the Affordable Housing Toolbox?," *Next City*, November 3, 2014, https://nextcity.org/daily/entry/should-community-land-trusts-be-higher-in-the-affordable-housing-toolbox.

68. Alexis Stephens, "D.C. Park Intends to Beat Gentrification Where Others Have Failed," *Next City*, May 5, 2015, https://nextcity.org/daily/entry/washington-dc-park-11thstreet-park-neighborhood-gentrification. Neil Flanagan, "Can a Park Bridging the Anacostia Bring Investment without Displacing Residents?" *Greater Greater Washington*, June 26, 2015, http://greatergreaterwashington.org/post/27235/can-a-park-bridging-the-anacostia-bring-investment-without-displacing-residents/. Franklin Cater, "Washington D.C. Pitches New Bridge Park as a 'Model for Social Equity,'" NPR, October 18, 2014, http://www.npr.org/sections/thetwo-way/2014/10/17/357003103/washington-d-c-pitches-new-bridge-park-as-a-model-for-social-equity.

69. Cater, "Washington D.C. Pitches New Bridge Park." 11th Street Bridge Park Project, "11th Street Bridge Park Equitable Development Plan," November 5, 2015, https://indd.adobe.com/view/f22c1340-3bc2-4fff-94da-cde1395bef99.

70. 11th Street Bridge Park, "Equitable Development Plan."

71. Stephens, "D.C. Park."

Chapter 7

1. James A. Clapp, *The City: A Dictionary of Quotable Thoughts on Cities and Urban Life* (New Brunswick, NJ: Center for Urban Policy Research, 1984), 114.

2. US Census, "Age and Sex Composition: 2010," http://www.census.gov /prod/cen2010/briefs/c2010br-03.pdf. "Movies Released in 1985," *The Numbers*, http://www.the-numbers.com/movies/year/1985. "List of Billboard Hot 100 Number One Singles," Wikipedia, https://en.wikipedia .org/wiki/List_of_Billboard_Hot_100_number-one_singles_of_1985. "1985," Wikipedia, https://en.wikipedia.org/wiki/1985.

3. Richard B. Rood, "30 Years of Above-Average Temperatures Means That the Climate Has Changed," *Phys.Org*, February 26, 2015, http://phys .org/news/2015-02-years-above-average-temperatures-climate.html. Bill McKibben, "Global Warming's Terrifying New Math," *Rolling Stone*, July 19, 2012, http://www.rollingstone.com/politics/news/global-warmings -terrifying-new-math-20120719.

4. Katie Herzog, "The Atmosphere Hit 400 ppm of CO^2 Earlier This Year. Yes, That's Terrible," *Grist*, November 9, 2015, http://grist.org/climate -energy/the-atmosphere-hit-400-ppm-of-co2-earlier-this-year-yes-thats -terrible/. National Aeronautics and Space Administration, "Publication Abstracts—Hansen et al. 2008," http://pubs.giss.nasa.gov/abs/ha00410c .html. Bill McKibben, "Remember This: 350 Parts per Million," *Washington Post*, December 28, 2007, http://www.washingtonpost.com/wp -dyn/content/article/2007/12/27/AR2007122701942.html.

5. McKibben, "Remember This."

6. Herzog, "The Atmosphere." Adam Vaughan, "Earth's Climate Entering New Permanent Reality as CO^2 Hits New High," *Guardian*, November 9, 2015, http://www.theguardian.com/environment/2015/nov/09 /earths-climate-entering-new-permanent-reality-as-co2-hits-new-high.

7. Steve Cole and Leslie McCarthy, "2014 Warmest Year in Modern Record," NASA, January 16, 2015, http://climate.nasa.gov/news/2221/. Mark Kinver, "2014 Warmest Year on Record, Say American Researchers," *BBC News*, January 16, 2015, http://www.bbc.com/news/science -environment-30852588. Justin Gillis, "2015 Hottest Year on Record, Scientists Say," *New York Times*, January 21, 2016, http://www.nytimes

.com/2016/01/21/science/earth/2015-hottest-year-global-warming .html. NOAA National Centers for Environmental Information, "Global Summary Information—December 2015," http://www.ncdc.noaa.gov /sotc/summary-info/global/201512.

8. Stephanie Meeks, "The Changing Climate," *Preservation*, Spring 2015, https://savingplaces.org/stories/presidents-notes-changing-climate. NPT Staff, "Climate Change Poses Risks of Flooding, Erosion, and Fires to National Park Units and Their Treasures," *National Parks Traveler*, May 30, 2014, http://www.nationalparkstraveler.com/2014/05/climate-change -poses-risks-flooding-erosion-and-fires-national-park-units-and-their-trea sures25135.

9. Stephanie Meeks, "Historic Boulder Annual Meeting," Boulder, Colo-rado, April 6, 2011, https://savingplaces.org/press-center/media-re sources/historic-boulder-annual-meeting

10. Preservation Green Lab, "The Greenest Building: Quantifying the Envi-ronmental Value of Building Reuse," http://www.preservationnation. org/information-center/sustainable-communities/green-lab/lca/The _Greenest_Building_lowres.pdf, 13. US Green Business Council, "Green Building Facts," February 23, 2015, http://www.usgbc.org/articles /green-building-facts. Energy Star, "2015 Energy Star Top Cities," https://www.energystar.gov/buildings/press_room/top_10_cities_2015 /about_epa%E2%80%99s_list_top_cities_most_energy_star_certified _buildings.

11. Preservation Green Lab, "Greenest Building," ix.

12. Diane Keaton, "Opinion: The Ambassador Hotel Lesson," *Los Angeles Times*, October 13, 2008, http://www.latimes.com/opinion/la-oe-kea ton13-2008oct13-story.html. Vancouver Heritage Foundation, "New Life, Old Buildings: Your Green Guide to Heritage Conservation," November 2014, http://www.vancouverheritagefoundation.org/wp-content/uploads /2014/11/VHF-GreenGuide-webbook.pdf. Lloyd Alter, "Preservation Is Sustainability," *Treehugger*, April 7, 2008, http://www.treehugger.com /sustainable-product-design/preservation-is-sustainability.html.

13. Carl Elefante, "Greenest Building," *Preservation Forum Journal* 27, no. 1 (Fall 2012): 62–72, http://www.preservationnation.org/forum/library /members-only/current-journal-issues/FJ_Fall12-compressed.pdf.

14. Robert Cassidy, "Chapter One Reconstruction: 'The 99% Solution' for Energy Savings in Buildings," *Building Design+Construction*, July 3, 2012,

http://www.bdcnetwork.com/chapter-1-reconstruction-%E2%80%98
-99-solution%E2%80%99-energy-savings-buildings. Elefante, "Greenest Building."

15. Preservation Green Lab, "Greenest Building."

16. Ibid.

17. Ibid., 20–21.

18. Ibid., vi.

19. Ibid., viii.

20. Compact of Mayors, September 2014, http://www.compactofmayor
s.org/. Sandy Dechert, "US & Chinese Cities Meet and Pledge Deeper
Carbon Cuts," *Clean Technica*, September 22, 2015, http://cleantechnica
.com/2015/09/22/us-chinese-cities-meet-pledge-deeper-carbon-cuts/.

21. Steve Mouzon, *Original Green*, http://www.originalgreen.org/. John A.
Burns, AIA, "Energy Conserving Features Inherent in Older Homes,"
Department of Housing and Urban Development, 1982, http://www
.nps.gov/tps/sustainability/greendocs/conservation-features-older
-homes.pdf.

22. National Park Service Technical Preservation Services, "Energy Efficiency
in Older Buildings," http://www.nps.gov/tps/sustainability/energy-effi
ciency.htm. Mireya Navarro, "City Law Tracking Energy Use Yields Some
Surprises," *New York Times*, December 24, 2012, http://www.nytimes
.com/2012/12/25/science/earth/new-york-citys-effort-to-track-energy
-efficiency-yields-some-surprises.html. Sustainable Business, "Why Some
NYC Buildings Are More Efficient than LEED-Certified Ones," *Green-
biz*, January 3, 2013, http://www.greenbiz.com/blog/2013/01/03/some
-nyc-buildings-more-efficient-leed-certified. Steve Mouzon, "Down the
Unlovable Carbon Stair-Steps," *Original Green*, May 19, 2009, http://
www.originalgreen.org/blog/down-the-unlovable-carbon.html.

23. Stephen Mouzon, *The Original Green: Unlocking the Mystery of True Sustainability* (Miami: Guild Foundation Press, 2010), 58–59.

24. Ibid.

25. Ibid., 62–63.

26. Preservation Green Lab, "Saving Windows, Saving Money: Achieving Home Energy Efficiency through Low-Cost Retrofit," http://www
.preservationnation.org/information-center/sustainable-communities
/green-lab/saving-windows-saving-money/WINDOWS_PGL_Fact
Sheet_100212.pdf. Preservation Green Lab, "Saving Windows, Sav-

ing Money," http://forum.savingplaces.org/connect/community-home /librarydocuments/viewdocument?DocumentKey=59eab0e4-f0f4-45c5 -97c8-147a8def82ae

27. Preservation Green Lab, "Saving Energy, Money, and Jobs: Realizing the Energy Efficiency of Small Buildings," http://forum.savingplaces .org/connect/community-home/librarydocuments/viewdocument? DocumentKey=afcd94e9-8670-4aaf-8525-b3a19feccaea.

28. Ibid. Preservation Green Lab, "America Saves!," http://forum.saving places.org/act/pgl/america-saves

29. Preservation Green Lab, "Saving Energy, Money, and Jobs."

30. Ibid.

31. Preservation Green Lab, "Outcome-Based Energy Codes," http://www .preservationnation.org/information-center/sustainable-communities /green-lab/outcome-based-energy-codes.html. New Buildings Institute, "Outcome-Based Energy Codes for Existing Buildings: Seattle Model Energy Code Project," May 16, 2011, http://newbuildings.org/resource /outcome-based-energy-codes-existing-buildings-seattle-model-energy -code-project/.

32. Preservation Green Lab, "Outcome-Based Energy Codes."

33. US Green Building Council, "LEED," http://www.usgbc.org/leed. Meeks, "Historic Boulder Annual Meeting."

34. Meeks, "Historic Boulder Annual Meeting." Preservation Green Lab, "District Energy and Eco-Districts," http://www.preservationnation.org /information-center/sustainable-communities/green-lab/district-energy .html.

35. Preservation Green Lab, "District Energy and Eco-Districts." Mark Boyer, "Frank Lloyd Wright's Taliesin West Aiming for Net-Zero Energy," *Inhabitat*, March 2, 2012, http://inhabitat.com/frank-lloyd-wrights -taliesin-west-aiming-for-net-zero-energy/.

36. National Trust for Historic Preservation, "Texas Courthouses," https:// savingplaces.org/places/texas-courthouses. James Lindberg, "Texas Courthouses Are Going Underground to Save Energy," *Preservation Leadership Forum*, September 14, 2012, http://blog.preservationleadershipforum .org/2012/09/14/texas-courthouses-are-going-underground-to-save-energy/.

37. National Trust for Historic Preservation, "About the Emerson School Project," http://www.preservationnation.org/information-center/sustainable

-communities/buildings/emerson-school-project/about.html. Meeks, "Historic Boulder Annual Meeting." Margaret Jackson, "1885 School to Be Revamped into Home for National Trust for Historic Preservation," *Denver Post*, September 6, 2010, http://www.denverpost.com/ci_16001128.

38. John Upton, "Sea Level Rise Making Floods Routine for Coastal Cities," *Climate Central*, October 8, 2014, http://www.climatecentral.org /news/coastal-flooding-us-cities-18148. Union of Concerned Scientists, "Encroaching Tides," October 2014, http://www.ucsusa.org/global _warming/impacts/effects-of-tidal-flooding-and-sea-level-rise-east-coast -gulf-of-mexico.

39. Union of Concerned Scientists, "Encroaching Tides."

40. Union of Concerned Scientists, "National Landmarks at Risk," May 2014, http://www.ucsusa.org/global_warming/science_and_impacts/impacts /national-landmarks-at-risk-from-climate-change.html. Rachel Hartigan Shea, "Climate Change Threatens National Landmarks," *National Geographic*, May 20, 2015, http://news.nationalgeographic.com/news /2014/05/140520-threatened-historic-landmarks-climate-change/.

41. Stephanie Meeks, "Step Forward Boldly, and Bring the Past Forward." November 12, 2014, http://forum.savingplaces.org/blogs/forum-online /2014/11/12/step-forward-boldly-and-bring-the-past-forward. National Park Service, "Capturing History in the Beach Ridges at Cape Krusenstern," http://www.nps.gov/articles/cakrbeachridges.htm. National Park Service, "Recent Climate Change Exposure of Tumacacori National Park," July 28, 2014, irmafiles.nps.gov/reference/holding/497118. Lisa W. Foderero, "Ellis Island Artifacts Still in Protective Custody after Storm," *New York Times*, June 28, 2014, http://www.nytimes.com/2014/06/28 /nyregion/ellis-island-artifacts-still-in-protective-custody-after-hurri cane-sandy.html. CBS New York, "Thousands of Artifacts, Removed after Superstorm Sandy, Return to Ellis Island," September 16, 2015, http:// newyork.cbslocal.com/2015/09/16/ellis-island-artifacts-return/.

42. Farnsworth House Flood Mitigation Project, http://farnsworthproject .org/. Blair Kamin, "Hydraulic Lifts May Hold Hope for Flood-Proof Farnsworth House," *Chicago Tribune*, June 5, 2014, http:// articles.chicagotribune.com/2014-06-05/news/ct-kamin-farnsworth -house-met-0605-20140605_1_chicago-doctor-edith-farnsworth-farn sworth-house-hydraulics-plan. Dennis Rodin, "National Trust Wants

to Give Farnsworth House a Lift," *Crain's Chicago Business*, November 10, 2015, http://www.chicagobusinesscom/realestate/20151110/CRED0701/151119999/national-trust-wants-to-give-farnsworth-house-a-lift.

43. Pocantico Call to Action on Climate Impacts and Cultural Heritage, April 29, 2015, http://www.ucsusa.org/sites/default/files/attach/2015/05/Pocantico-Call-to-Action-on-Climate-Impacts-Cultural-Heritage-4-29-2015.pdf.

Conclusion

1. Mike Sweeney, "Protecting What We're Afraid Of," *Nature Conservancy*, August 5, 2013, http://blog.nature.org/conservancy/2013/08/05/protecting-what-were-afraid-of/.

2. Tom Mayes, "Why Old Places Matter—Community," *Preservation Nation*, March 10, 2015, http://forum.savingplaces.org/blogs/forum-online/2015/03/10/why-do-old-places-matter-community. Pope Francis, "Encyclical Letter Laudato Si of the Holy Father Francis on Care for Our Common Home," May 24, 2015, http://w2.vatican.va/content/francesco/en/encyclicals/documents/papa-francesco_20150524_enciclica-laudato-si.html.

3. National Park Service Technical Preservation Standards, "A History of the Secretary of the Interior's Standards," http://www.nps.gov/tps/standards/history-of-standards.htm. Brown Morton, "Beyond History: Success and Failure in Preservation," February 20, 2014, https://www.youtube.com/watch?v=H-M4TZhASmg.

4. Morton, "Beyond History."

Bibliography

Books and Reports

Ballon, Hilary. *New York's Pennsylvania Stations*. New York: W. W. Norton, 2002.

Ballon, Hilary, and Kenneth T. Jackson, eds. *Robert Moses and the Modern City: The Transformation of New York*. New York: W. W. Norton, 2007.

Basso, Keith H. *Wisdom Sits in Places: Landscape and Language among the Western Apache*. Albuquerque: University of New Mexico Press, 1996.

Blight, David. *Race and Reunion: The Civil War in American Memory*. Cambridge: Harvard University Press, 2001.

Brand, Stewart. *How Buildings Learn: What Happens after They're Built*. New York: Penguin, 1994.

Byrne, J. Peter. *Historic Preservation and Its Cultured Despisers: Reflections on the Contemporary Role of Preservation Law in Urban Development*. Washington, DC: Georgetown University Law Center, 2012.

Caro, Robert. *The Power Broker: Robert Moses and the Fall of New York*. New York: Vintage, 1974.

Clapp, James A. *The City: A Dictionary of Quotable Thoughts on Cities and Urban Life*. New Brunswick, NJ: Center for Urban Policy Research, 1984.

Corbusier, Le. *The City of Tomorrow and Its Planning*. Trans. Frederick Etchells. New York: Payson and Clarke Ltd., 1929.

Ehrenhalt, Alan. *The Great Inversion and the Future of the American City*. New York: Alfred A. Knopf, 2012.

Faust, Drew Gilpin. *This Republic of Suffering: Death and the American Civil War*. New York: Alfred A. Knopf, 2008.

Flint, Anthony. *Wrestling with Moses: How Jane Jacobs Took on New York's Master Builder and Transformed the American City*. New York: Random House, 2009.

————. *Modern Man: The Life of Le Corbusier, Architect of Tomorrow*. New York: New Harvest, 2014.

Gallagher, Leigh. *The End of the Suburbs: Where the American Dream Is Moving*. New York: Penguin, 2013.

Gehl, Jan. *Life between Buildings*. Washington, DC: Island Press, 2011.

Glaeser, Edward. *Triumph of the City: How Our Greatest Invention Makes Us Richer, Smarter, Greener, Healthier, and Happier*. New York: Penguin, 2011.

Harris, Donna Ann. *New Solutions for House Museums*. Lanham, MD: Altamira Press, 2007.

Hippocrates. *On Air, Water, and Places*. Trans. Francis Adams. MIT Internet Classics Archive. http://classics.mit.edu/Hippocrates/airwatpl.html.

Hirt, Sonia. *Zoned in the U.S.A.: The Origins and Implications of American Land-Use Regulation*. Ithaca, NY: Cornell University Press, 2015.

Howard, J. Myrick. *Buying Time for Heritage: How to Save an Endangered Historic Property*. Chapel Hill: University of North Carolina Press, 2007.

Hyden, Carl T., and Theodore F. Sheckels. *Public Places: Sites of Political Communication*. New York: Rowman and Littlefield, 2016.

Jackson, Kenneth T. *Crabgrass Frontier: The Suburbanization of the United States*. New York: Oxford University Press, 1985.

Jacobs, Jane. "Downtown Is for People." *Fortune*, 1958.

————. *The Death and Life of Great American Cities*. New York: Vintage Books, 1961.

————. *Dark Age Ahead*. New York: First Vintage Books, 2004.

Kaufman, Ned. *Race, Place, and Story: Essays on the Past and Future of Historic Preservation*. New York: Routledge, 2009.

King, Martin Luther, Jr. *Where Do We Go from Here—Chaos or Community?* Boston: Beacon Press, 2010.

Kunstler, James Howard. *The Geography of Nowhere: The Rise and Decline of America's Man-Made Landscape*. New York: Touchstone, 1993.

Lerner, Jaime. *Urban Acupuncture: Celebrating Pinpricks of Change That Enrich City Life*. Washington, DC: Island Press, 2014.

Leuchtenberg, William, ed. *American Places: Encounters with History*. New York: Oxford University Press, 2000.

Lubeck, Aaron. *Green Restorations: Sustainable Building and Historic Homes*. Gabriola Island, BC: New Society, 2010.

Lydon, Mike, and Anthony Garcia. *Tactical Urbanism: Short-Term Action for Long-Term Change*. Washington, DC: Island Press, 2015.

McCann, Barbara. *Completing Our Streets: The Transition to Safe and Inclusive Transportation*. Washington, DC: Island Press, 2013.

McElya, Micki. *Clinging to Mammy: The Faithful Slave in Twentieth-Century America*. Cambridge: Harvard University Press, 2007.

Moe, Richard, and Carter Wilkie. *Changing Places: Rebuilding Community in the Age of Sprawl*. New York: Henry Holt & Co., 1997.

Mohl, Raymond. *The Interstates and the Cities: Highways, Housing, and the Freeway Revolt*. Poverty and Race Research Action Council, 2002.

Montgomery, Charles. *Happy City: Transforming Our Lives through Urban Design*. New York: Farrar, Straus, and Giroux, 2013.

Mouzon, Stephen. *The Original Green: Unlocking the Mystery of True Sustainability*. Miami: Guild Foundation Press, 2010.

Murphy, Kevin C. "Uphill All the Way: The Fortunes of Progressivism," *1920–1929*. February 2013.

Page, Max, and Randall Mason, eds. *Giving Preservation a History: Histories of Historic Preservation*. New York: Routledge, 2004.

Page, Max, and Timothy Mennel. *Reconsidering Jane Jacobs*. Chicago: American Planning Association, 2011.

Page, Max, and Marla Miller, eds. *Bending the Future: Fifty Ideas for the Next Fifty Years of Preservation*. Amherst: University of Massachusetts Press, 2016.

Partnership for Building Reuse. "Learning from Los Angeles." October 2013.

———. "Retrofitting Philadelphia." September 2014.

———. "Building on Baltimore's History." November 2014.

Place Economics and the National Trust for Historic Preservation. "The Federal Historic Tax Credit: Transforming Communities." June 2014.

Preservation Green Lab. "The Greenest Building: Quantifying the Environmental Value of Building Reuse." January 2012.

———. "Saving Windows, Saving Money: Achieving Home Energy Efficiency through Low-Cost Retrofit." October 2012.

———, "Saving Energy, Money, and Jobs: Realizing the Energy Efficiency of Small Buildings." June 2013.

———. *Older, Smaller, Better: Measuring How the Character of Buildings and Blocks Influences Urban Vitality*. May 2014.

Special Committee on Historic Preservation. *With Heritage So Rich*. New York: Random House, 1966.

Speck, Jeff. *Walkable City: How Downtown Can Save America, One Step at a Time*. New York: Northpoint Press, 2012.

SPUR and San Francisco Architectural Heritage. "Historic Preservation in San Francisco: Making the Preservation Process Work for Everyone." July 2013.

Steinbeck, John. *The Grapes of Wrath*. 1939. Reprint, New York: Penguin, 2006.

Stipe, Robert. *A Richer Heritage: Historic Preservation in the Twenty-First Century*. Chapel Hill: University of North Carolina Press, 2003.

Trigg, Dylan. *The Memory of Place: A Phenomenology of the Uncanny*. Athens: Ohio University Press, 2013.

Vancouver Heritage Foundation. "New Life, Old Buildings: Your Green Guide to Heritage Conservation." November 2014.

Verney, Kevern, and Lee Sartain, eds. *Long Is the Way and Hard: One Hundred Years of the NAACP*. Fayetteville: University of Arkansas Press, 2009.

Willson, Richard. *Parking Reform Made Easy*. Washington, DC: Island Press, 2013.

Journals, Newspapers, and Websites

AIArchitect

All Other Persons

Arch Daily

The Atlantic

Baltimore Sun

BBC News

Bedford and Bowery

Big Box Reuse

Bloomberg

The Boston Globe

Buffalo News

Business Insider

CBS News

Charleston City Paper

Christian Science Monitor

CityLab

Clean Technica

CNBC

CNN

Construction Law Depot

Curbed

Daily Beast

Daily Journal of Commerce

Daily Mail

Dallas Magazine

DCist

Denver Post

Deseret News

De Zeen

Discovering Urbanism

The Eastsider LA

Fast Company

Forbes

Foreign Affairs

Fortune

FOX News Latino

Free Enterprise

Gothamist

Greater Greater Washington

Grist

The Guardian

Hidden City

The Hill
HillNow
History Channel
History Matters
Hoodline
H Street Neighborhood News
Huffington Post
Inhabitat
*International Journal of Urban and
    Regional Research*
Jeremiah's Vanishing New York
Journal of Environmental Psychology
Kansas City Star
KPCC
KUSA
Latina
The Los Angeles Times
Mashable
Medium
Mendocino Beacon-Journal
The Millions
Milwaukee Business-Journal
Minneapolis Post
Miss Representation
National Geographic
NBC News
New Orleans Time-Picayune
New Yorker
New York Magazine
New York Observer
New York Post
New York Times
Next City
NPR
NRDC Switchboard
Observer
Original Green

Paris Review
Philadelphia Inquirer
Philadelphia Magazine
Place Promotion
Planetizen
Playgroundology
Politico
Preservation
Preservation Law Reporter
Preservation Leadership Forum
ProPublica
Providence Journal Bulletin
Real Clear Politics
Roll Call
The Root
San Francisco Chronicle
San Francisco Examiner
Savannah Morning News
Seattle Post-Intelligencer
Seattle Times
Slate
Teachadelphia
TechCrunch
The Telegraph
ThinkProgress
TIME
Topia
Treehugger
USA Today
Used to Be a Pizza Hut
Vice
Voice of America
Vox
Wall Street Journal
Washington Business Journal
Washington City Paper
Washington DC Eater

Washingtonian   *Wired*
Washington Post   *YES*
Where Traveler

Organizations and Municipalities
11th Street Bridge Park Project
Acme Feed and Seed Nashville
Advisory Council on Historic Preservation
America Saves
American Institute of Architects
Architect of the Capitol
Artspace
Baltimore Design School
Brookings Institution
Brucemore
California Office of Historic Preservation
Center for an Urban Future
Centers for Disease Control
Chicago Metropolitan Agency for Planning
City Observatory
City of Boulder
City of Philadelphia
City of Phoenix
City of San Antonio
Civil War Trust
Compact of Mayors
Congress for a New Urbanism
DC United
East Bay Asian Local Development Corporation
Farnsworth House
First Hill Streetcar
Fox Oakland Theatre
Freemason Abbey
Friends of La Laguna
Friends of Miami Marine Stadium
Gehl Architects

Government Accountability Office
Heartland Housing
Historic Charleston
Historic England
Historic Hudson River Towns
Historic Macon Foundation
Historic New England
Historic Savannah Foundation
History Colorado
Howard Theatre
Humanim
Indiana Economic Development Corporation
Kings Theatre
Knight Foundation
LA Conservancy
Mapos LLC
Massachusetts Office of Housing and Economic Development
McMenamins
Monticello
Montpelier
Mount Vernon
Nantucket Preservation Trust
National Aeronautics and Space Administration
National Community Land Trust Network
National Complete Streets Coalition
National Geographic
National Housing Institute
National Main Street Center
National Oceanic and Atmospheric Administration
National Park Service
National Trust for Historic Preservation
Natural Resources Defense Council
Neighborhood Service Organization
New Jersey Department of Community Affairs
New York Landmarks Conservancy
Park Avenue Armory
Partnership for Urban Reuse

Partnership for Working Families
Pauli Murray Project
Poverty and Race Research Action Council
San Francisco Ferry Building Marketplace
San Francisco Heritage
Sasaki Associates
Savannah College of Art and Design
Skylight One Hanson
Smart Growth America
South Carolina Association for Community and Economic Development
South Carolina State Historic Preservation Office
SPUR
SurveyLA
Take Back NYC
The Nature Conservancy
Tinner Hill Heritage Foundation
Union of Concerned Scientists
Urban Land Institute
US Census
US Congress
US Green Business Council
Vancouver Heritage Foundation

About the Authors

Stephanie Meeks has been the president and chief executive officer of the National Trust for Historic Preservation since July 2010. During her tenure, the National Trust has expanded its work to highlight the critical connection between older buildings and vibrant cities and has spearheaded research reflecting the benefits of historic preservation in today's urban areas.

Before joining the National Trust, Meeks served in several senior executive positions, including chief operating officer as well as acting president and chief executive officer, during her almost eighteen years at The Nature Conservancy. She currently serves as chair of the board of the Potomac Conservancy.

She holds a BA in English from the University of Colorado and an MBA from the George Washington University.

Kevin C. Murphy is the speechwriter at the National Trust for Historic Preservation. For nearly two decades, he has worked behind the scenes as a speechwriter, ghostwriter, researcher, editor, and advisor. Over that time, he has written for pundits, strategists, historians, business and nonprofit leaders, cabinet officials, and members of Congress. He holds an AB in History from Harvard University and a PhD in history from Columbia University, and lives in Washington, D.C.

Index

Figures/photos/illustrations are indicated by a "f" and tables by a "t"